SPY vs SPY

FIGHT TO THE FINISH!

WRITTEN AND ILLUSTRATED BY
PETER KUPER

MAD
NEW YORK
BOOKS

D0129210

MAD BOOKS

William Gaines Founder
John Ficarra VP & Executive Editor
Charlie Kadau, Joe Raiola Senior Editors
Dave Croatto Editor
Jacob Lambert Associate Editor
Sam Viviano Art Director
Ryan Flanders Associate Art Director
Doug Thomson Assistant Art Director
Lana Limón Production Artist

ADMINISTRATION

Diane Nelson President
Dan DiDio and Jim Lee Co-Publishers
Geoff Johns Chief Creative Officer
John Rood Executive VP – Sales, Marketing and Business Development
Amy Genkins Senior VP – Business and Legal Affairs
Nairi Gardiner Senior VP – Finance
Jeff Boison VP – Publishing Planning
John Cunningham VP – Marketing
Terri Cunningham VP – Editorial Administration
Anne DePies VP – Strategy Planning and Reporting
Amit Desai Senior VP – Franchise Management
Alison Gill Senior VP – Manufacturing and Operations
Bob Harras VP – Editor in Chief, DC Comics
Jason James VP – Interactive Marketing
Hank Kanalz Senior VP – Vertigo and Integrated Publishing
Jay Kogan VP – Business and Legal Affairs, Publishing
Jack Mahan VP – Business Affairs, Talent
Nick Napolitano VP – Manufacturing Administration
Rich Palermo VP – Business Affairs, Media
Sue Pohja VP – Book Sales
Courtney Simmons Senior VP – Publicity
Bob Wayne Senior VP – Sales

"Drawn Out Dramas" Throughout By Sergio Aragonés

Compilation and new material © 2013 by E.C. Publications, Inc. All Rights Reserved.

MAD, Boy's Head Design, and all related indicia are trademarks of E.C. Publications, Inc.

Published by MAD Books. An imprint of E.C. Publications, Inc., 1700 Broadway, New York, NY 10019.
A Warner Bros. Entertainment Company.

CARTOON NETWORK and the logo TM & © Cartoon Network.

No part of this book may be reproduced in any form or by any electronic or mechanical means, including information storage and retrieval systems, without permission in writing from the publisher, except in the case of brief quotations embodied in critical articles and reviews.

The names and characters used in MAD fiction and semi-fiction are fictitious. A similarity without satiric purpose to a living person is a coincidence.

Printed by RR Donnelley, Crawfordsville, IN, USA. 10/11/13. First Printing.
ISBN: 978-1-4012-4814-7

SUSTAINABLE FORESTRY INITIATIVE

Certified Chain of Custody
At Least 20% Certified Forest Content
www.sfiprogram.org
SFI-01042
APPLIES TO TEXT STOCK ONLY

Spy vs. Spy created by Antonio Prohias

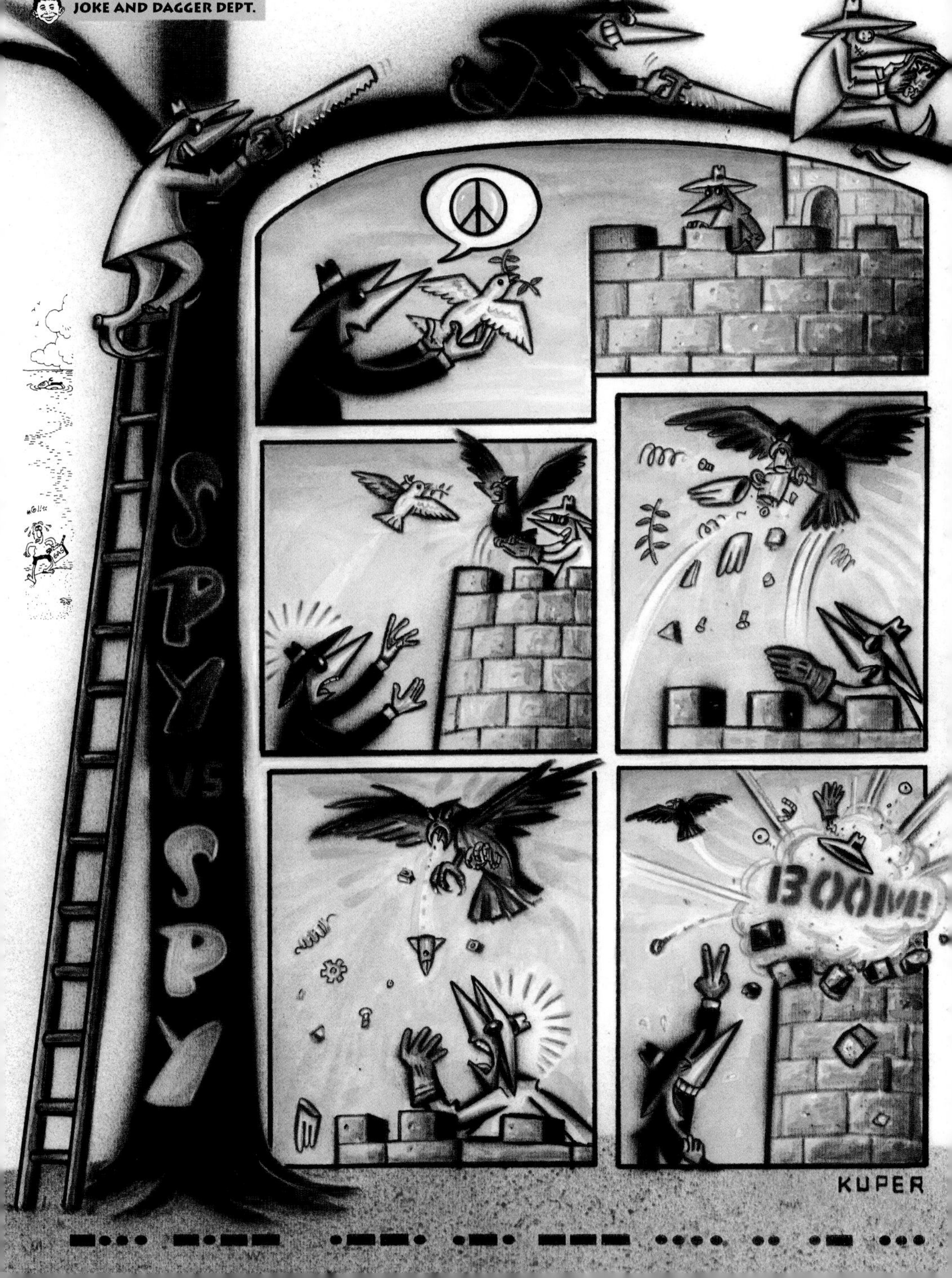
SPY
VS
SPY
BOOM!
KUPER

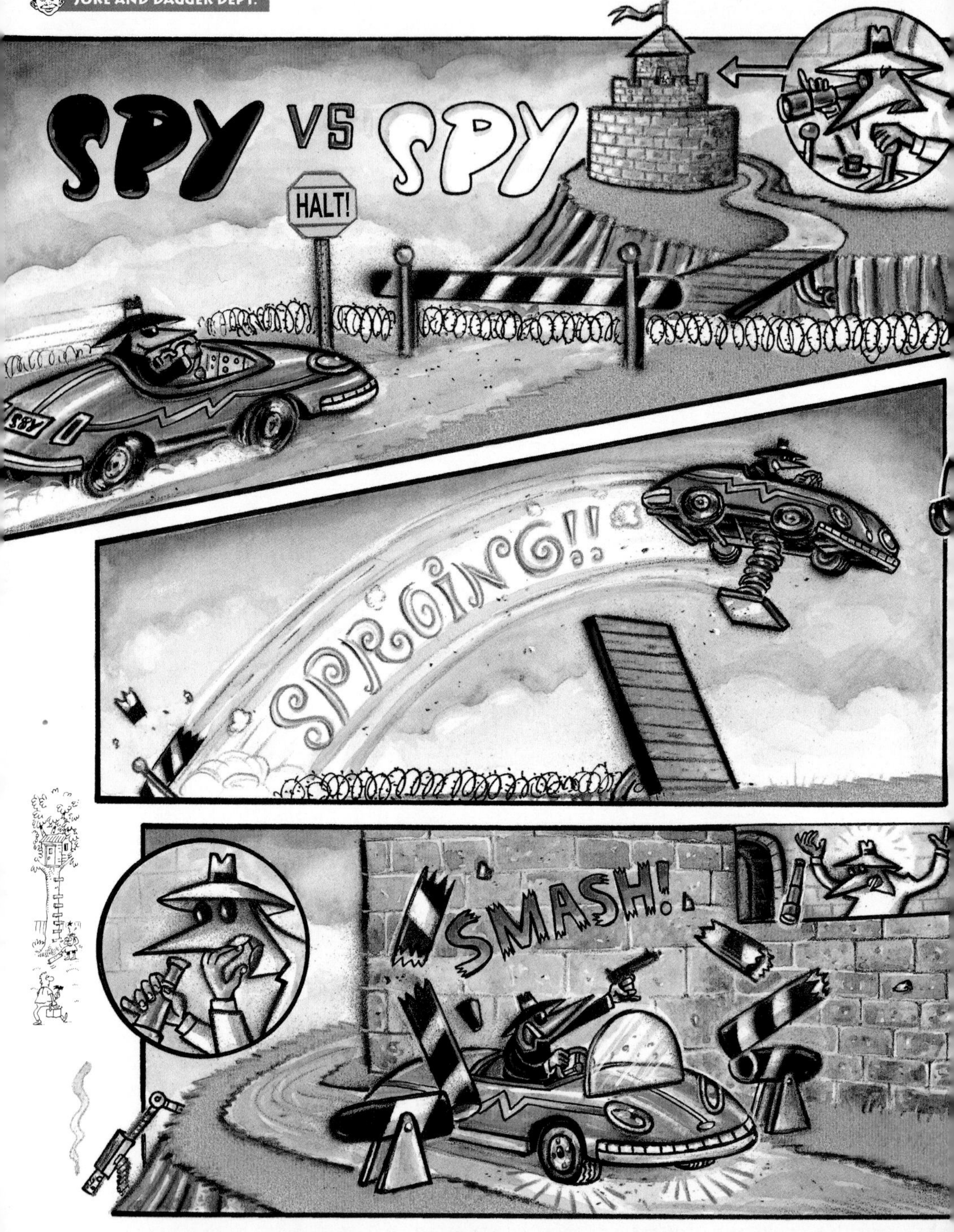
SPY VS SPY
HALT!
SPROING!!
SMASH!

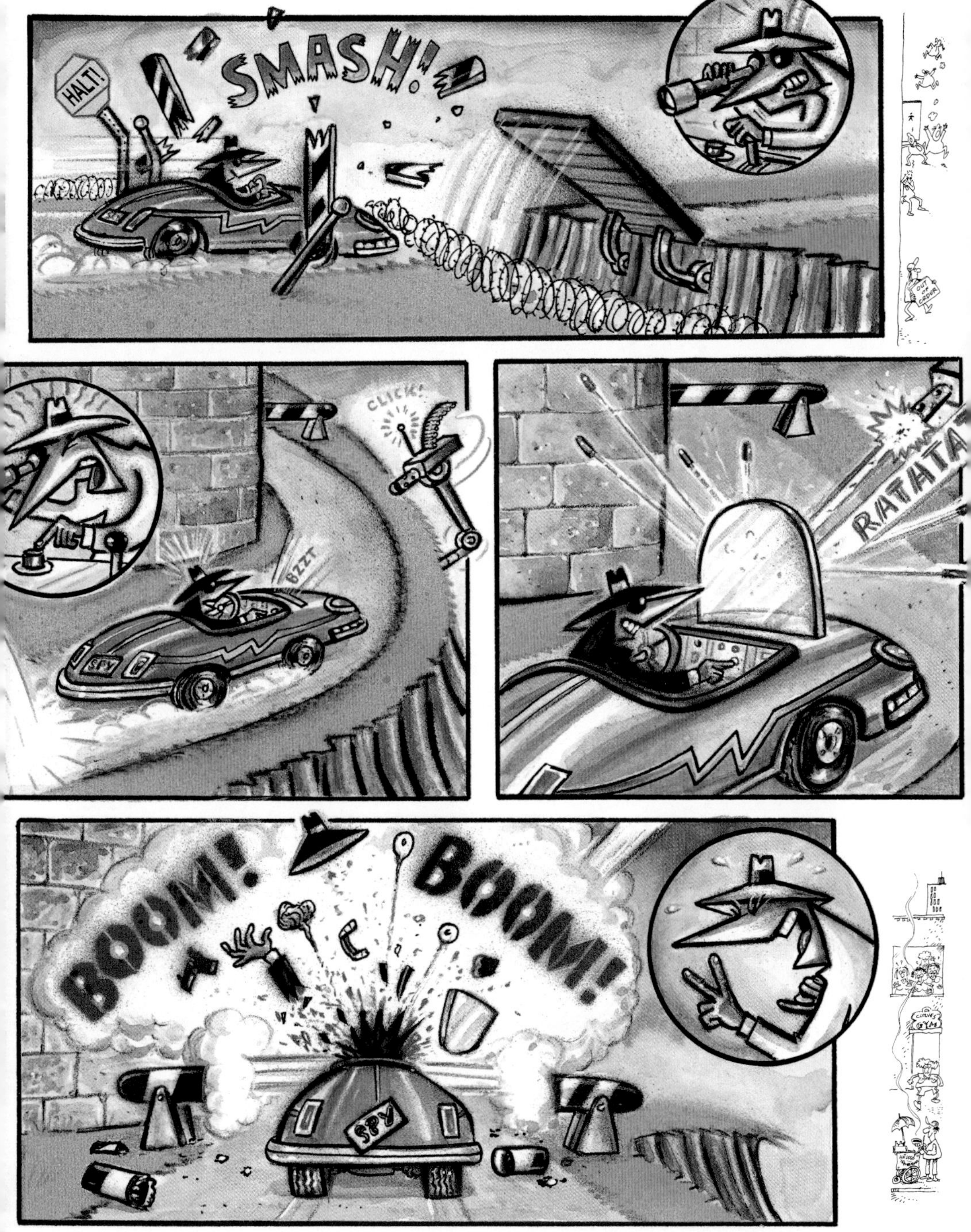
HALT!
SMASH!
CLICK!
BZZT
SPY
RATATAT
BOOM!
BOOM!
SPY
OUT OF ORDER
CURVES GYM
KUPER

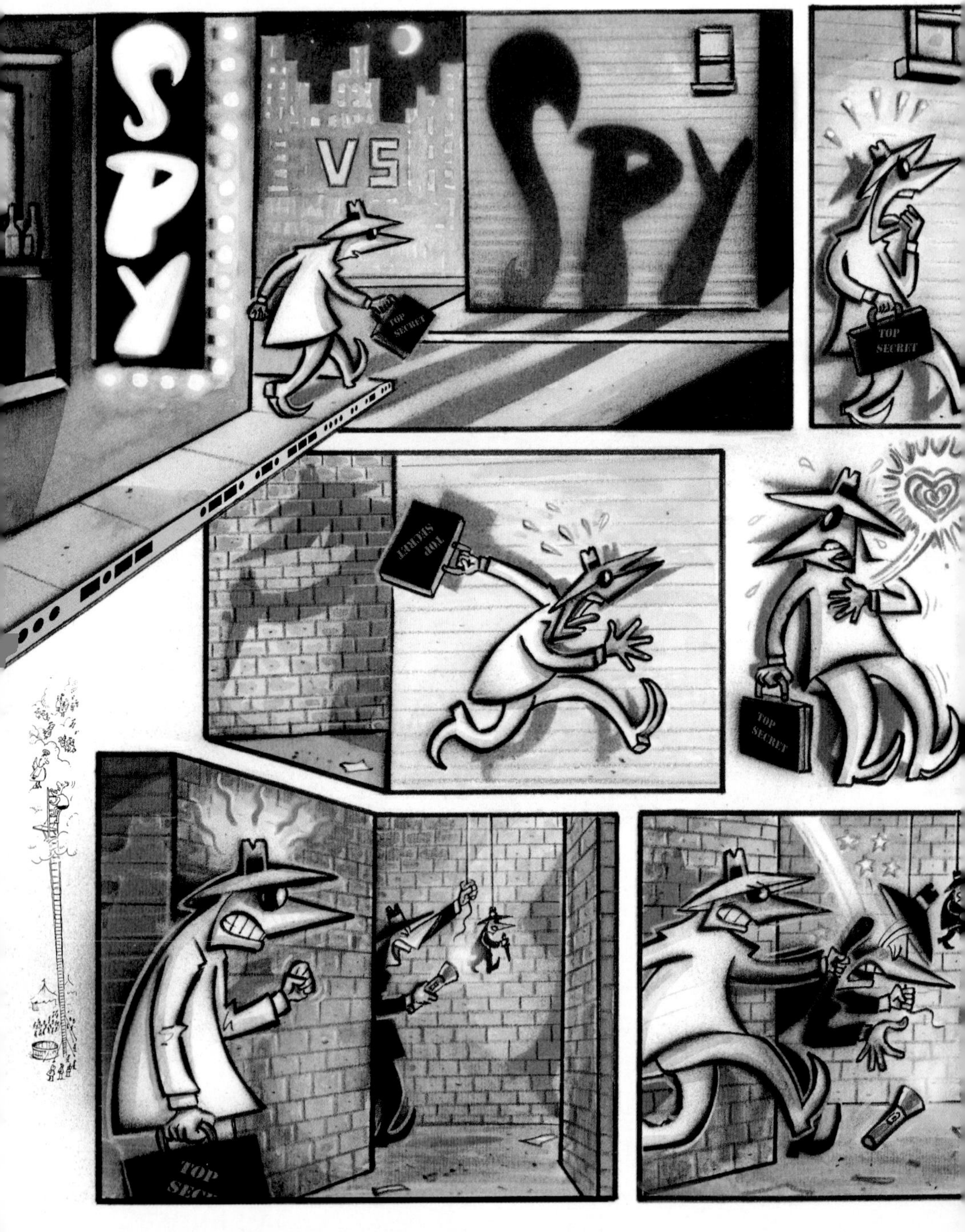
SPY VS SPY
TOP SECRET
TOP SECRET
TOP SECRET
TOP SECRET
TOP SECRET

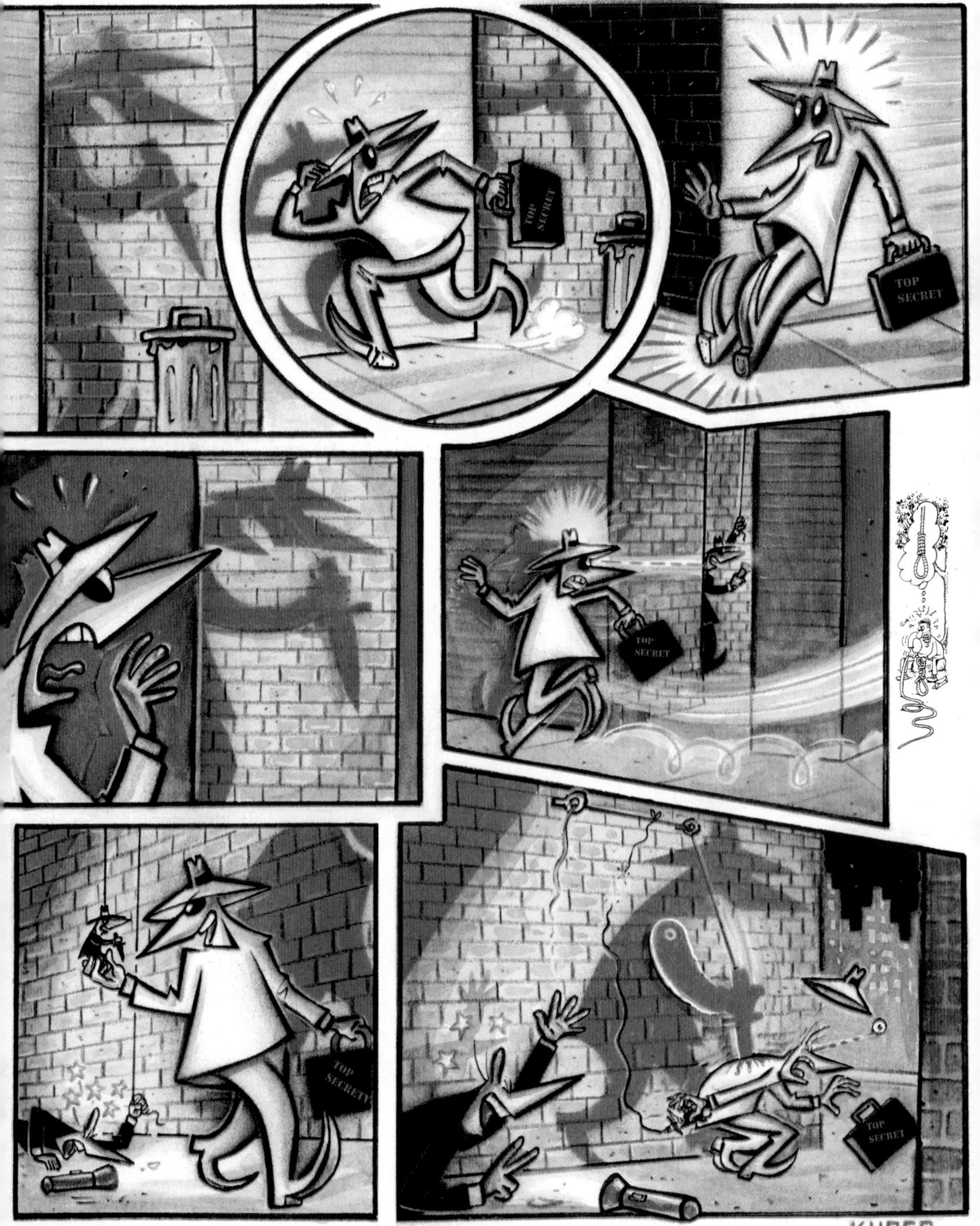
TOP SECRET
TOP SECRET
TOP SECRET
TOP SECRET
TOP SECRET
KUPER

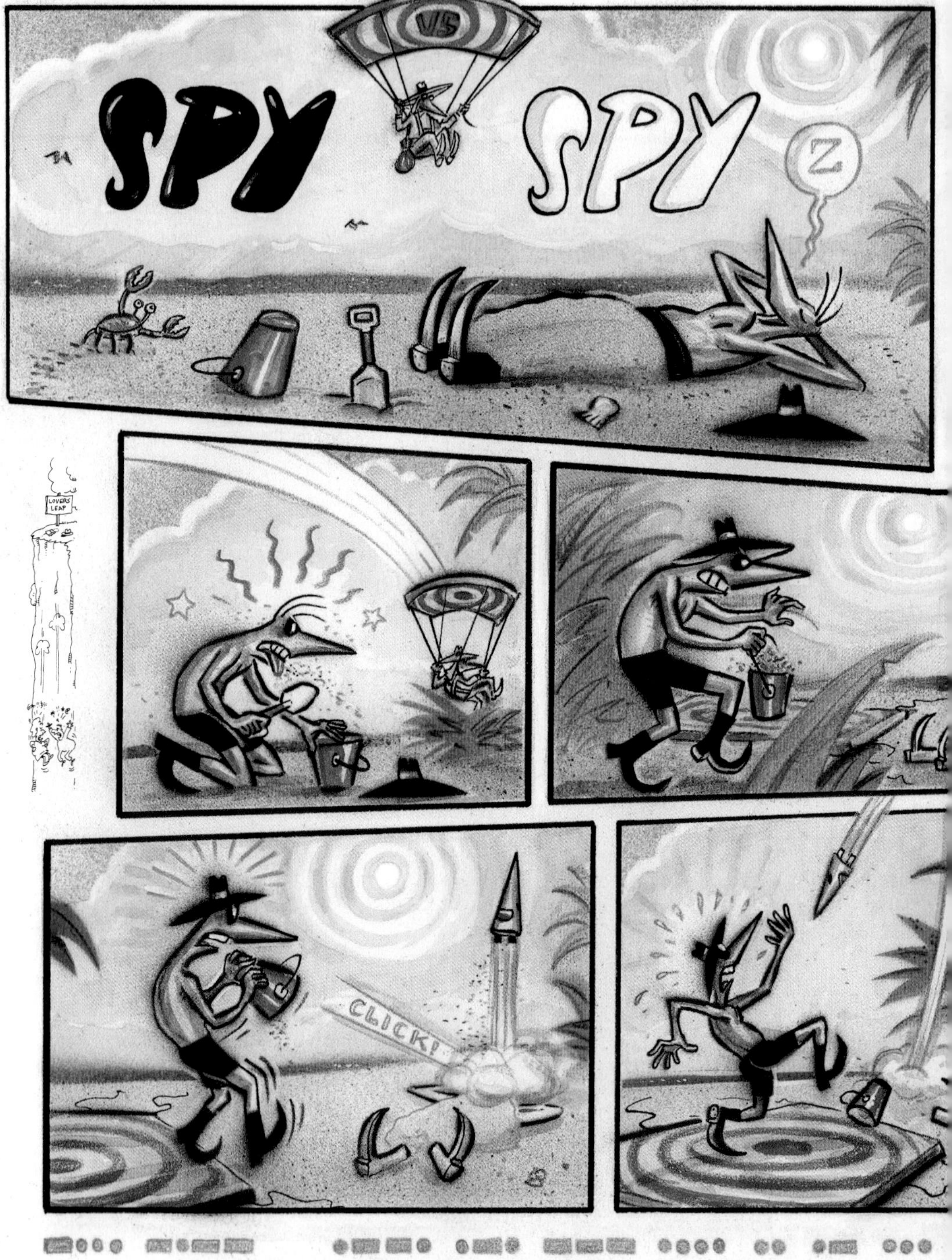
SPY
VS
SPY
Z
LOVERS LEAP
CLICK!

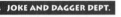

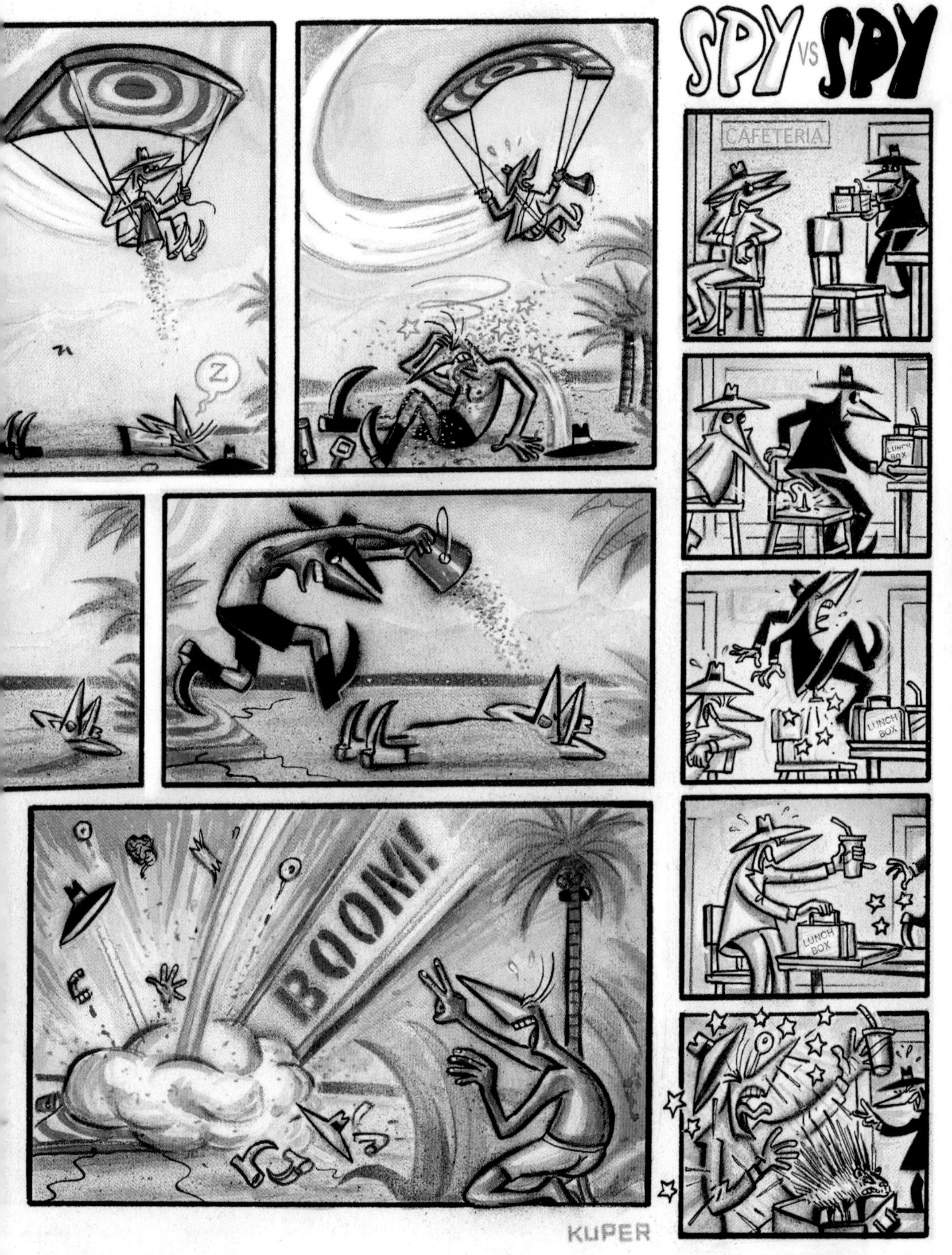
SPY VS SPY
CAFETERIA
Z
LUNCH BOX
LUNCH BOX
LUNCH BOX
BOOM!
KUPER

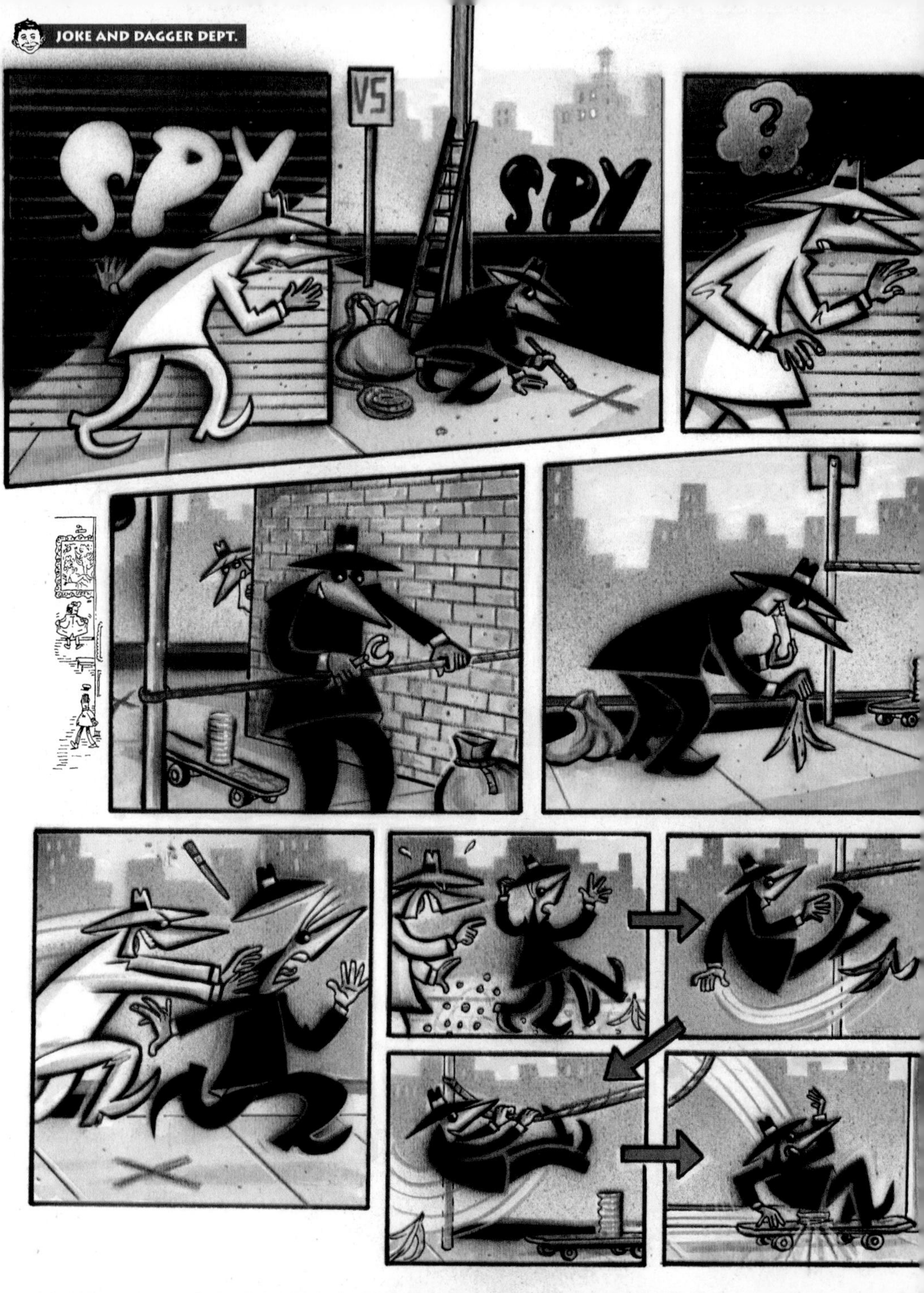
SPY
VS
SPY

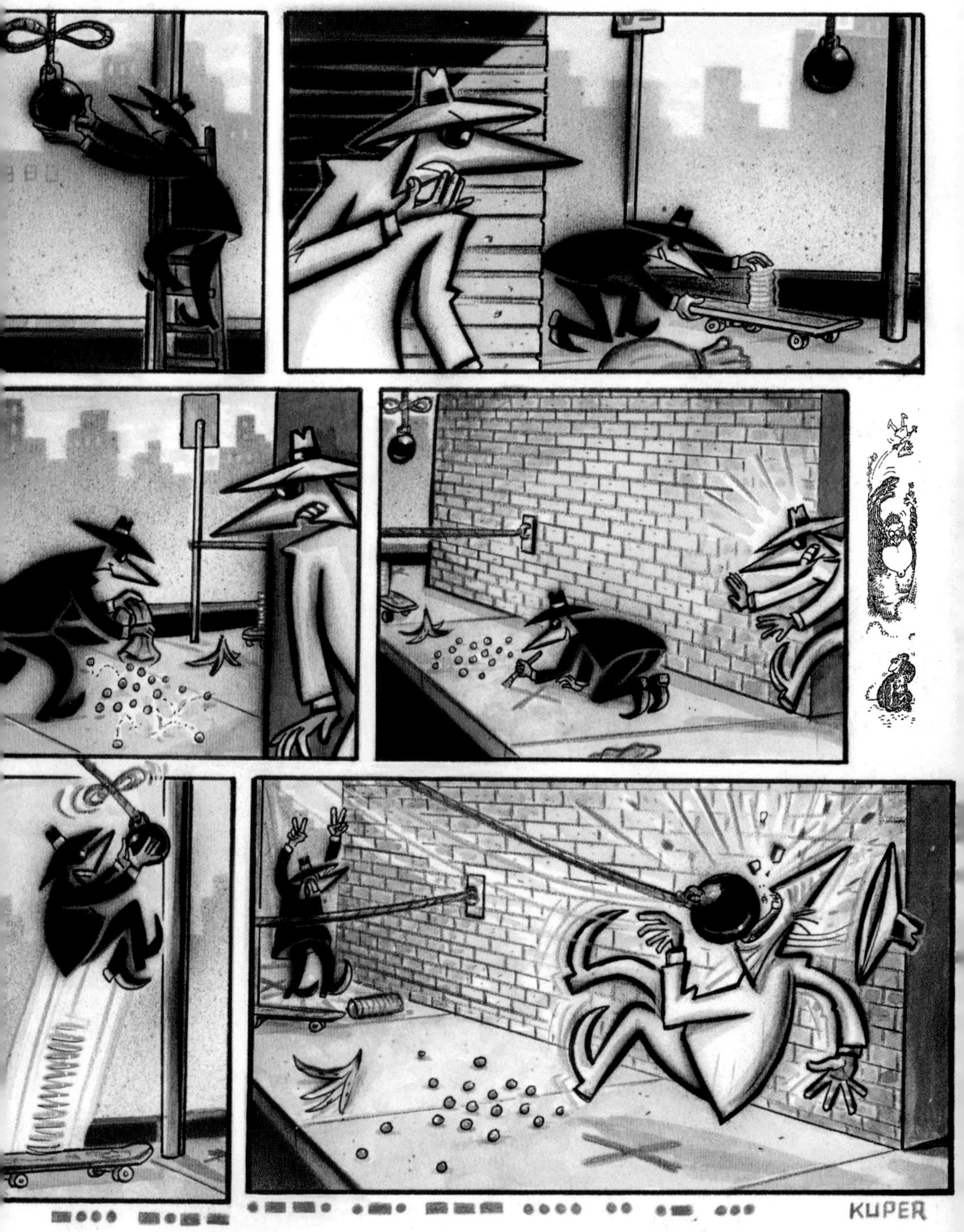
KUPER

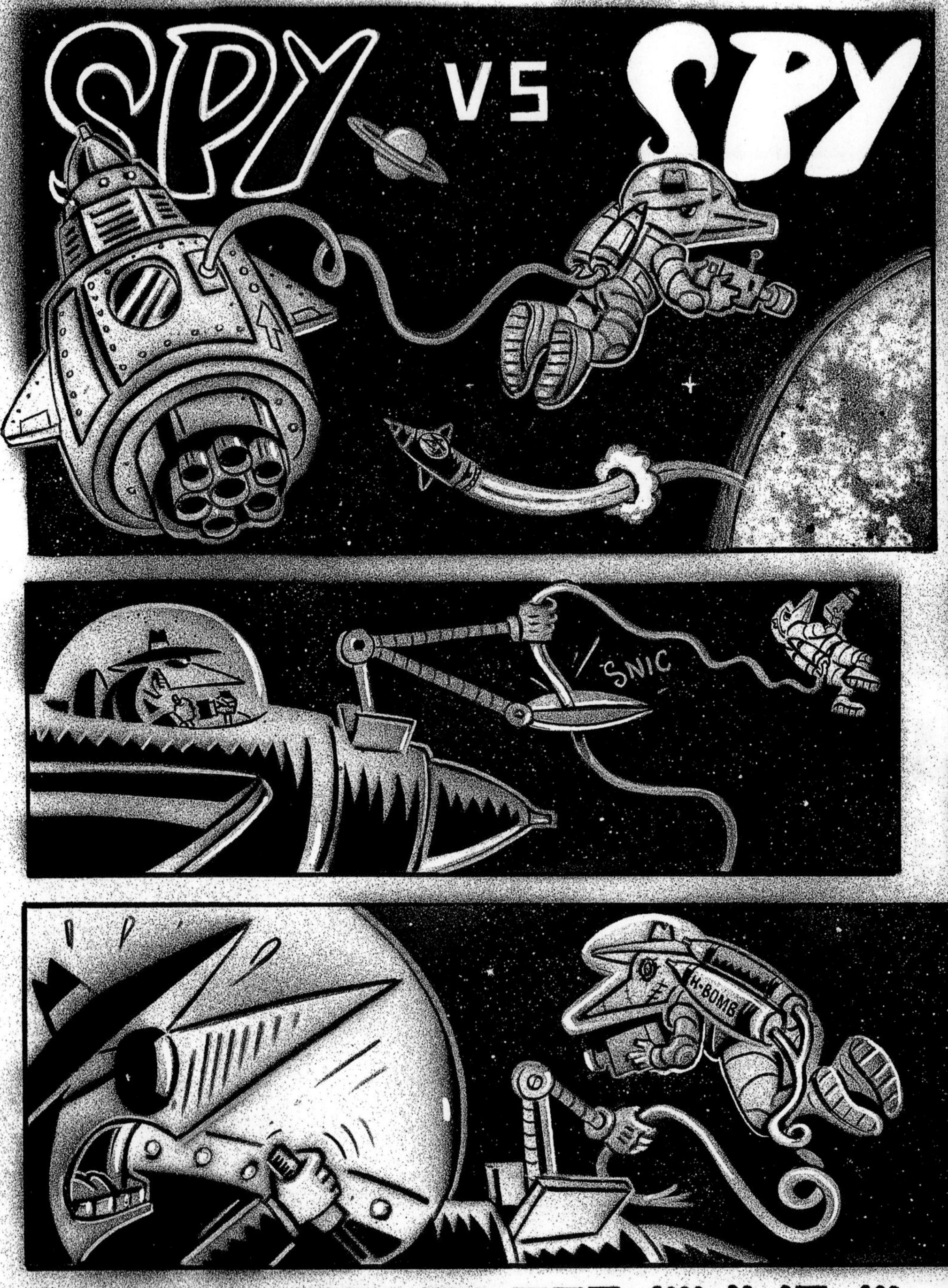
SPY VS SPY
SNIC
H-BOMB

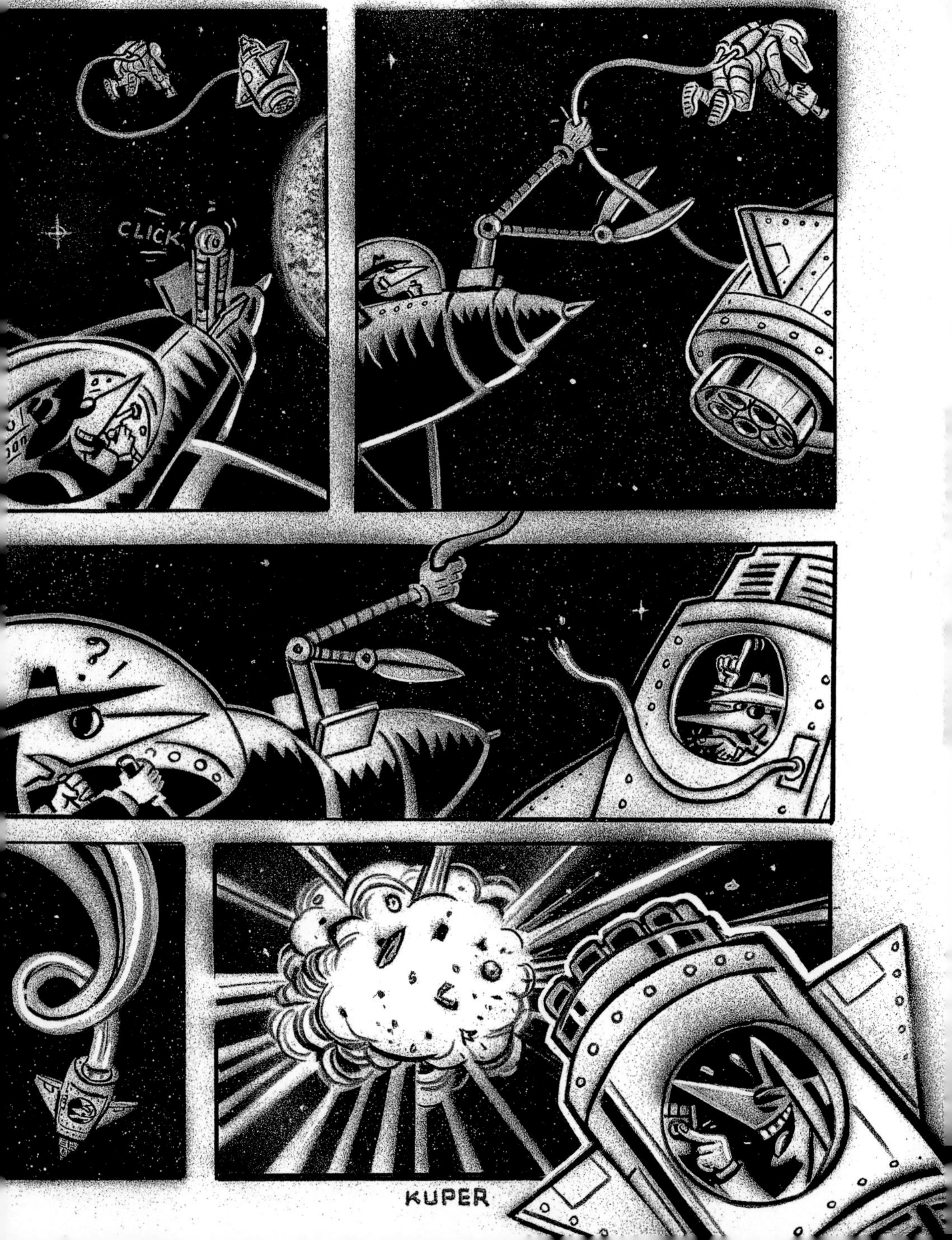
CLICK
?!
KUPER

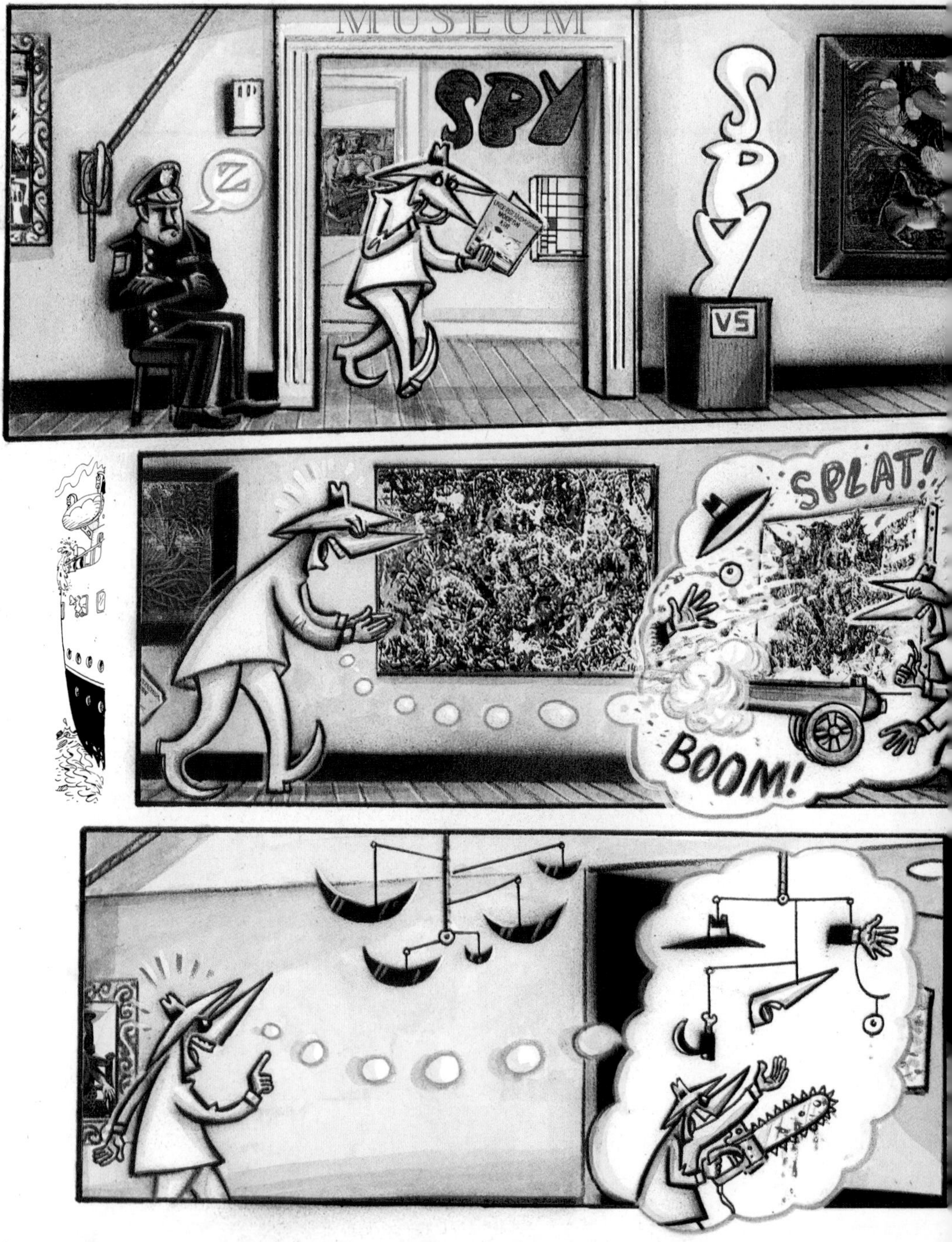
MUSEUM
SPY
Z
SPY
VS
SPLAT!
BOOM!

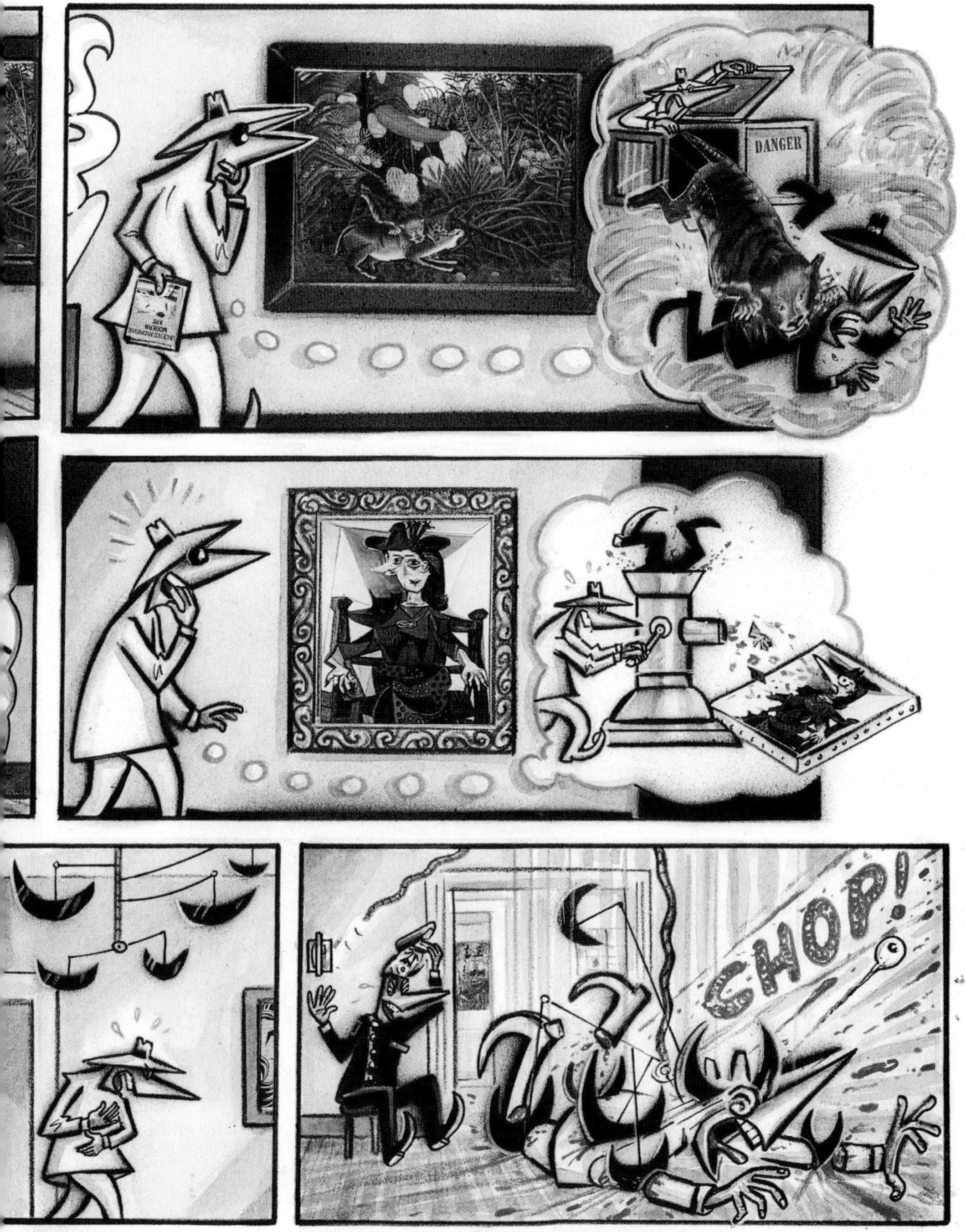
DANGER
CHOP!

KUPER

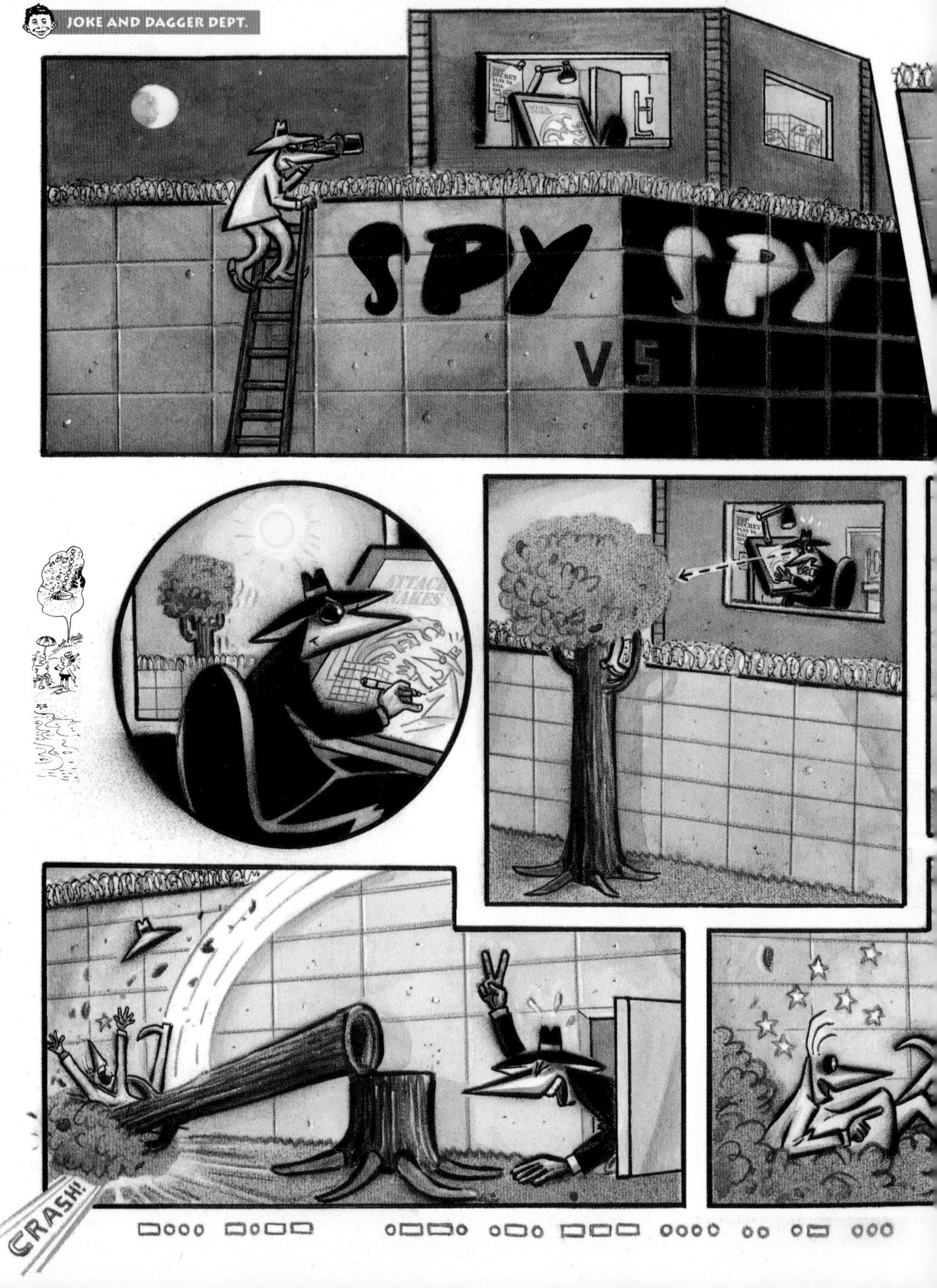
SPY
VS
SPY
TOP SECRET PLAN TO KILL
CRASH!

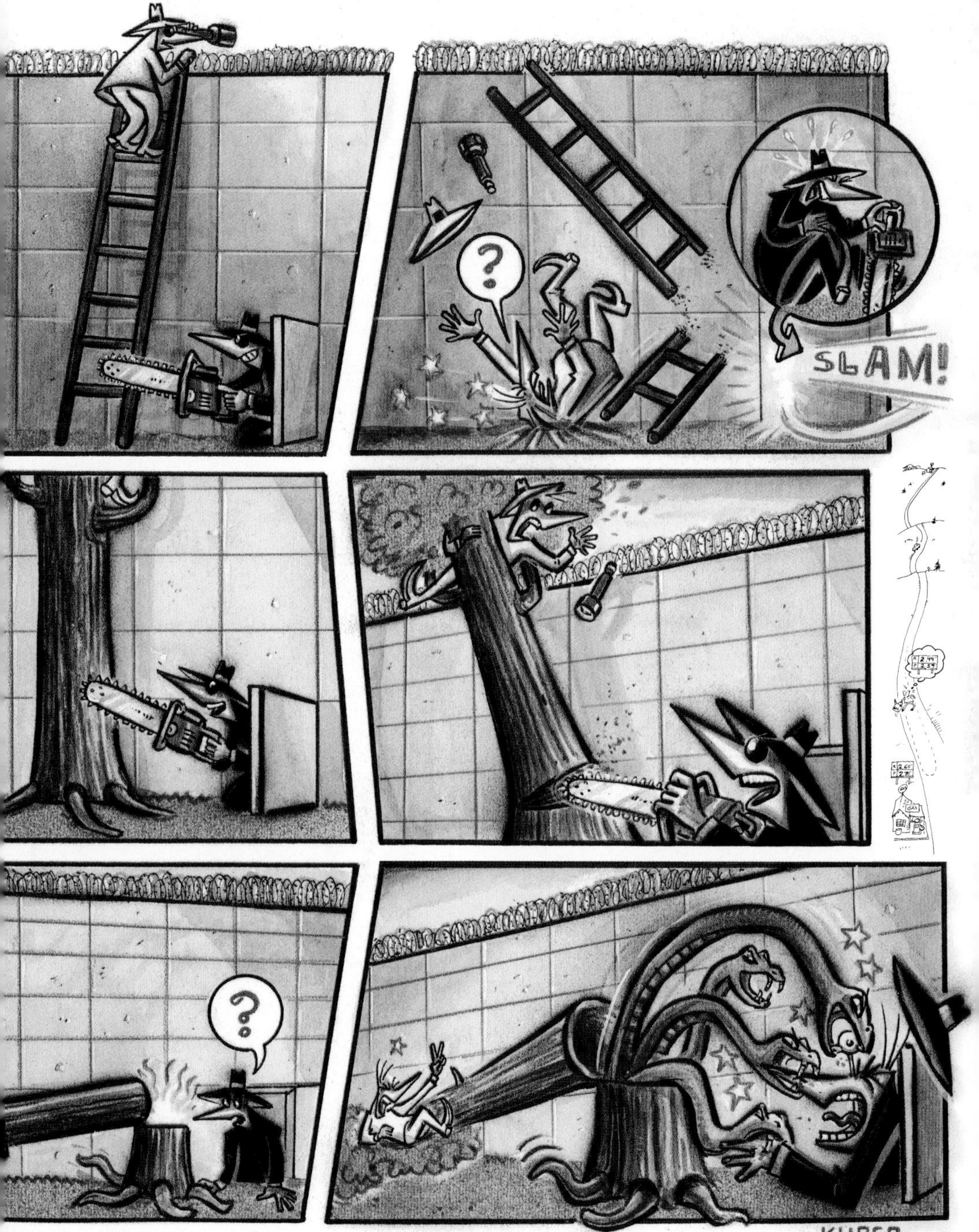
?
SLAM!
?
KUPER

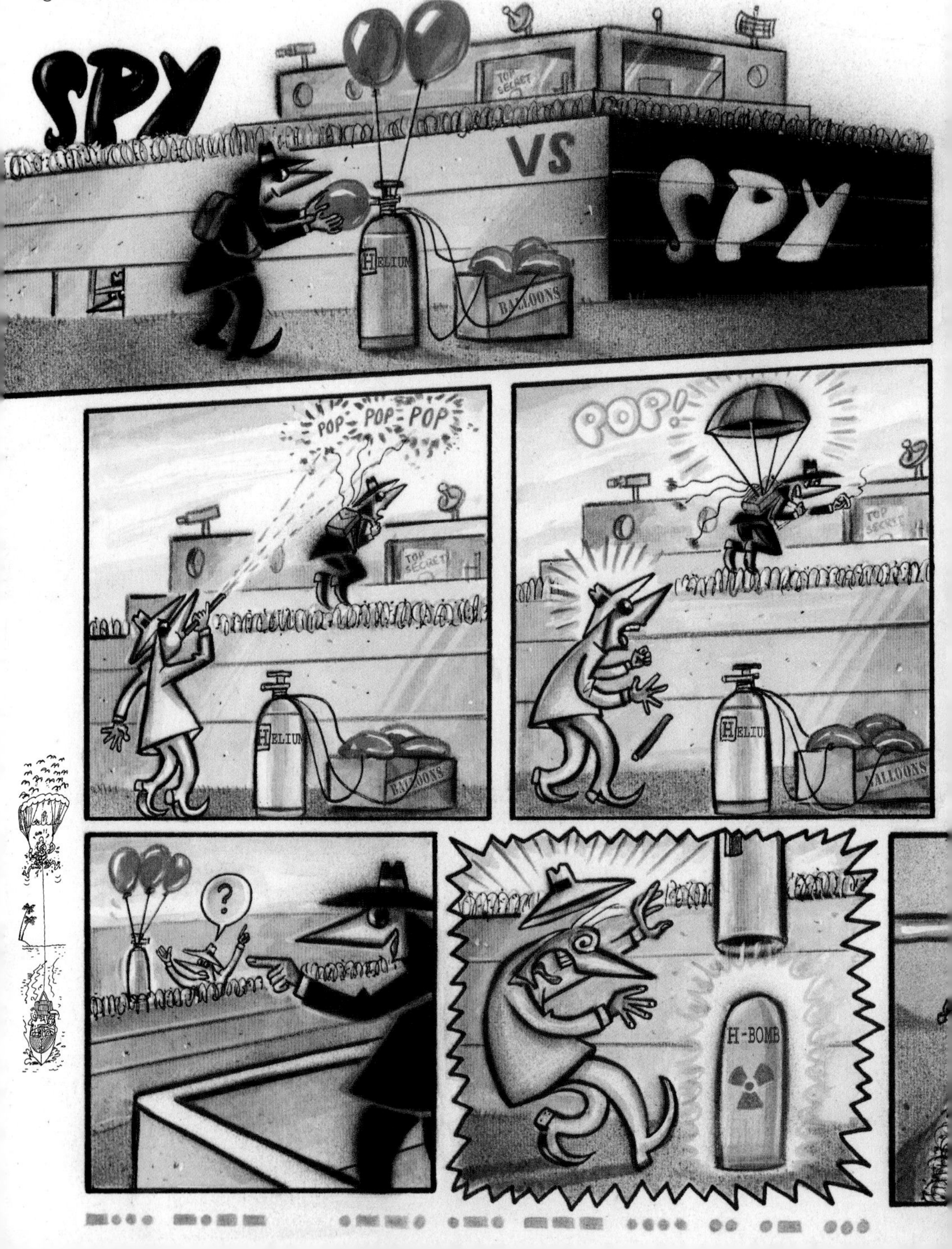
SPY
VS
SPY
TOP SECRET
HELIUM
BALLOONS
POP POP POP
TOP SECRET
HELIUM
BALLOONS
POP!
TOP SECRET
HELIUM
BALLOONS
?
H-BOMB

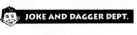

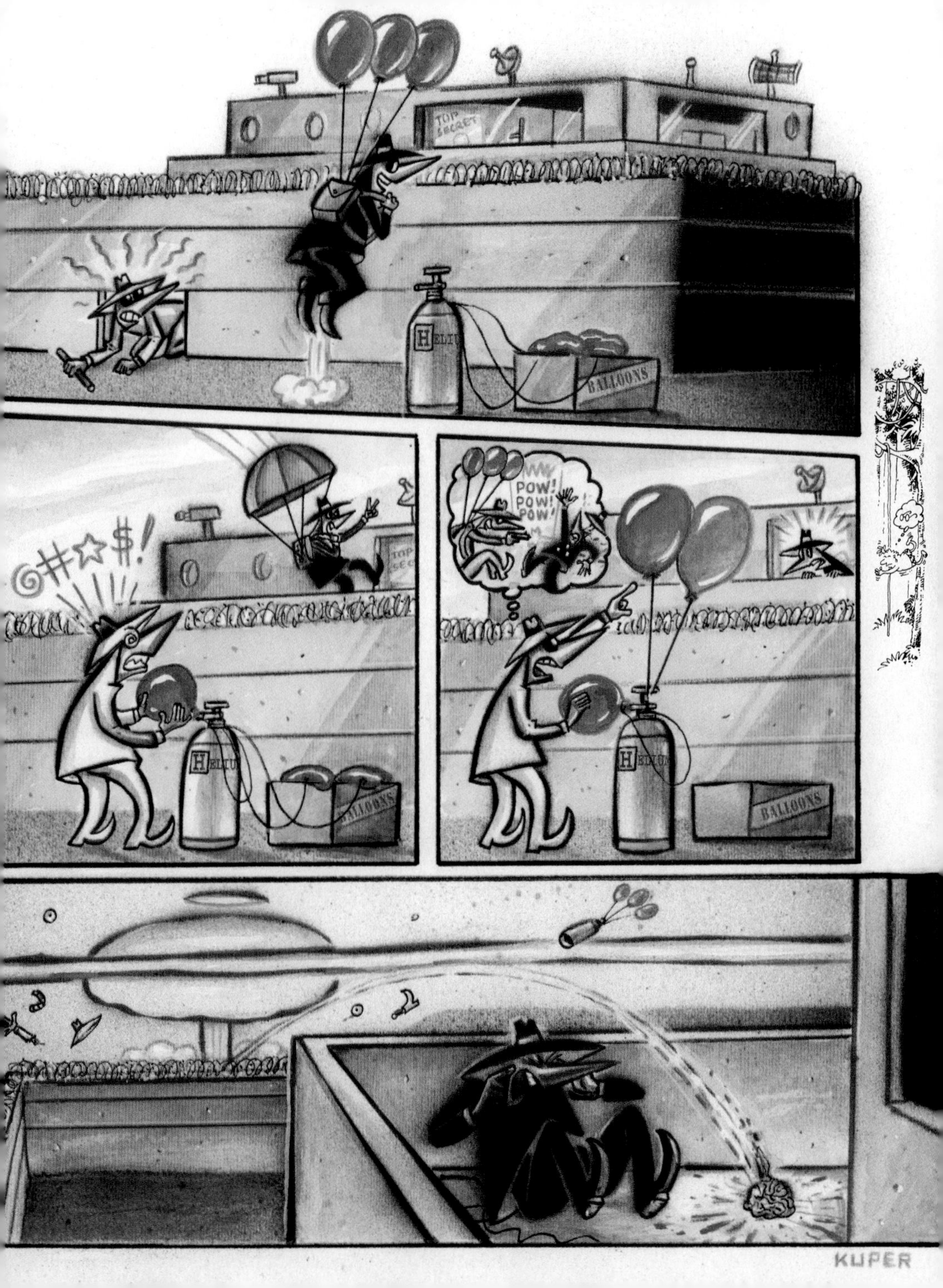
TOP SECRET
BALLOONS
POW!
POW!
POW!
KUPER

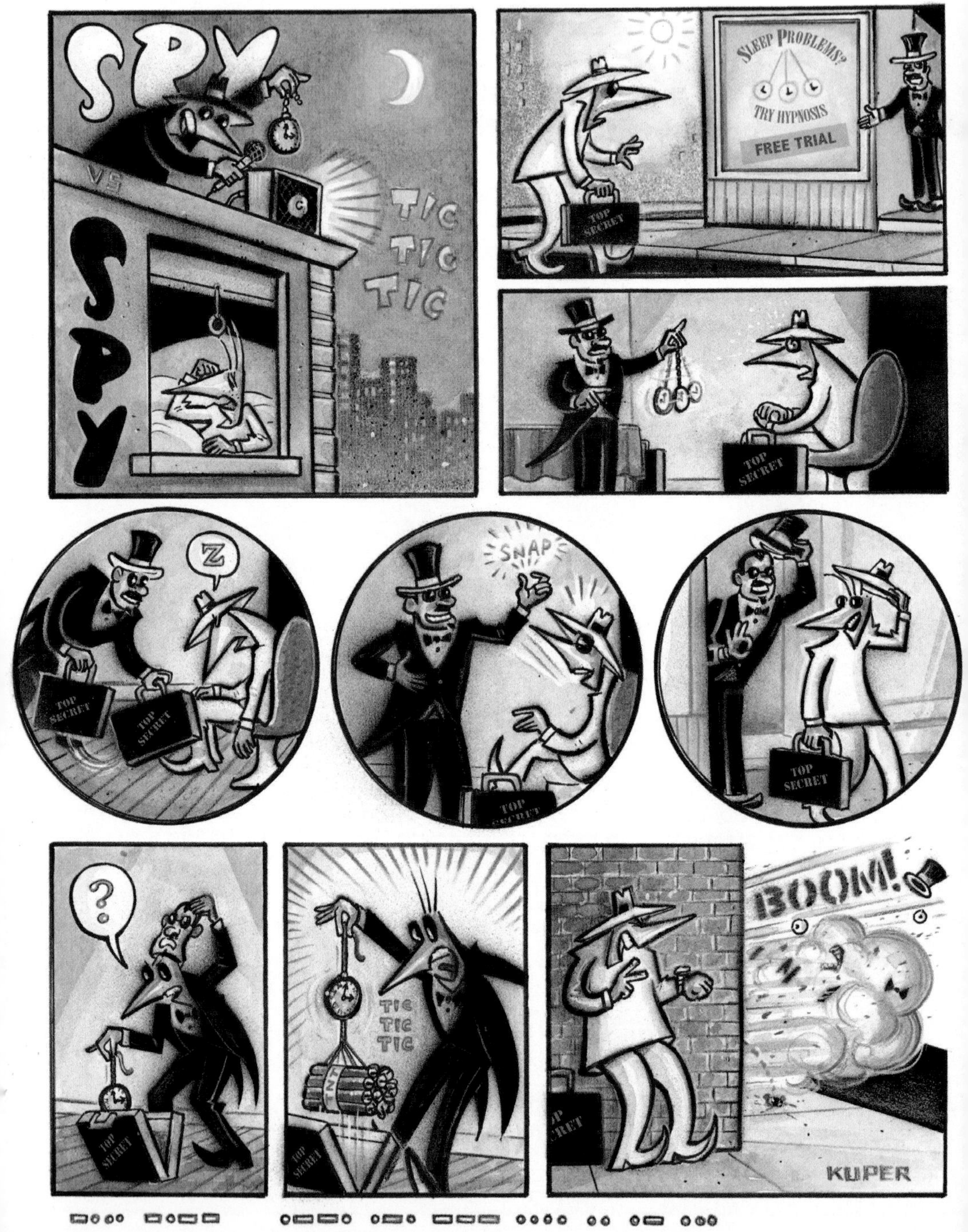
SPY
VS
SPY
TIC
TIC
TIC
SLEEP PROBLEMS?
TRY HYPNOSIS
FREE TRIAL
TOP SECRET
TOP SECRET
Z
TOP SECRET
TOP SECRET
SNAP
TOP SECRET
TOP SECRET
?
TOP SECRET
TIC
TIC
TIC
TOP SECRET
BOOM!
KUPER

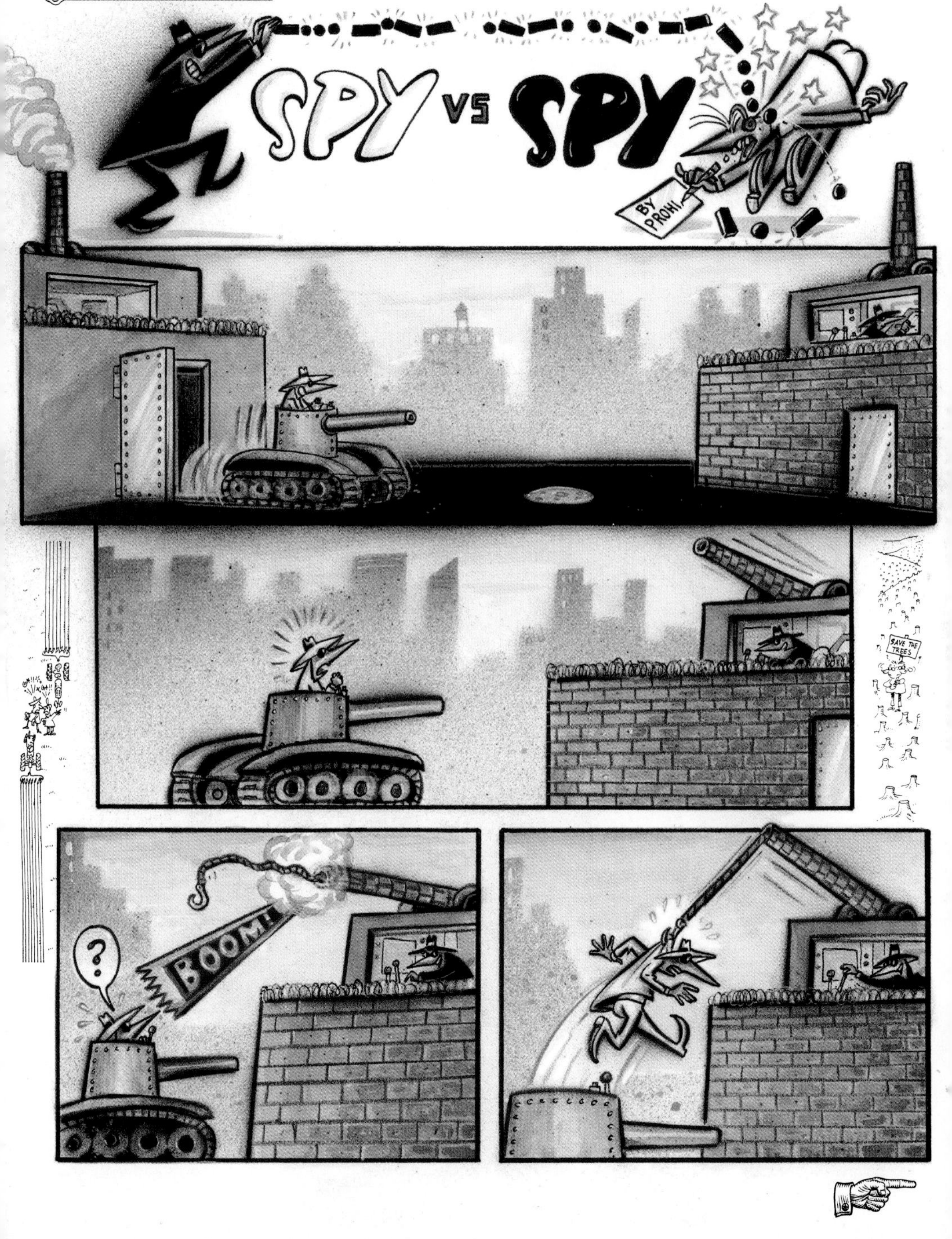
SPY vs SPY
BY PROHIAS
SAVE THE TREES
?
BOOM!

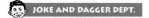

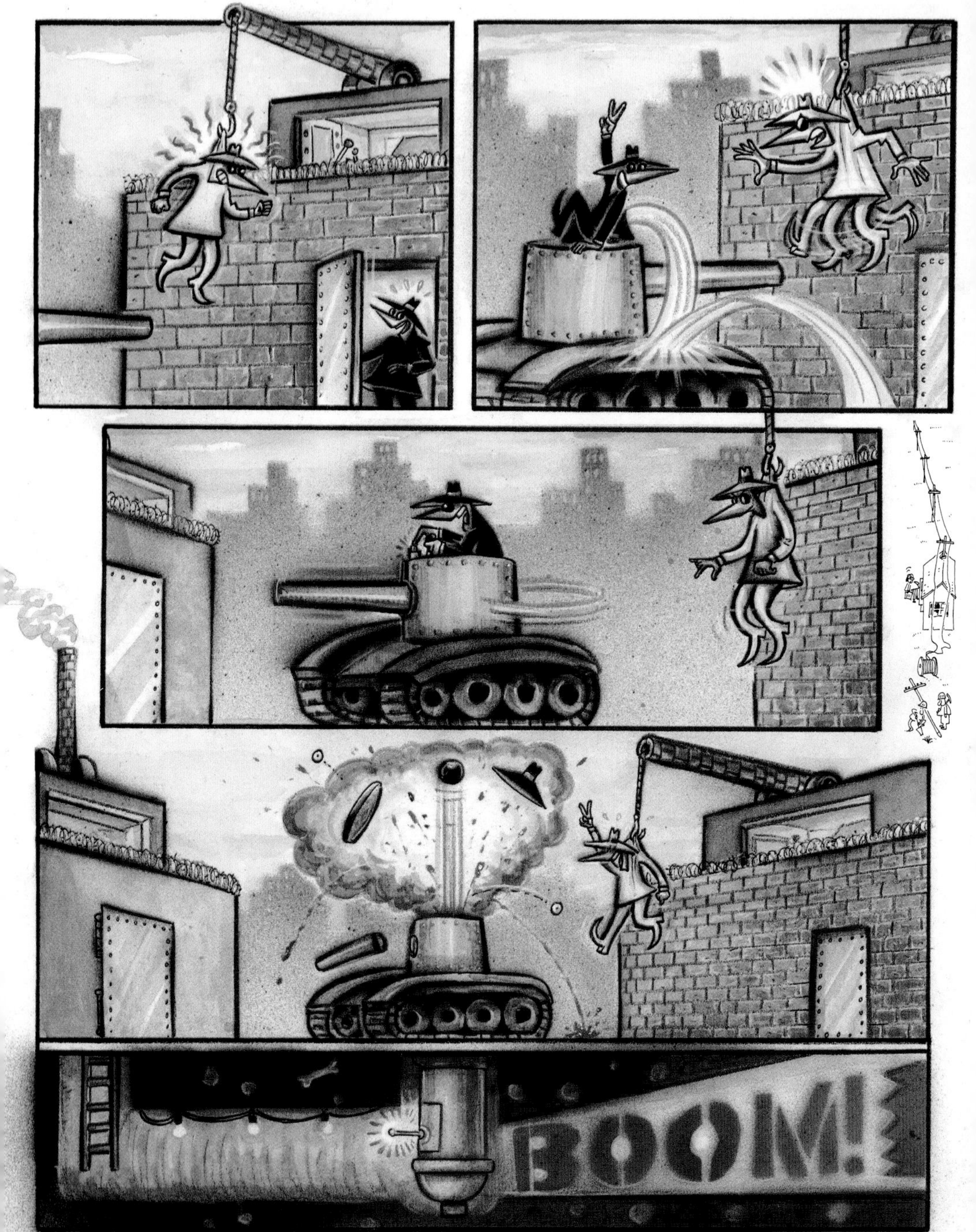
BOOM!
KUPER

JOKE AND DAGGER DEPT.

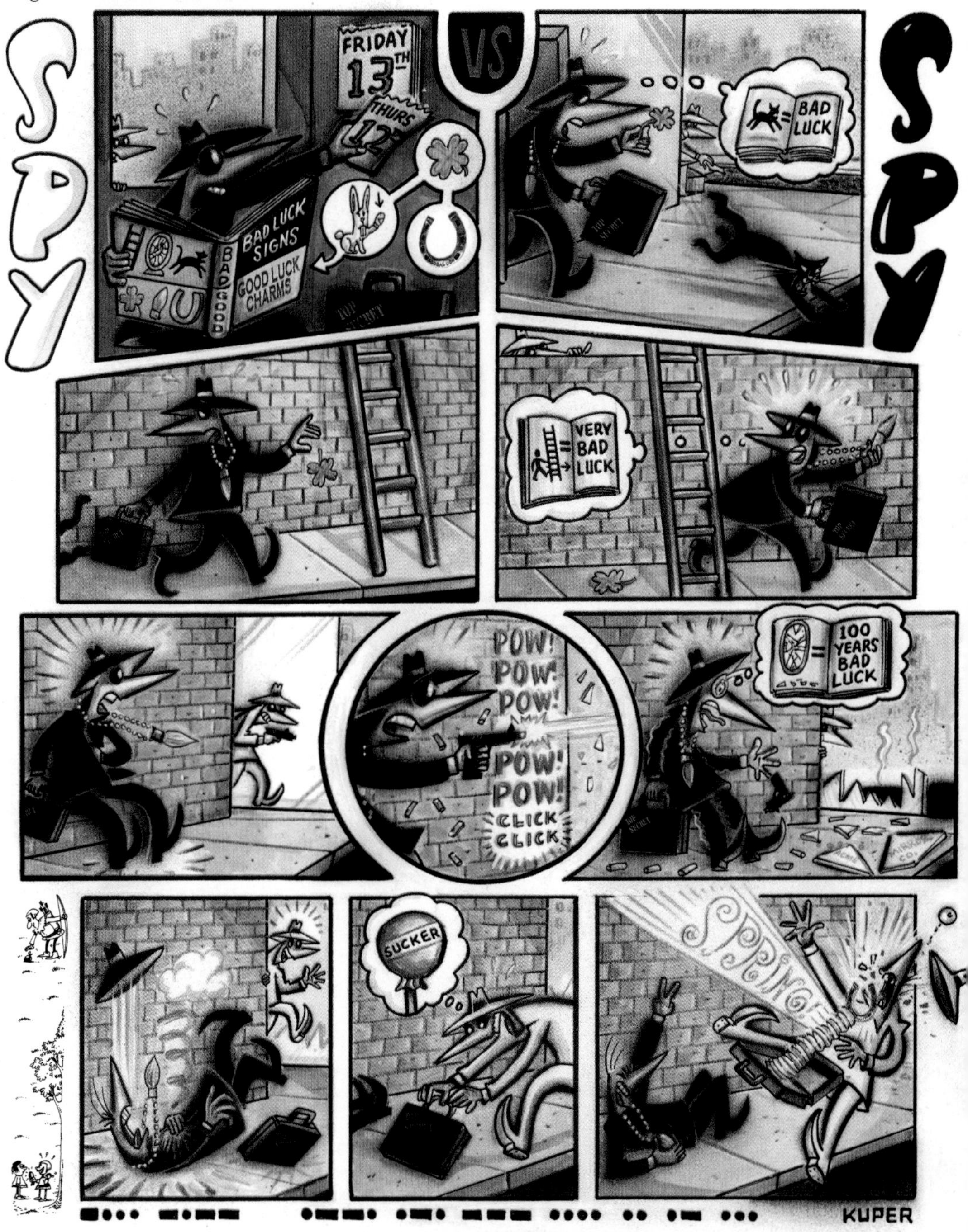
SPY
VS
SPY
FRIDAY 13TH
THURS 12
BAD LUCK SIGNS
GOOD LUCK CHARMS
BAD
GOOD
TOP SECRET
= BAD LUCK
TOP SECRET
= VERY BAD LUCK
POW! POW! POW!
POW! POW!
CLICK CLICK
= 100 YEARS BAD LUCK
MIRROR CO.
SUCKER
SPRING!
KUPER

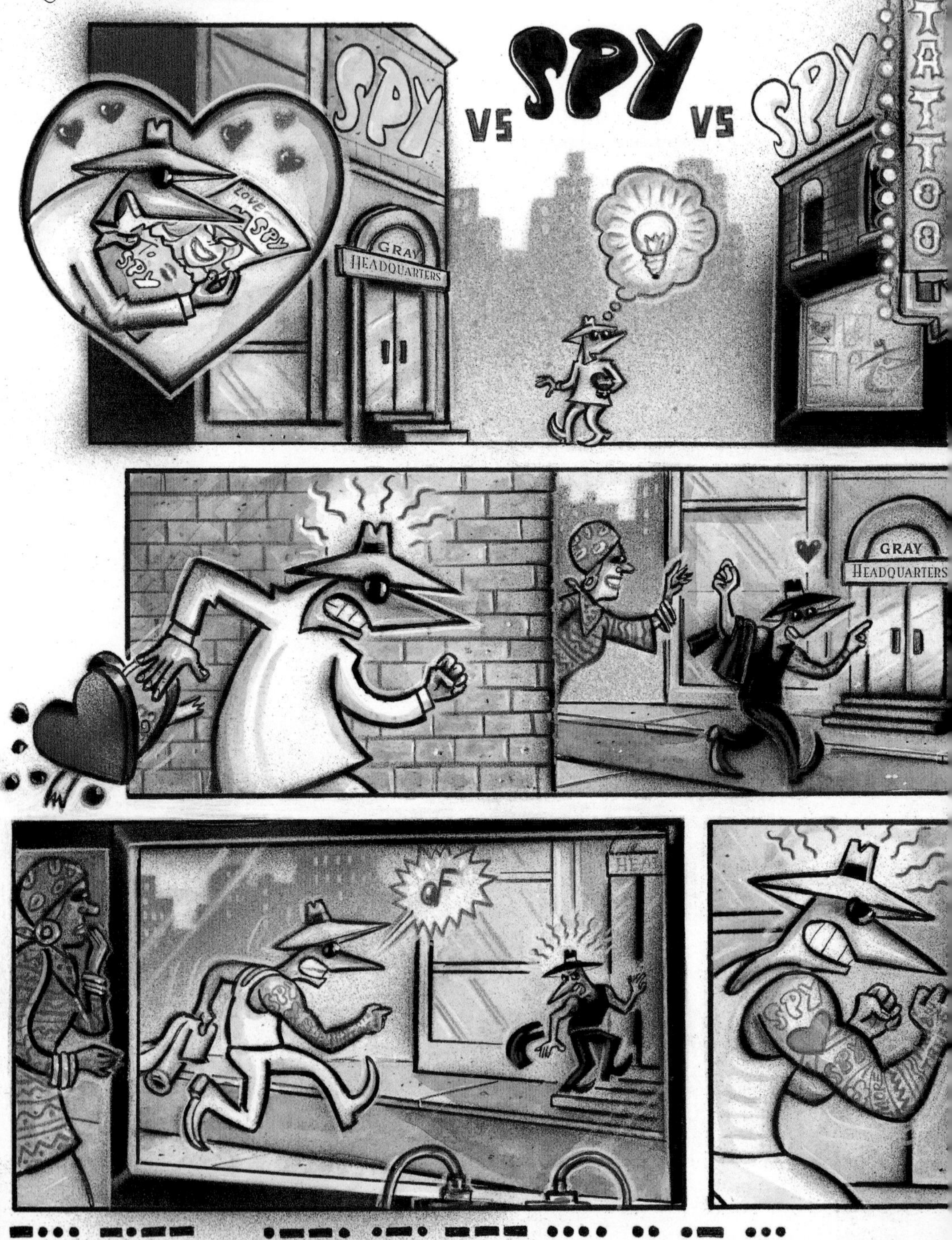
SPY
VS
SPY
VS
SPY
TATTOO
LOVE SPY
TO SPY
GRAY
HEADQUARTERS
GRAY
HEADQUARTERS
SPY

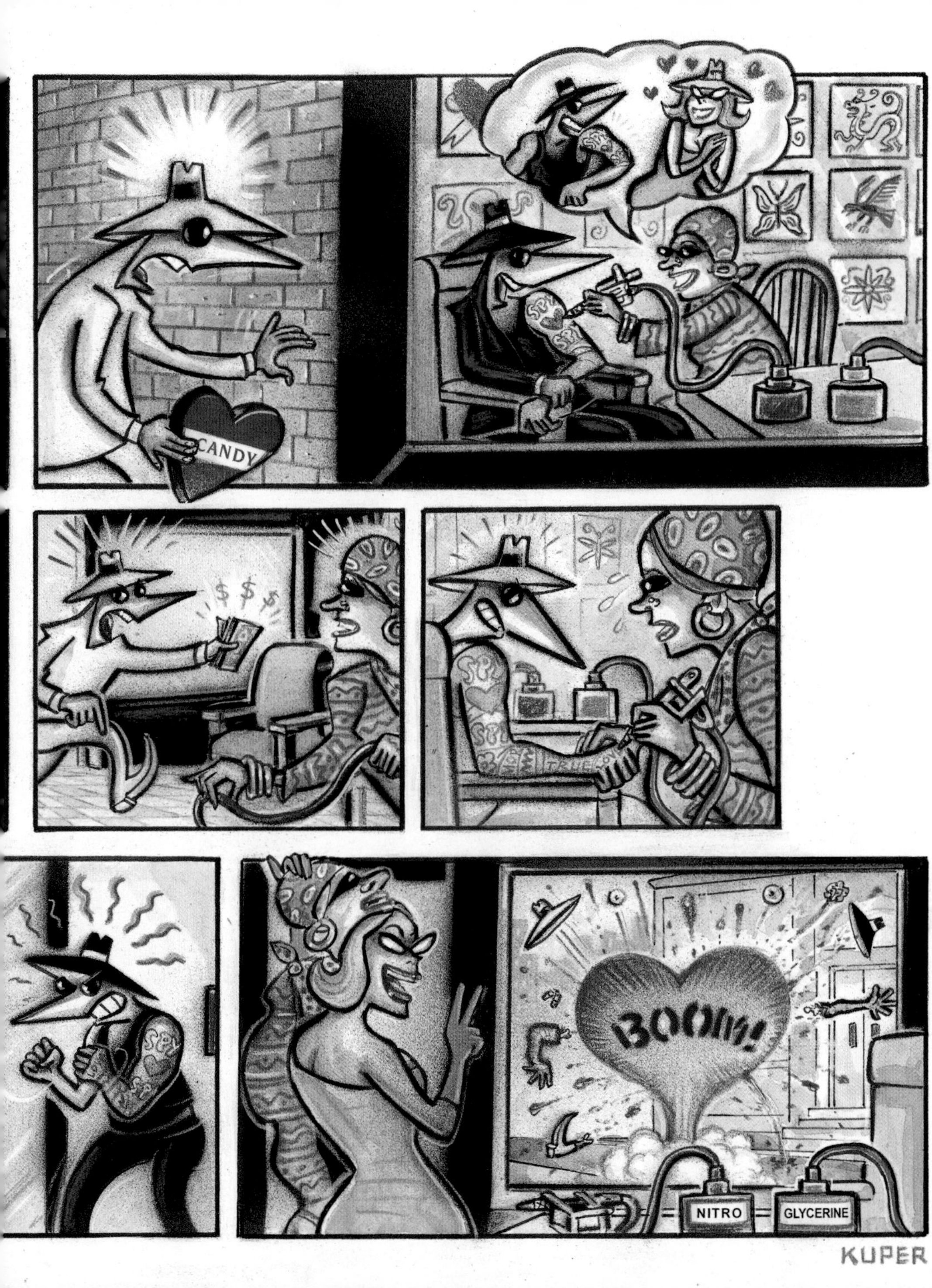
CANDY
$ $ $
BOOM!
NITRO
GLYCERINE
KUPER

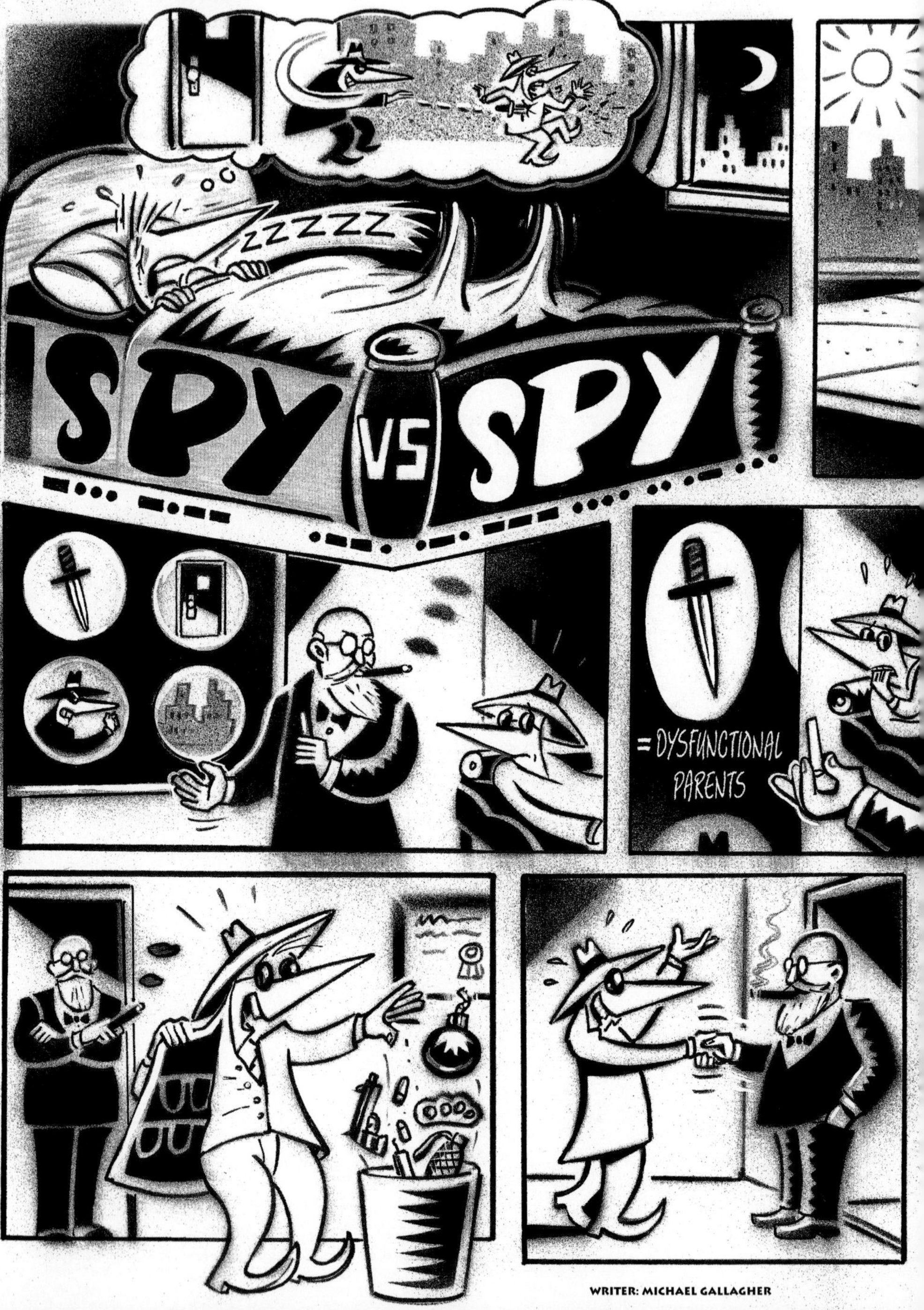
ZZZZZZ
SPY VS SPY
= DYSFUNCTIONAL PARENTS

WRITER: MICHAEL GALLAGHER

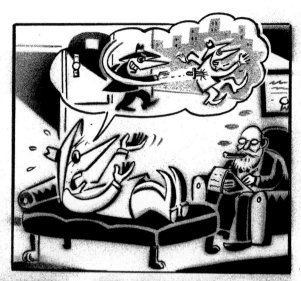

= REPRESSED SEXUALITY

= INNER CHILD'S ALTER-EGO

= SOCIAL, RELIGIOUS, AND ECONOMIC STRESS

KUPER

JOKE AND DAGGER DEPT.

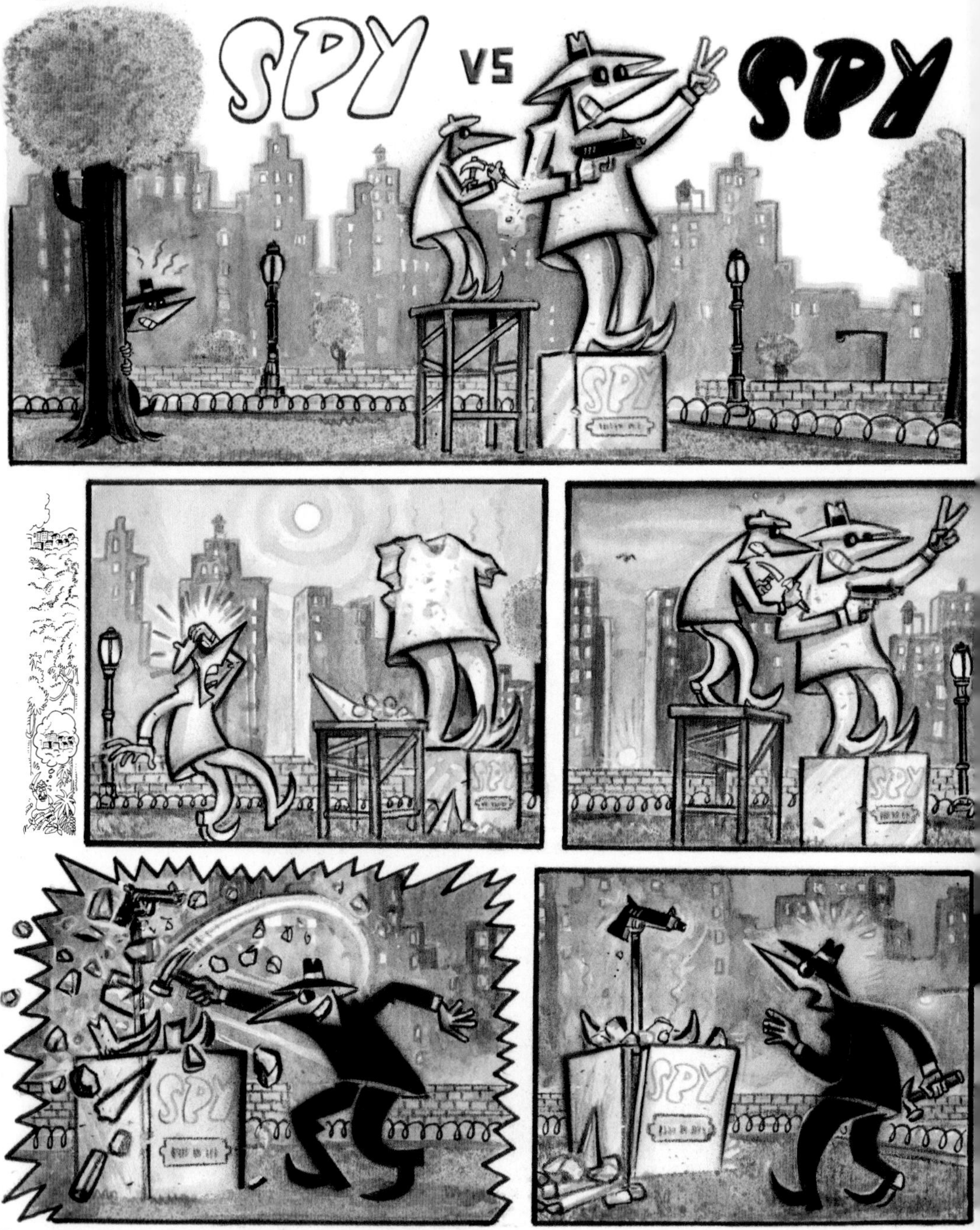
SPY VS SPY
SPY
SPY
SPY
SPY
SPY

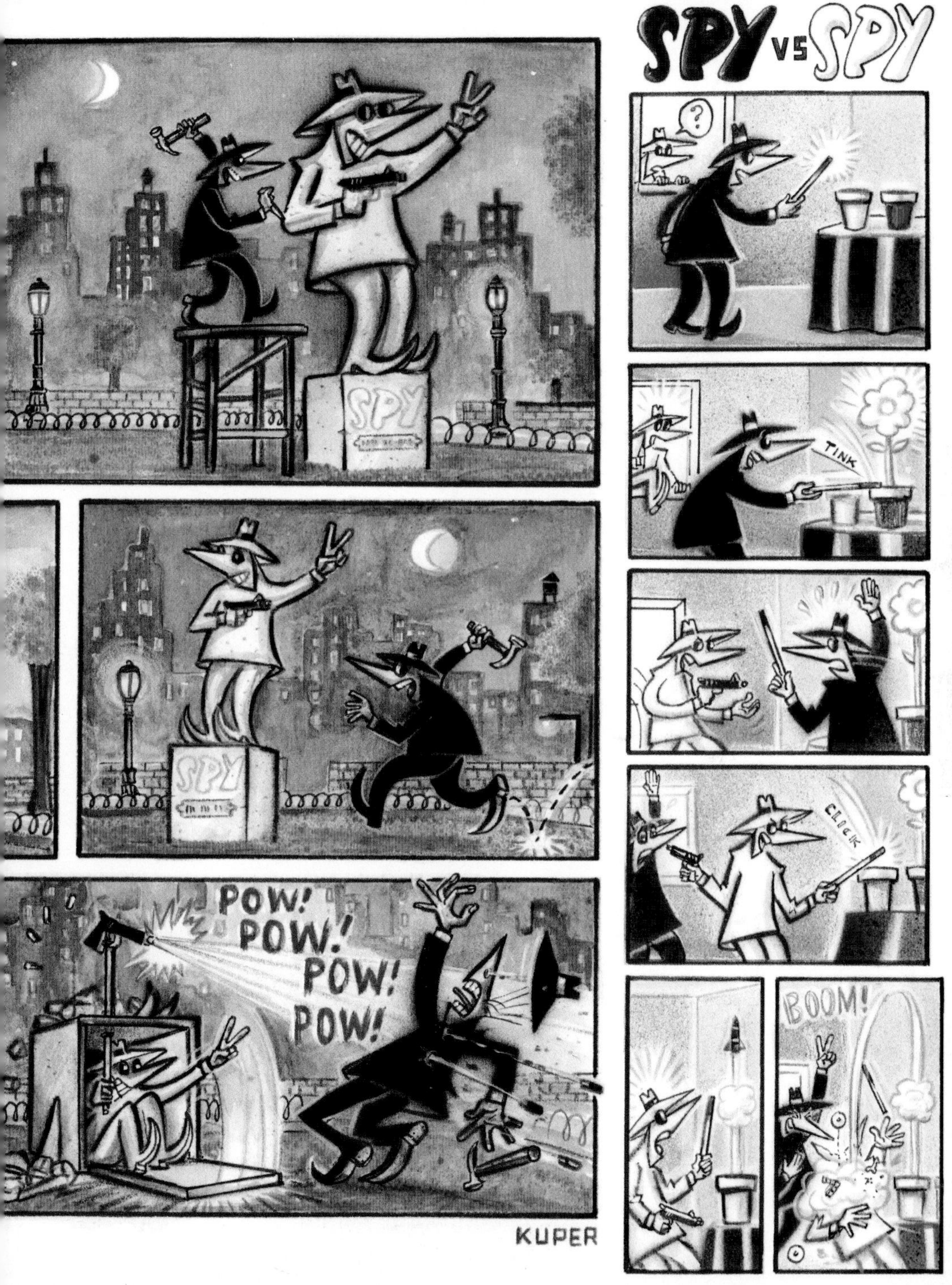
SPY vs SPY
?
TINK
CLICK
BOOM!
SPY
SPY
POW!
POW!
POW!
POW!
KUPER

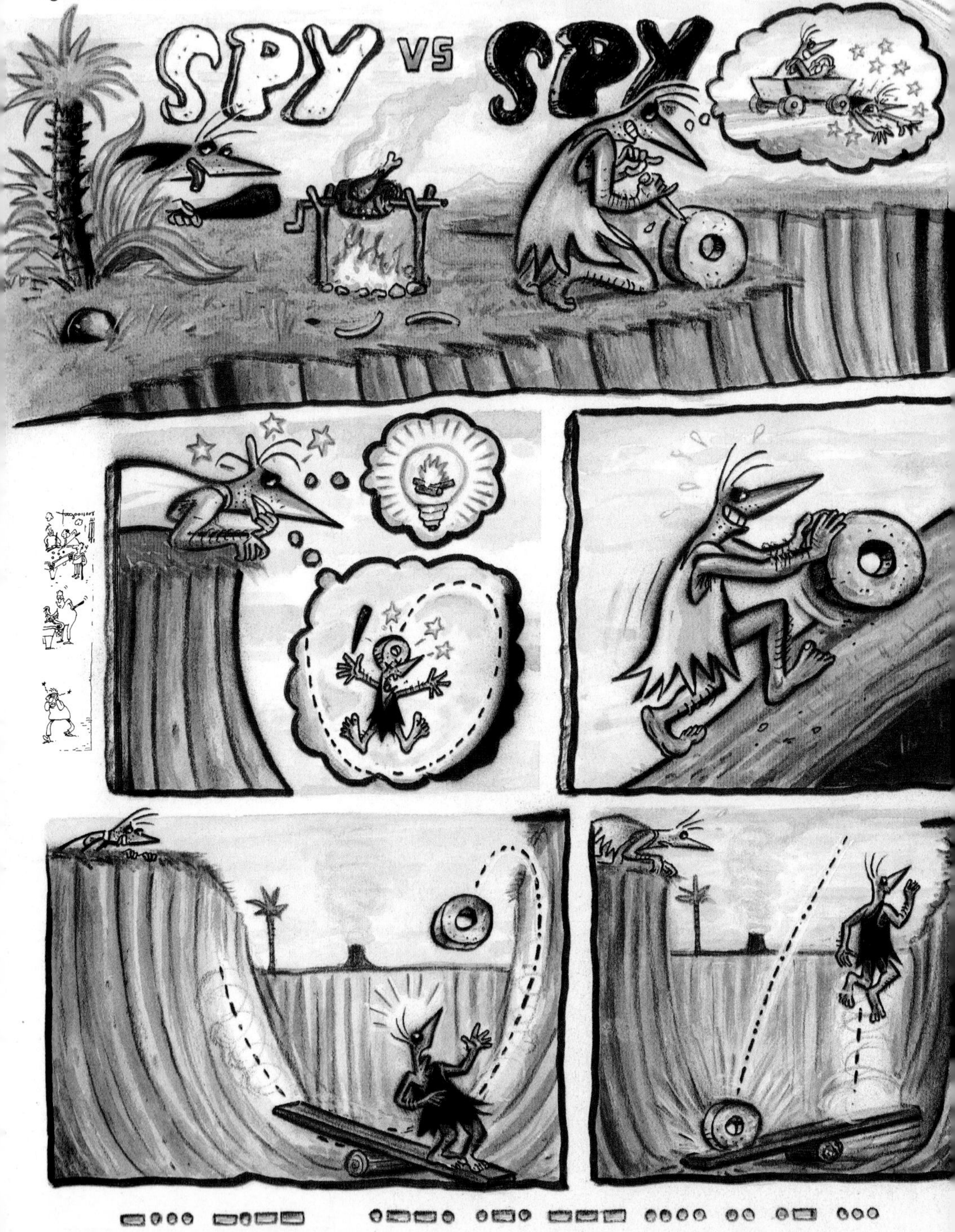
SPY VS SPY

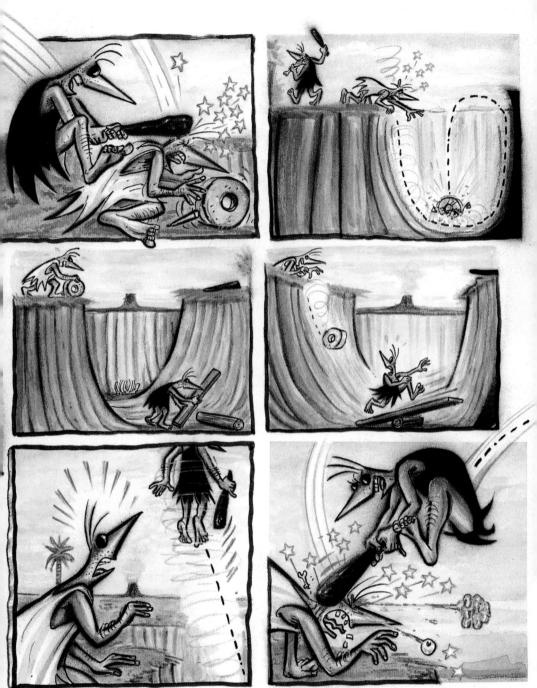

KUPER

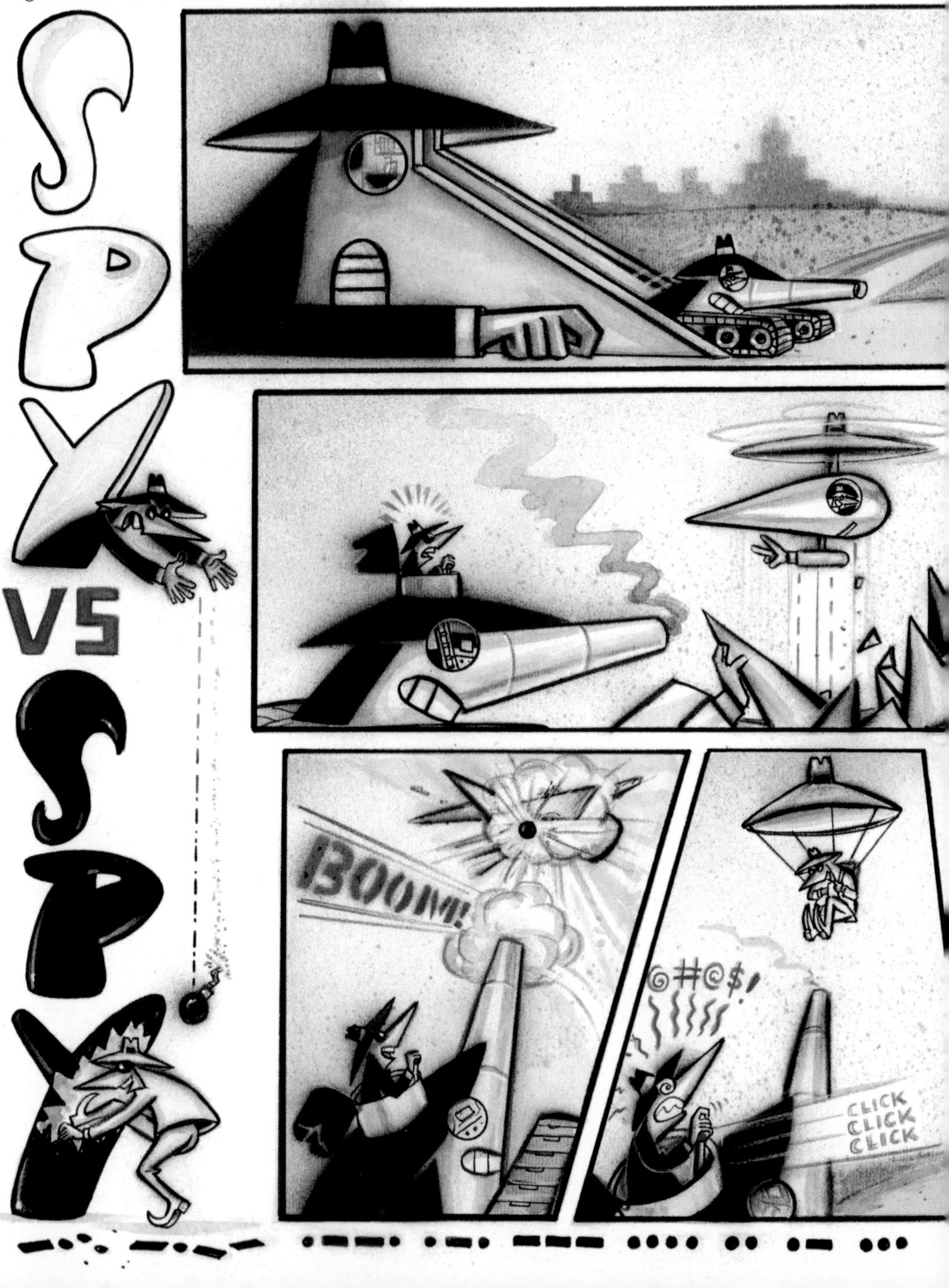
SPY
VS
SPY
BOOM!
@#@$!
CLICK
CLICK
CLICK

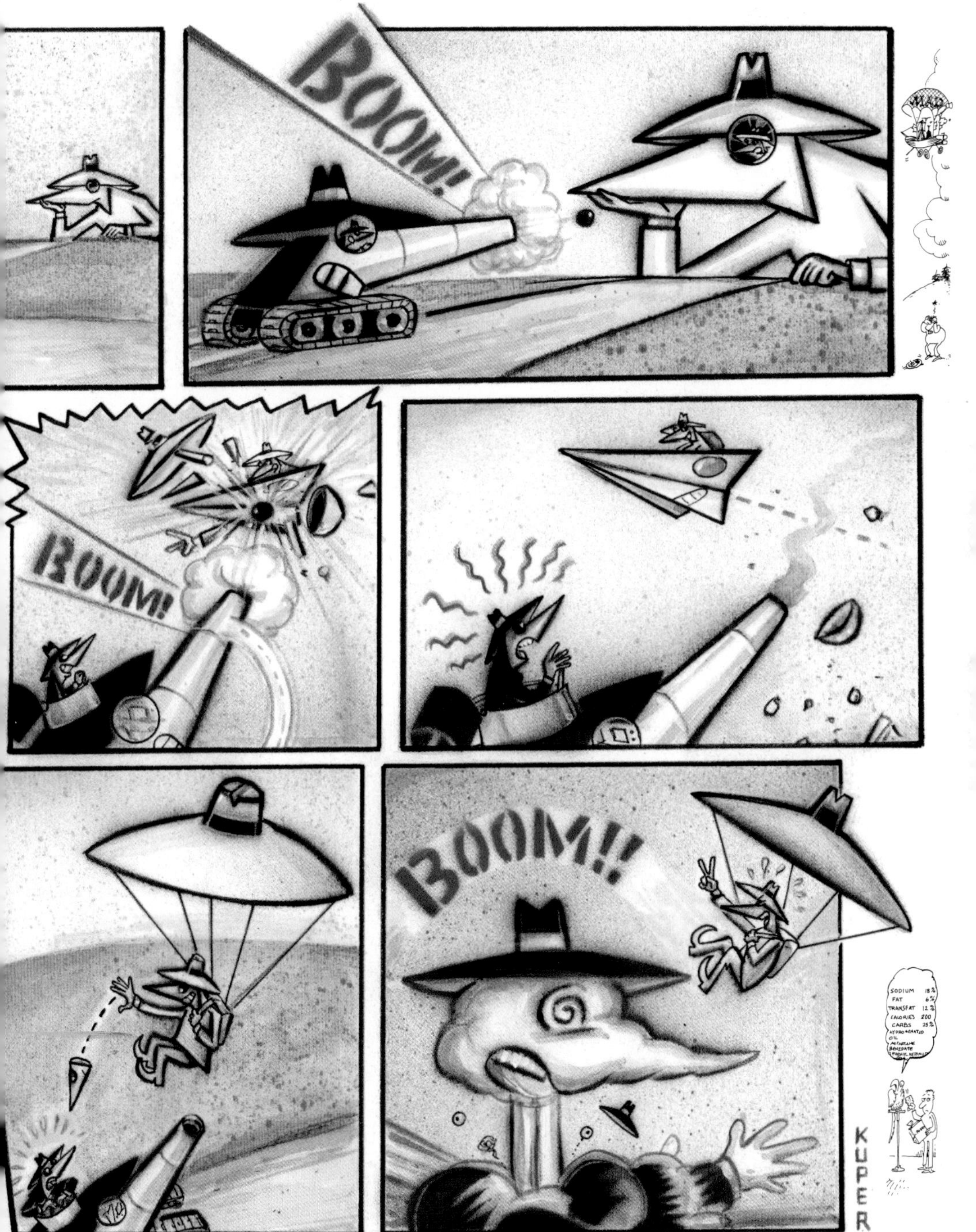
BOOM!
BOOM!
BOOM!!
SODIUM 18%
FAT 6%
TRANSFAT 12%
CALORIES 200
CARBS 25%
KUPER

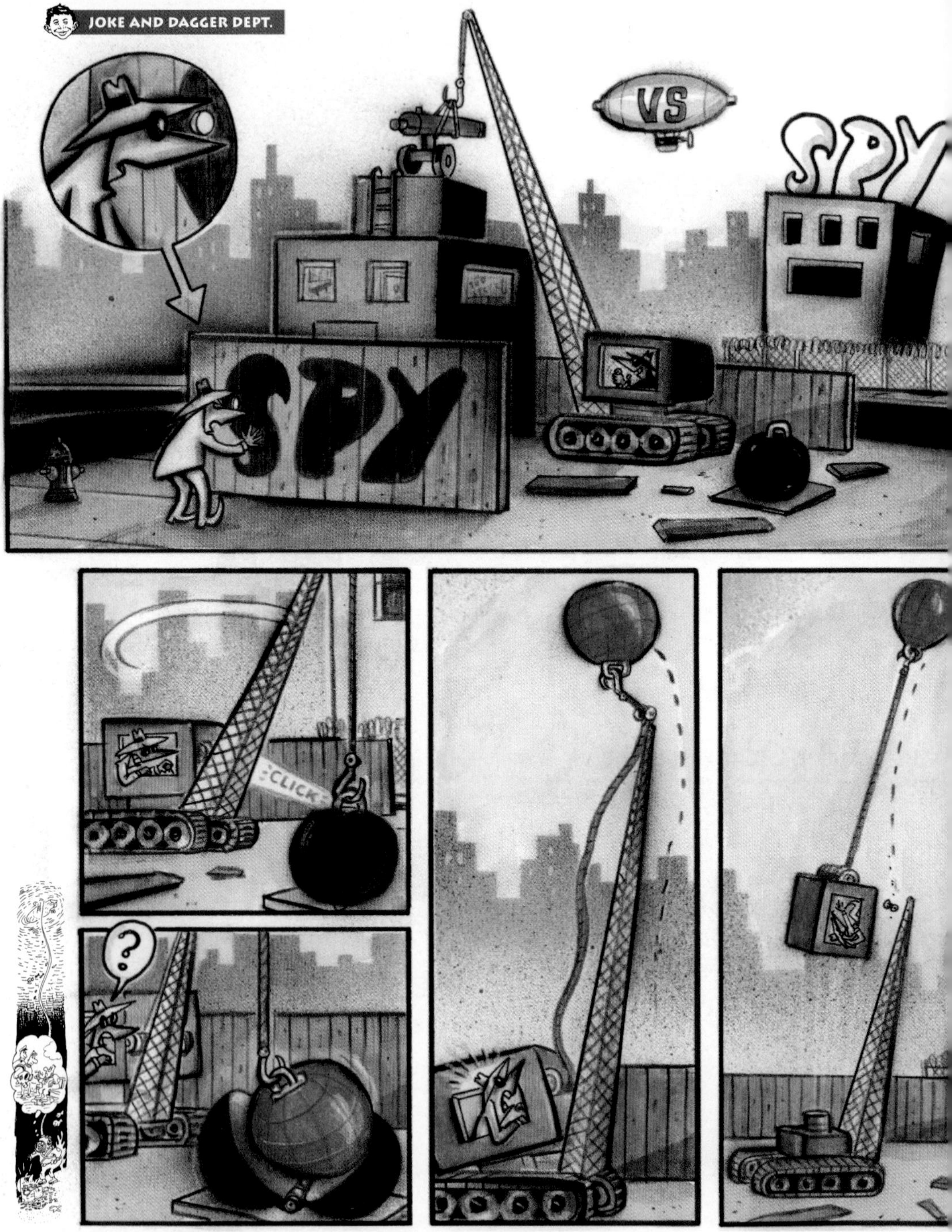
VS
SPY
SPY
CLICK
?

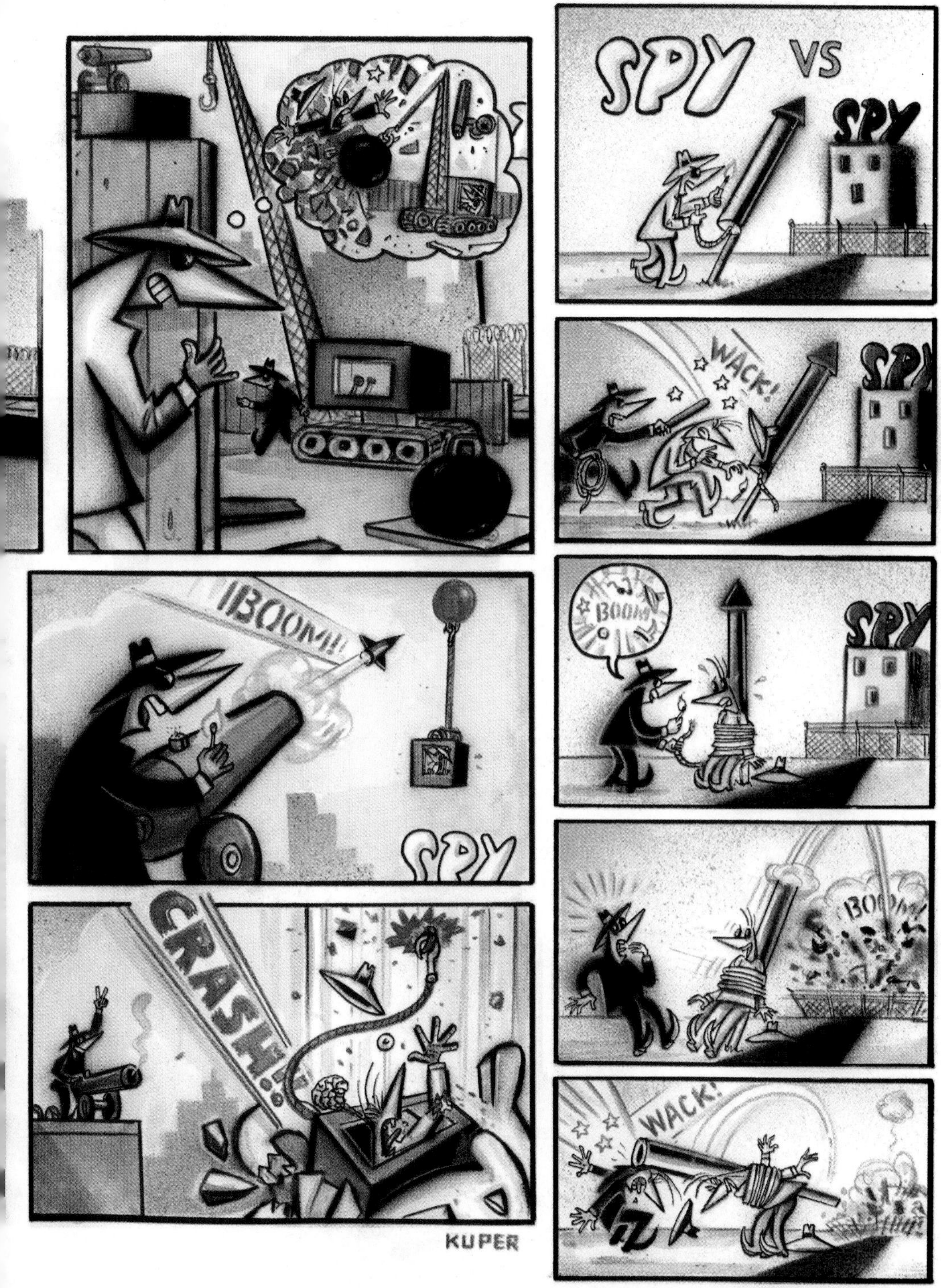

SPY VS SPY
WACK!
BOOM
BOOM!
WACK!
BOOM!!
SPY
CRASH!
KUPER

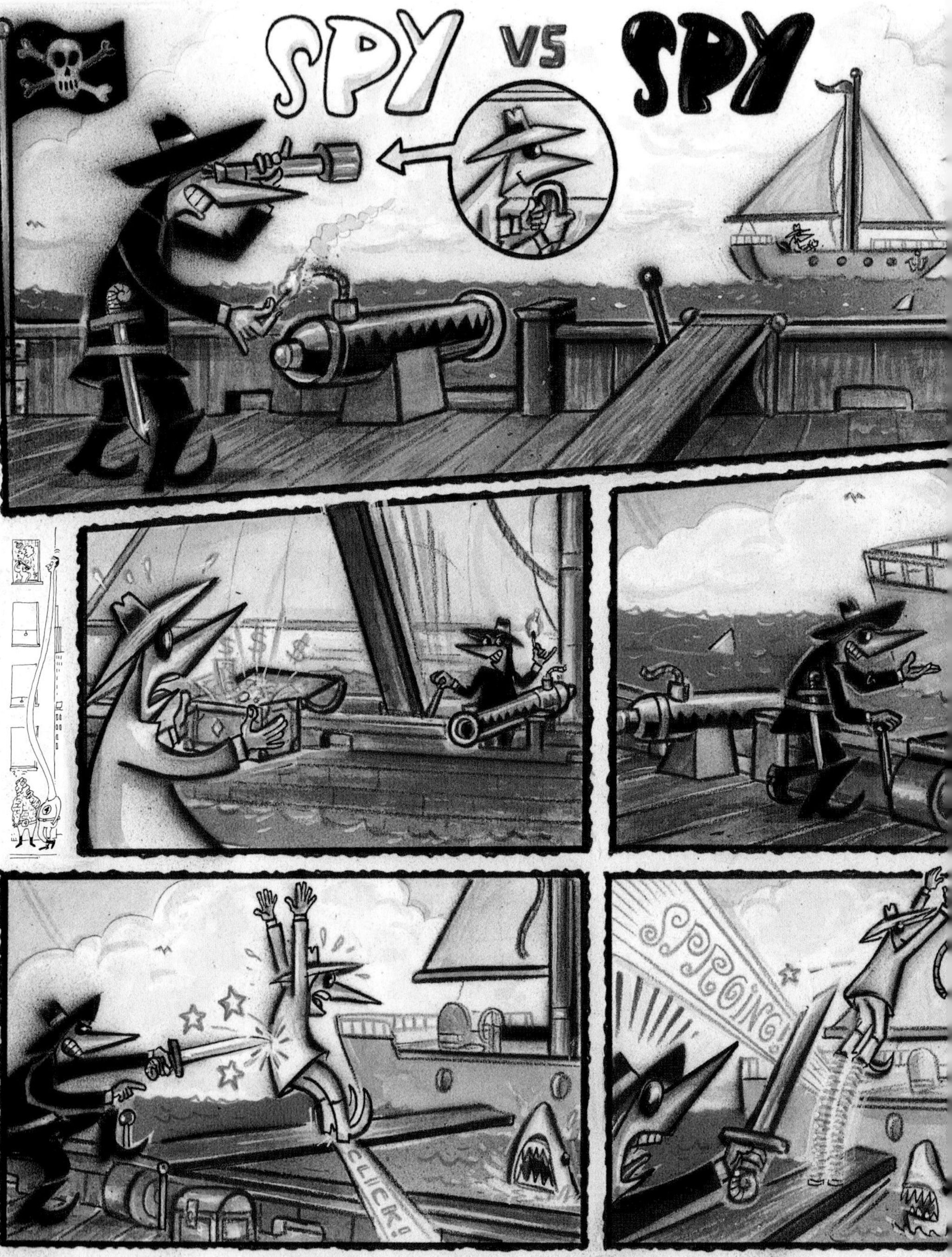
SPY VS SPY
CLICK!
SPROING!

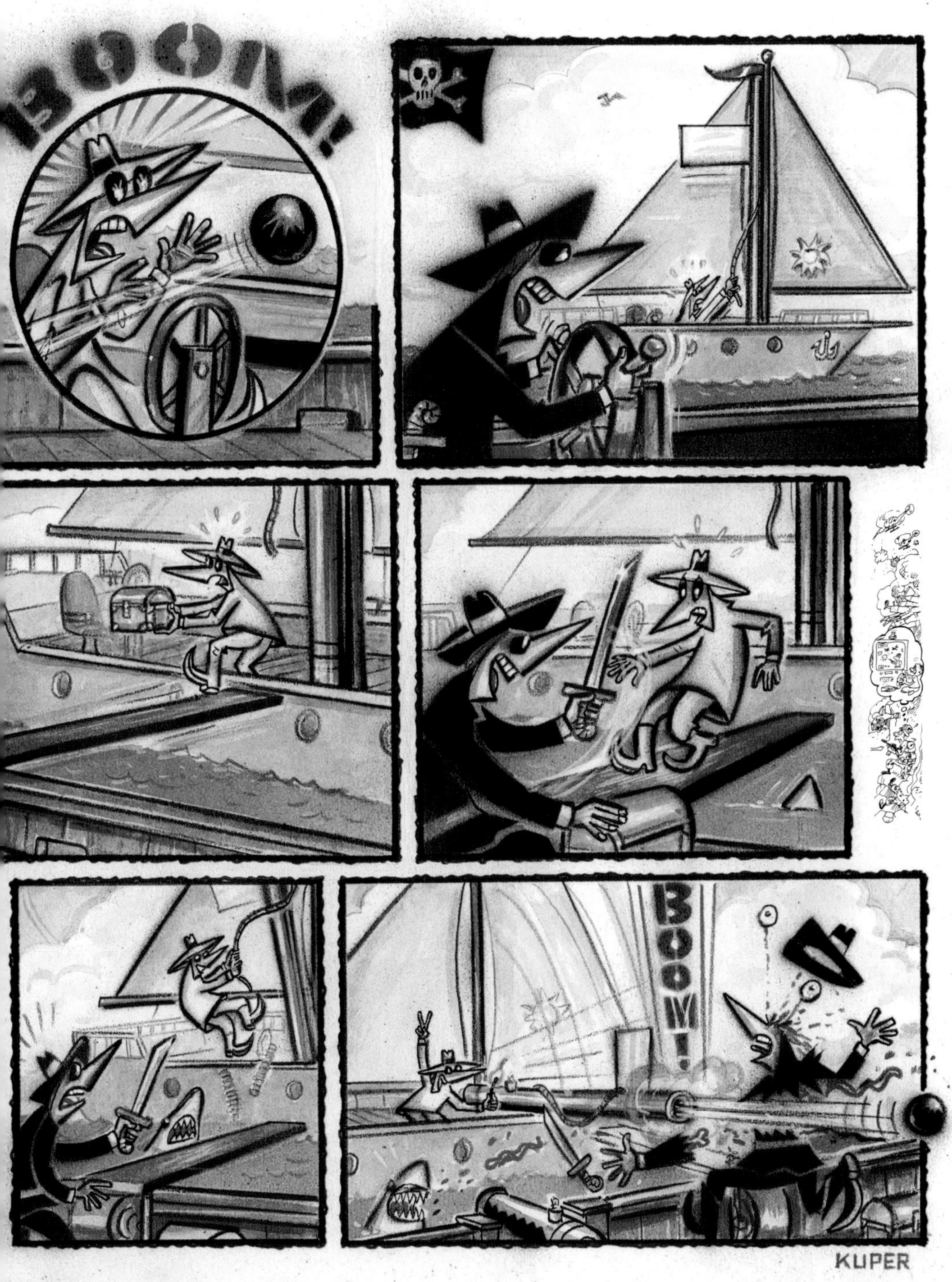
BOOM!
BOOM!
KUPER

JOKE AND DAGGER DEPT.

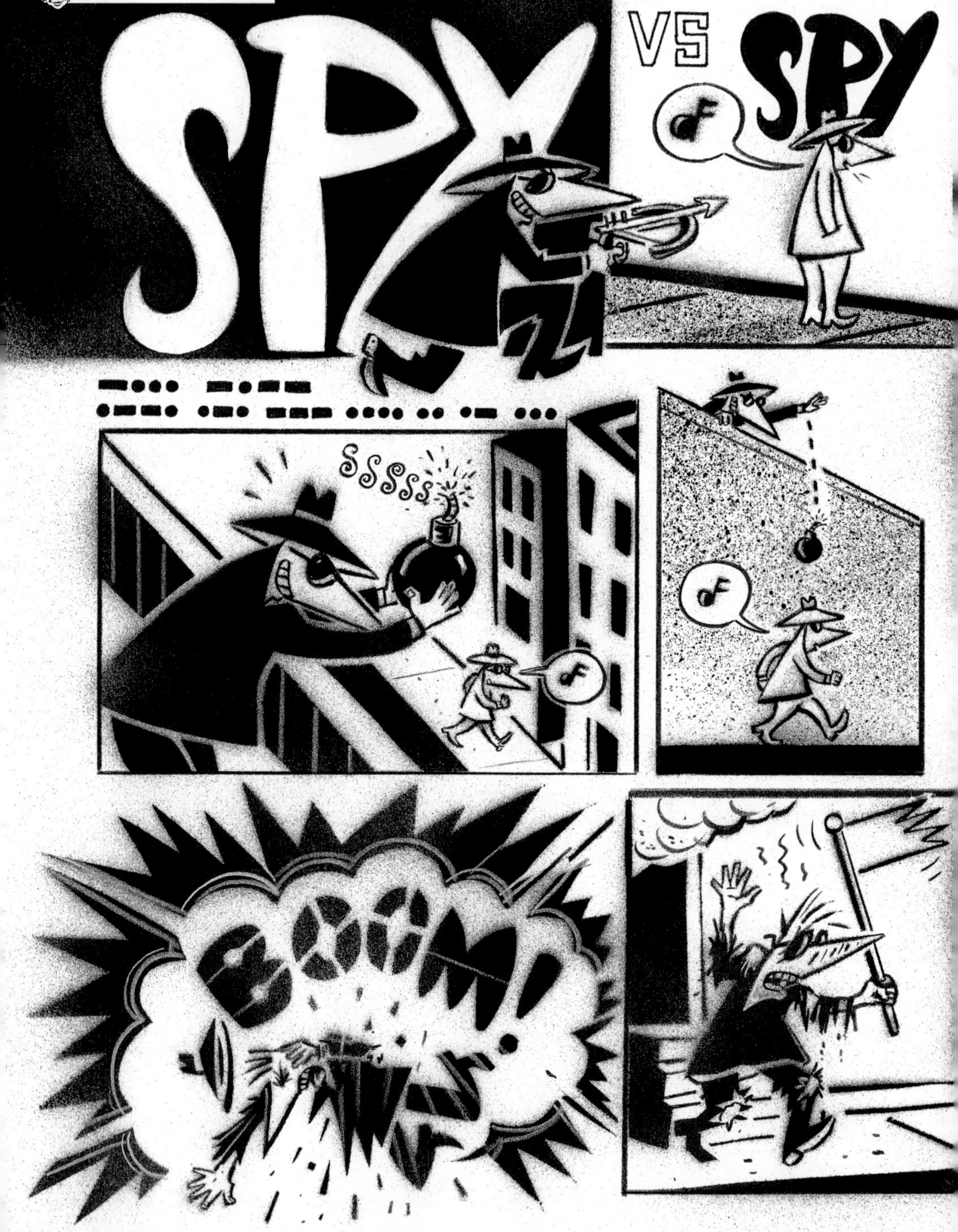
SPY VS SPY
SSSSS
BOOM!

WRITER: BILL JANOCHA

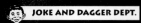

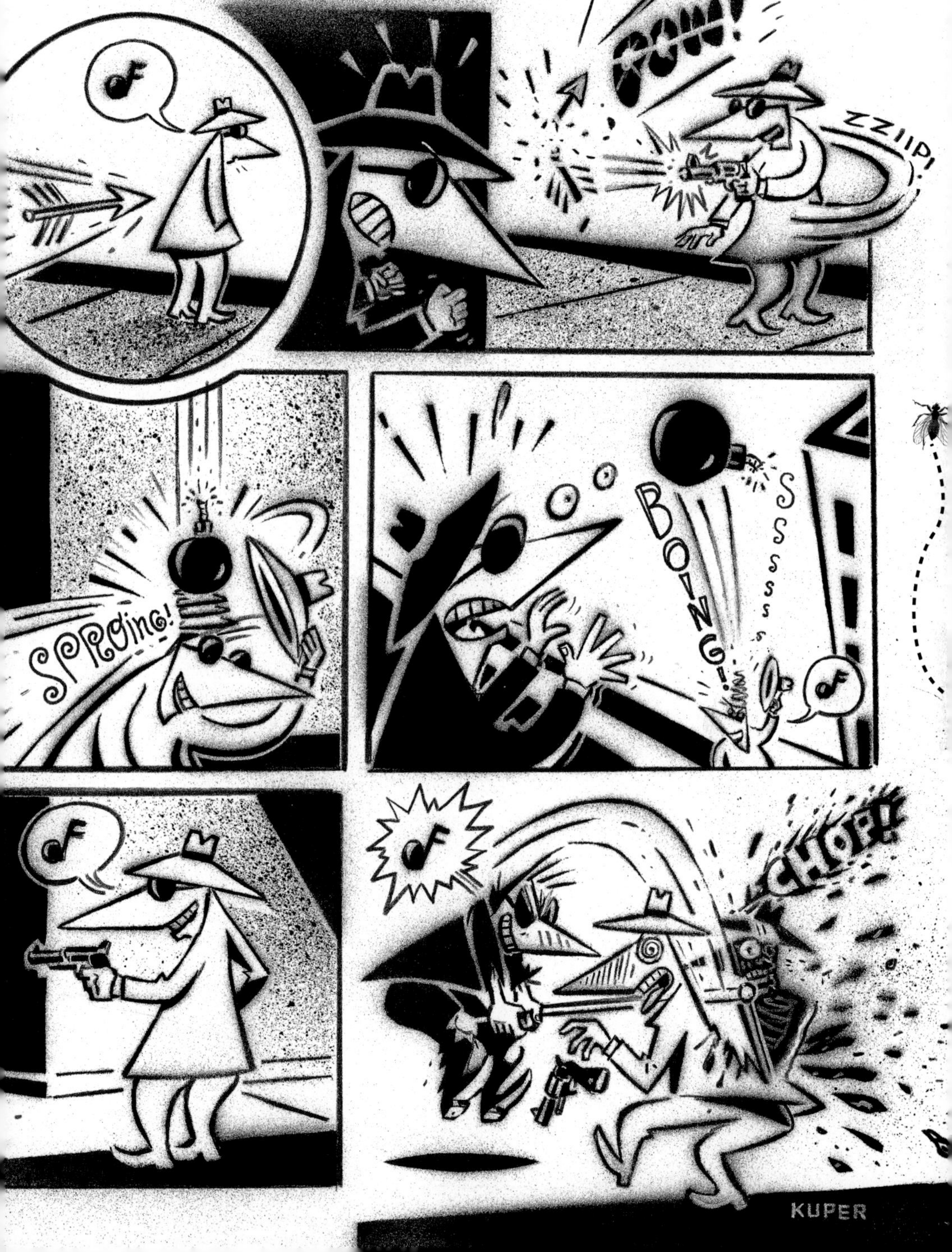
POW!
ZZIIP!
SPPROING!
BOING!
SSSSSS
CHOP!
KUPER

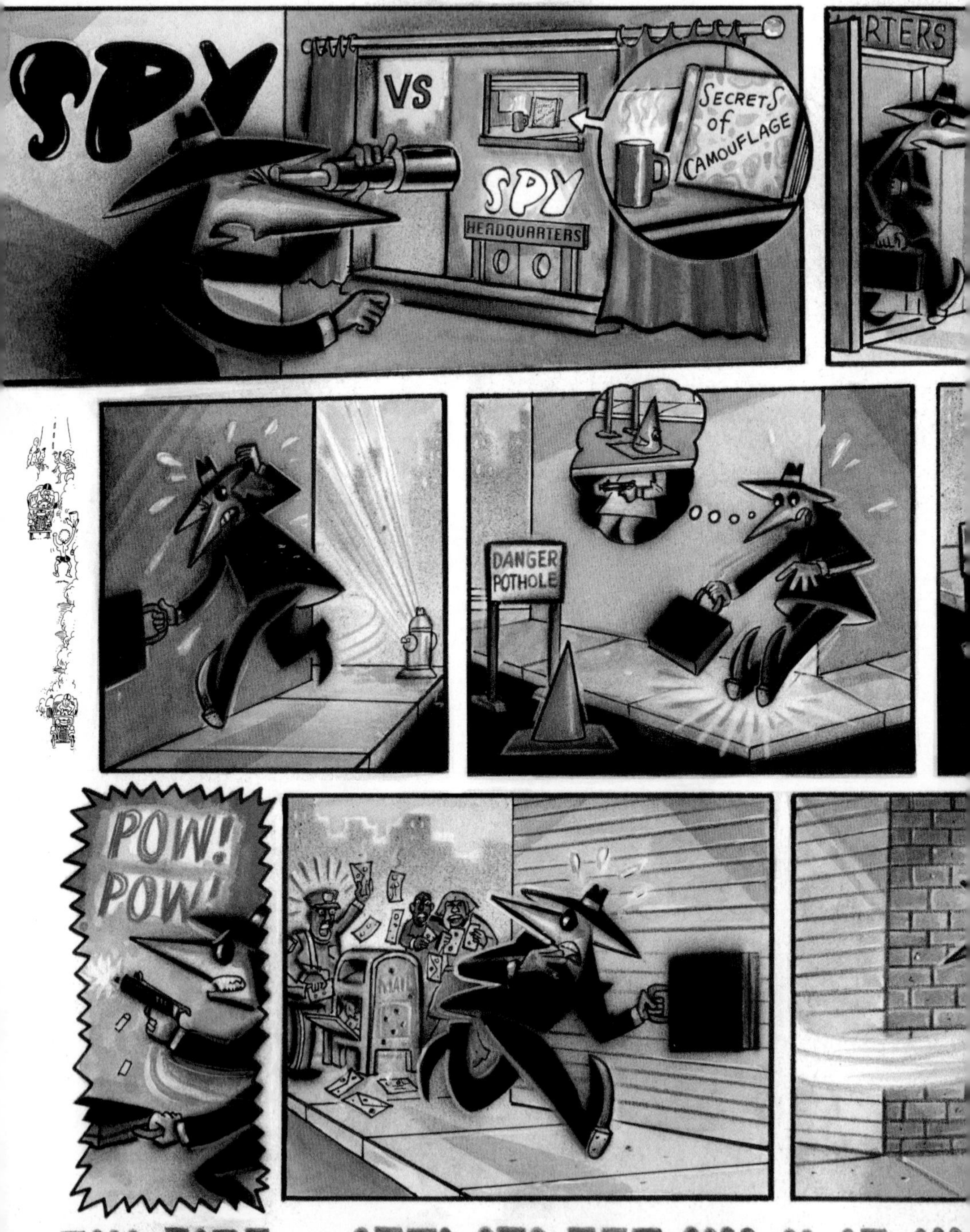
SPY
VS
SPY
HEADQUARTERS
SECRETS of CAMOUFLAGE
RTERS
DANGER POTHOLE
POW! POW!
MAIL

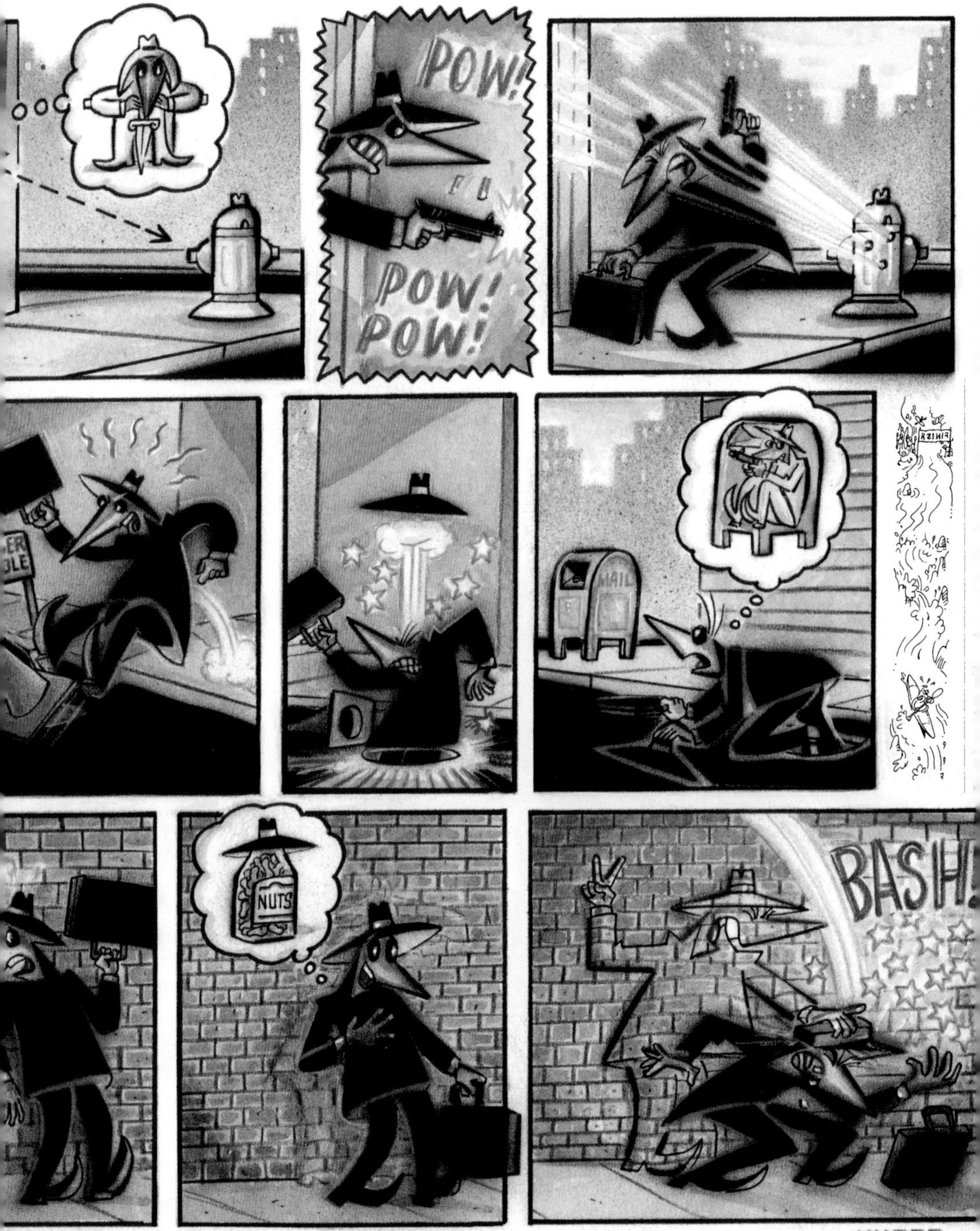
POW!
POW!
POW!
MAIL
NUTS
BASH!
KUPER

JOKE AND DAGGER DEPT.

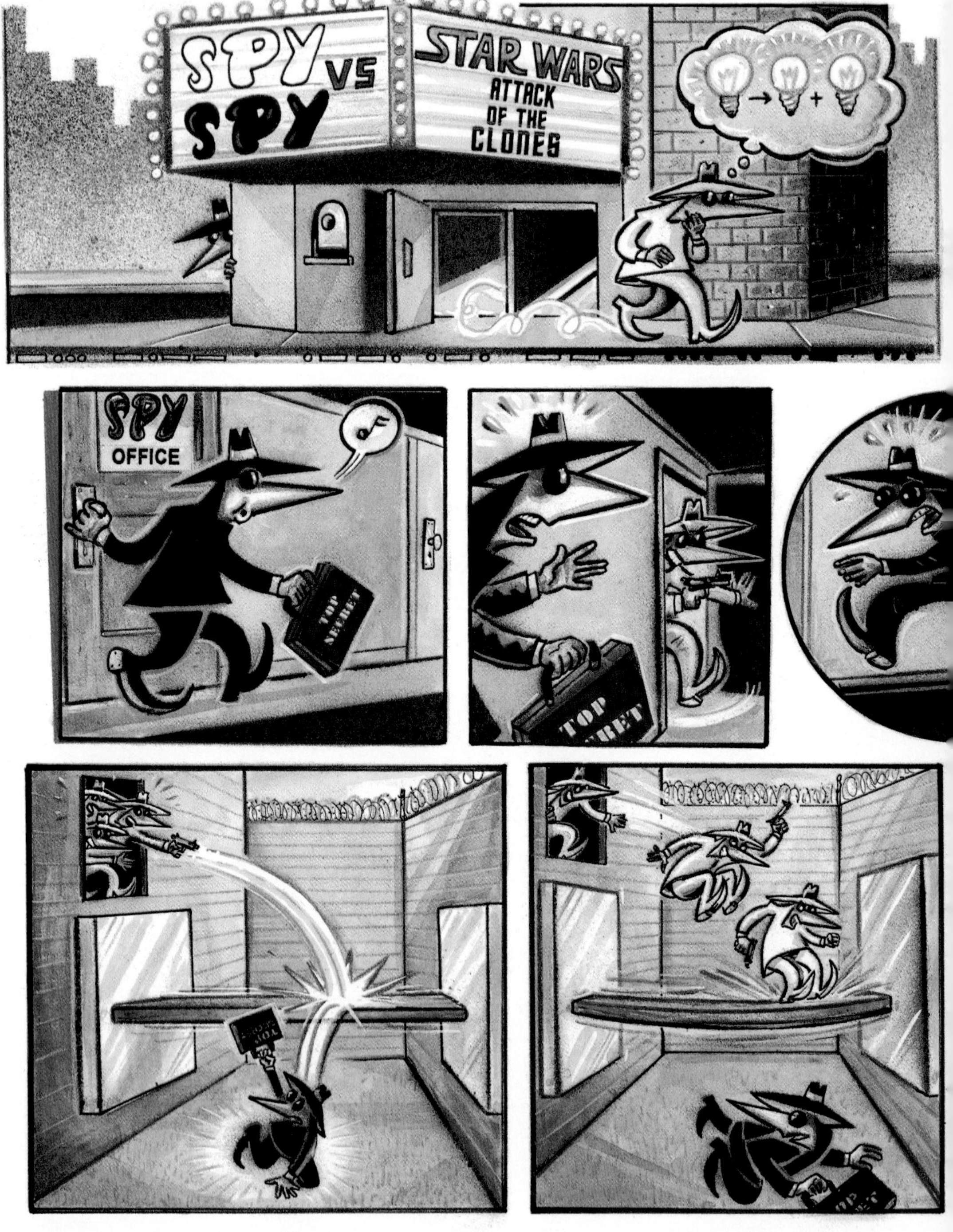
SPY VS SPY
STAR WARS
ATTACK OF THE CLONES
SPY
OFFICE
TOP SECRET
TOP SECRET

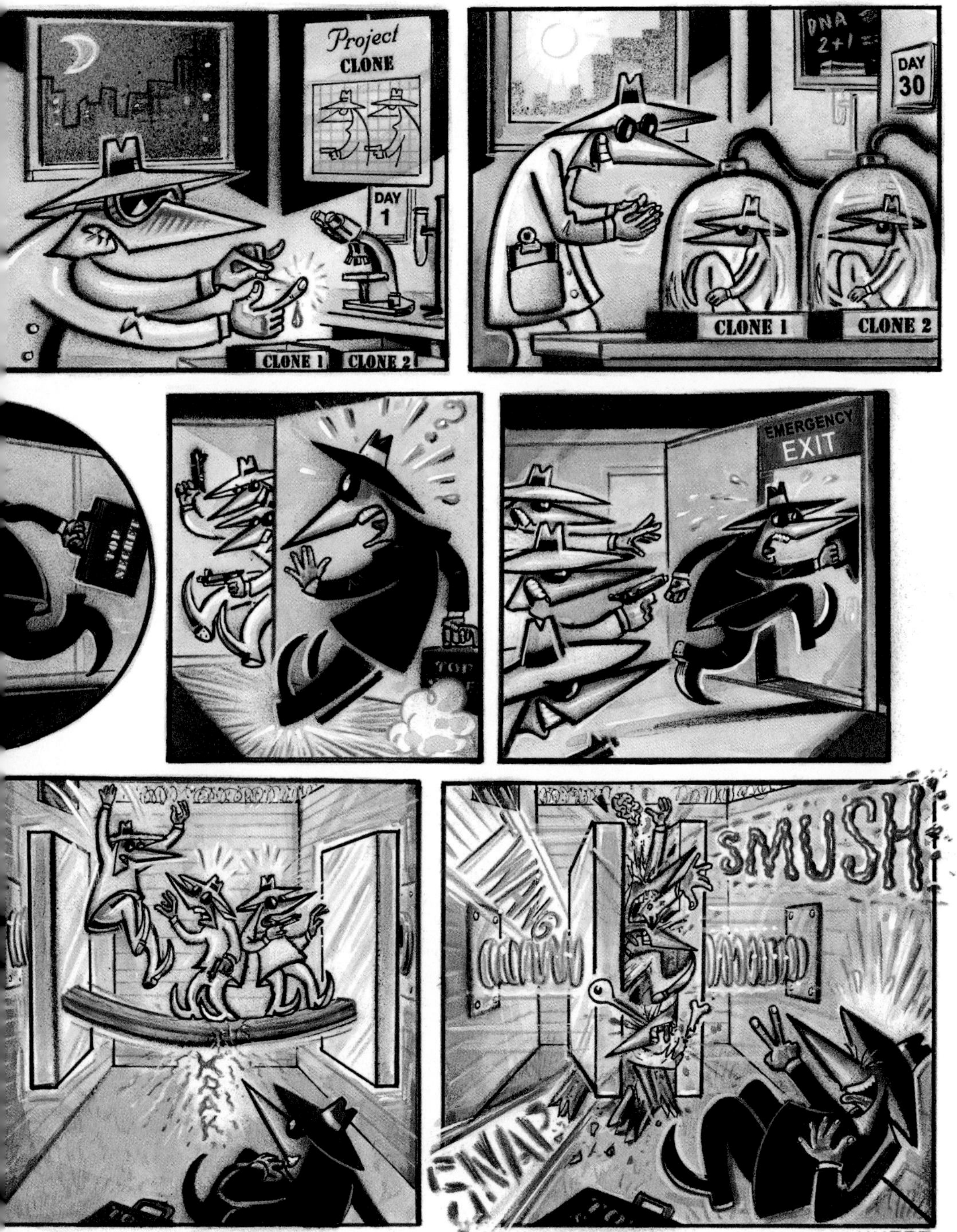
Project
CLONE
DAY
1
CLONE 1
CLONE 2
DNA
2+1
DAY
30
CLONE 1
CLONE 2
TOP
SECRET
TOP
EMERGENCY
EXIT
KRAK
SMUSH
SNAP

IDEA: JONATHAN BRESMAN

KUPER

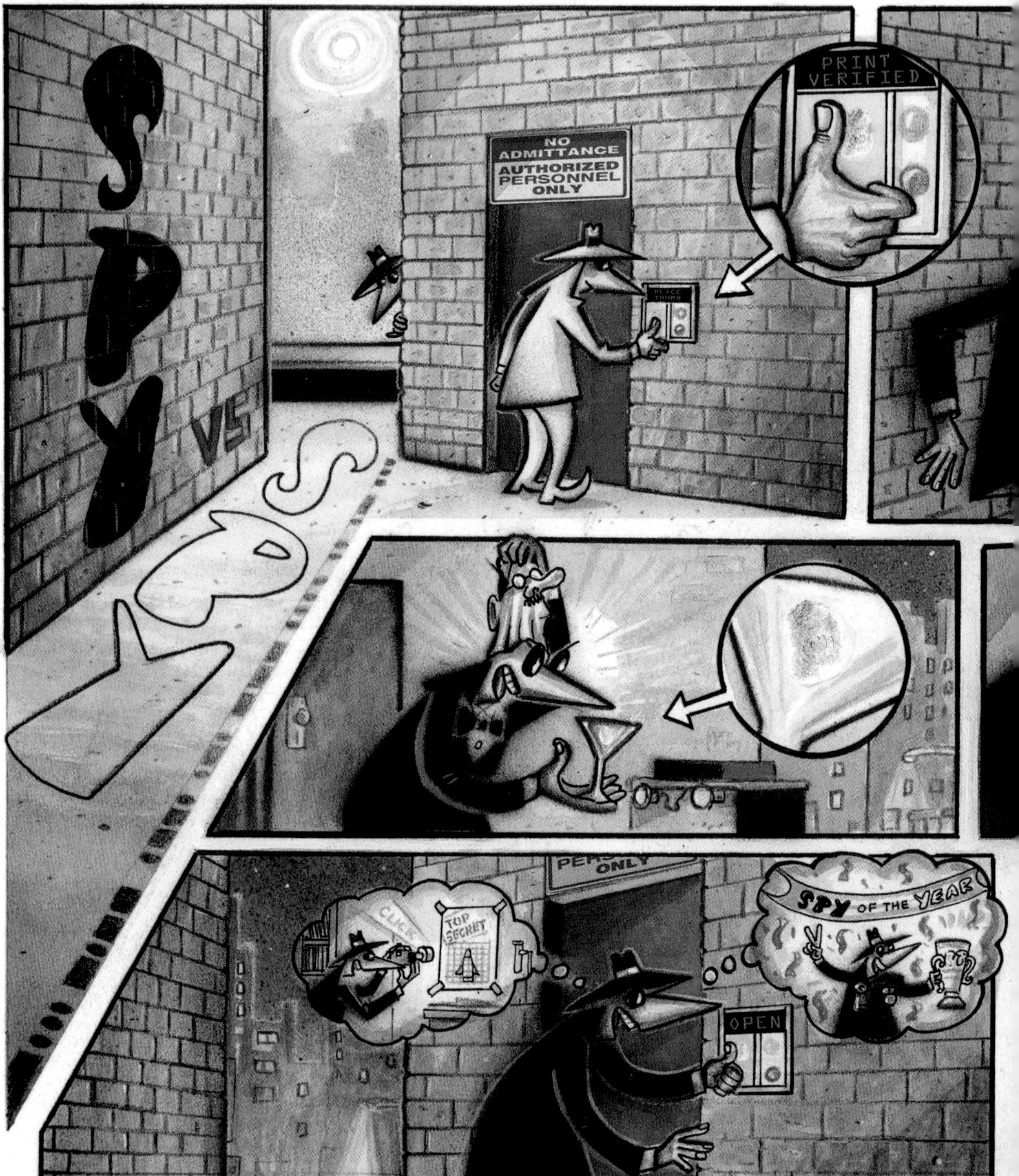
SPY vs SPY
NO ADMITTANCE
AUTHORIZED PERSONNEL ONLY
PRINT VERIFIED
CLICK
TOP SECRET
ONLY
SPY OF THE YEAR
OPEN

KUPER

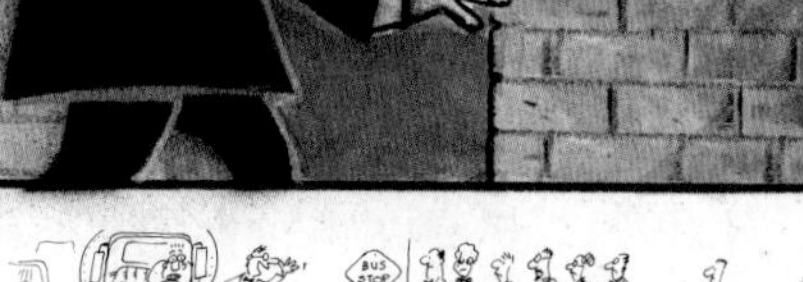
BUS STOP

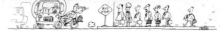

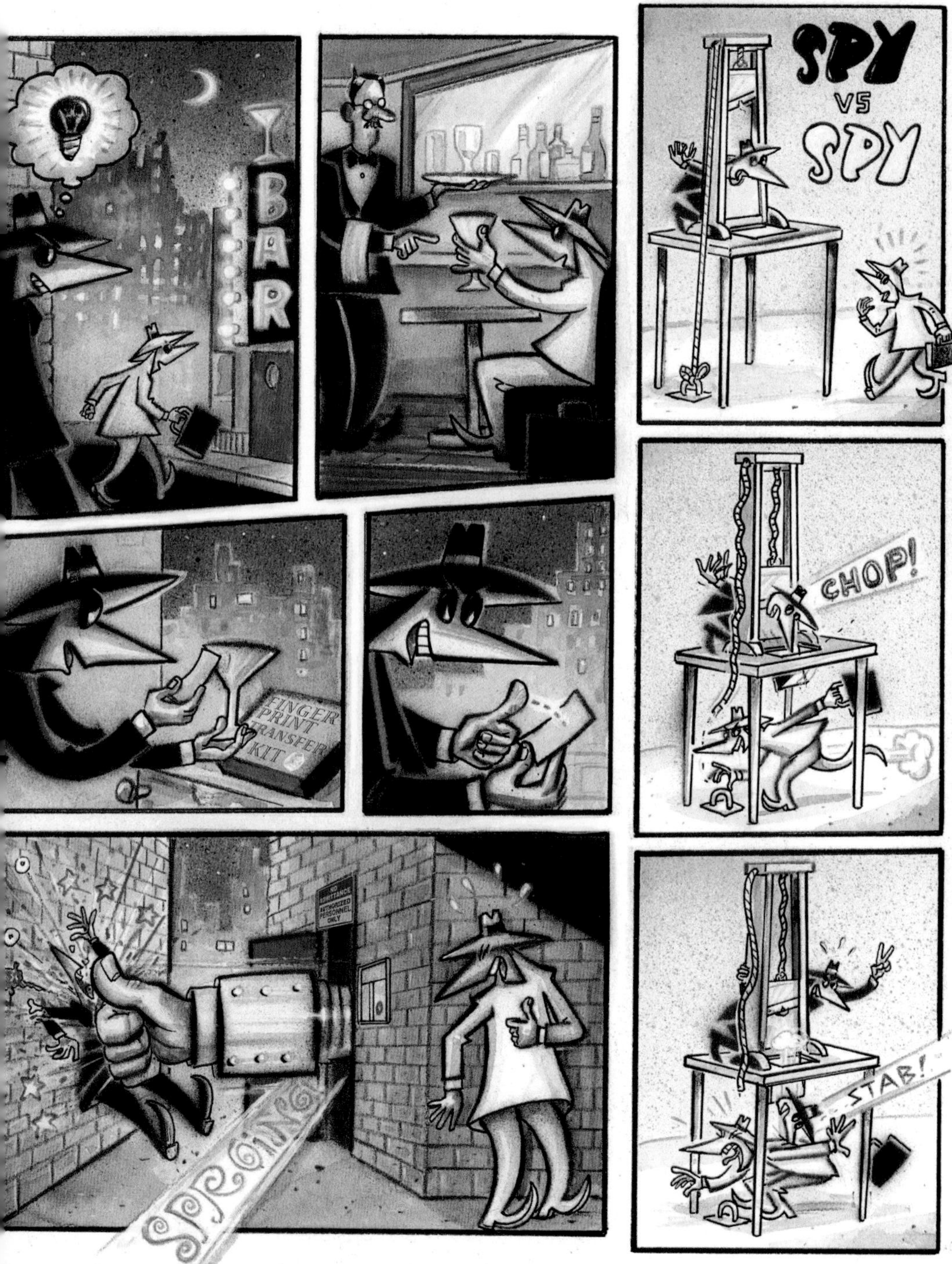

SPY vs SPY
BAR
FINGER PRINT TRANSFER KIT
CHOP!
NO ADMITTANCE
AUTHORIZED PERSONNEL ONLY
SPROING
STAB!

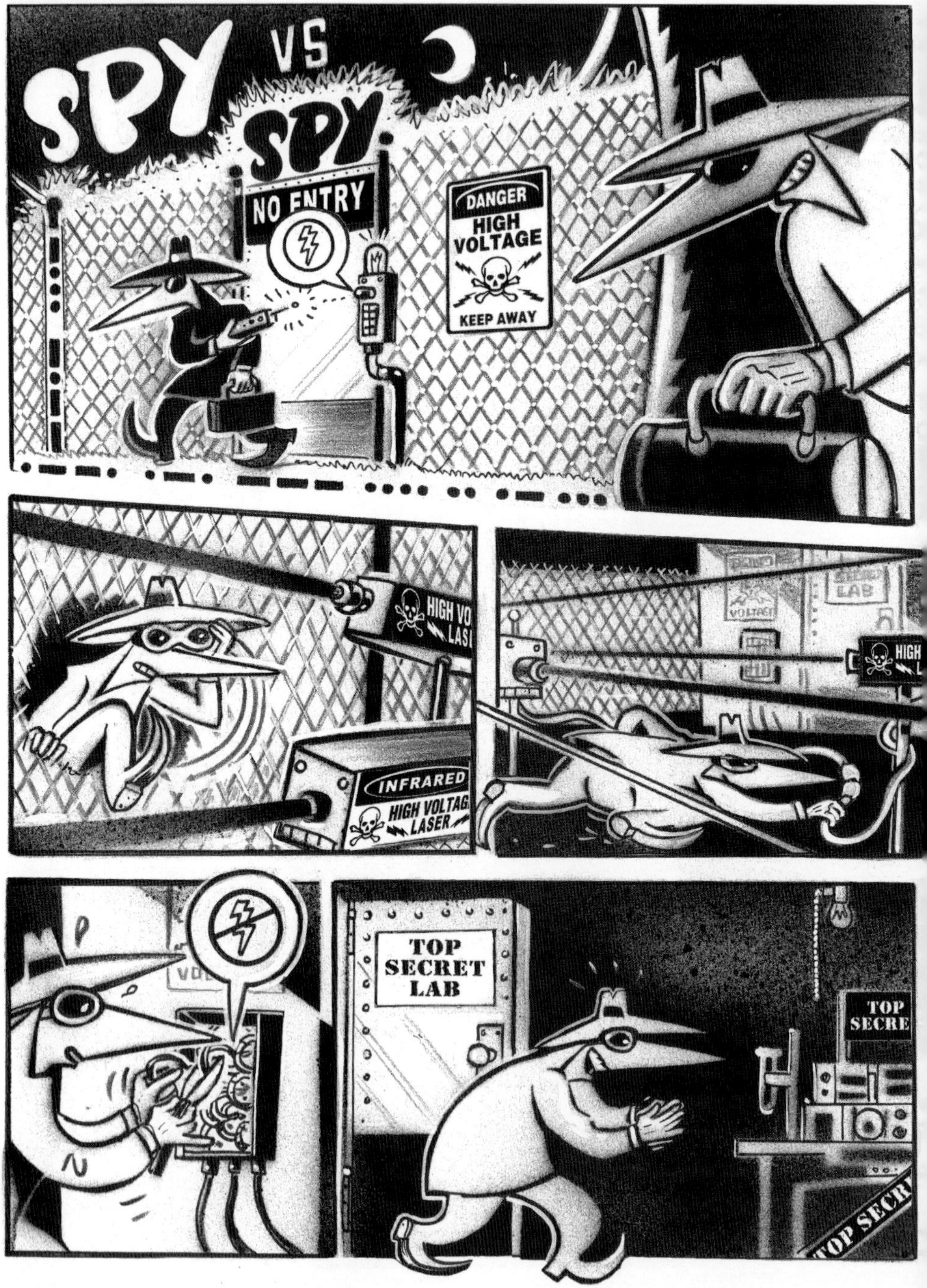
SPY VS SPY
NO ENTRY
DANGER
HIGH VOLTAGE
KEEP AWAY
INFRARED
LASER
TOP SECRET LAB

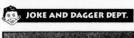

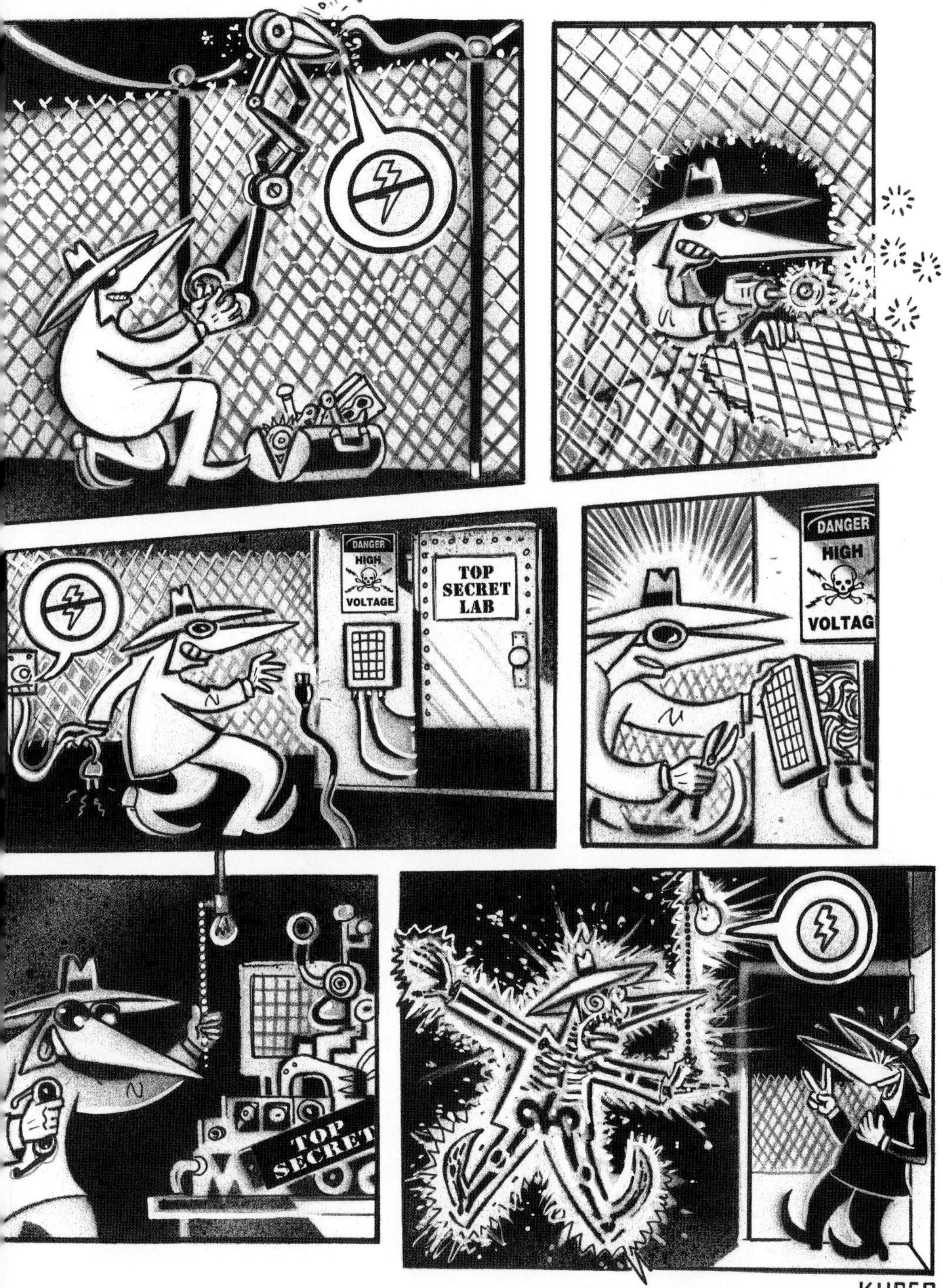
DANGER
HIGH
VOLTAGE
TOP
SECRET
LAB
DANGER
HIGH
VOLTAG
TOP
SECRET
KUPER

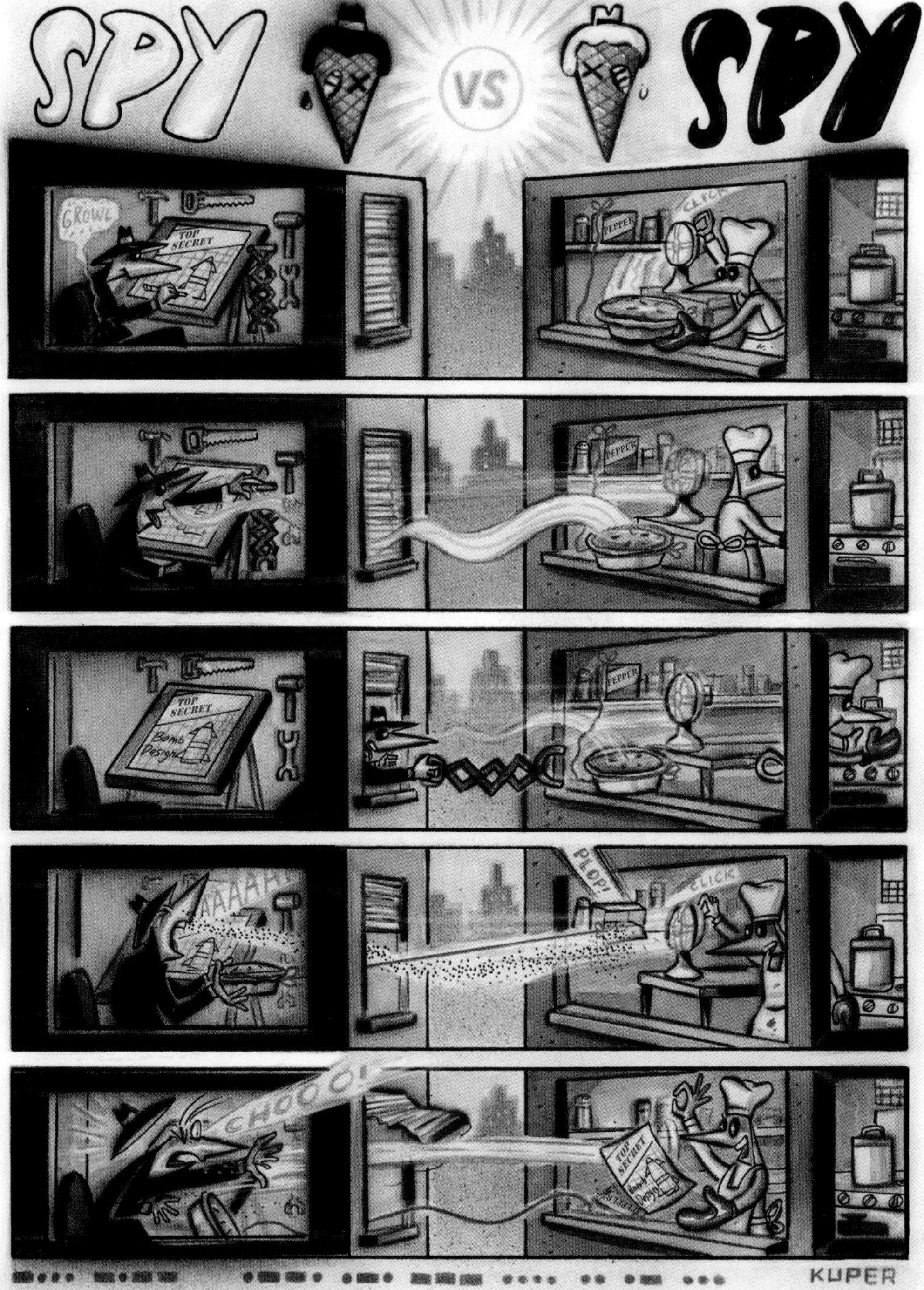
SPY VS SPY
GROWL
TOP SECRET
CLICK
PEPPER
TOP SECRET
Bomb Design
PEPPER
AAAAH!
PLOP!
CLICK
CHOOO!
TOP SECRET
Bomb Design
KUPER

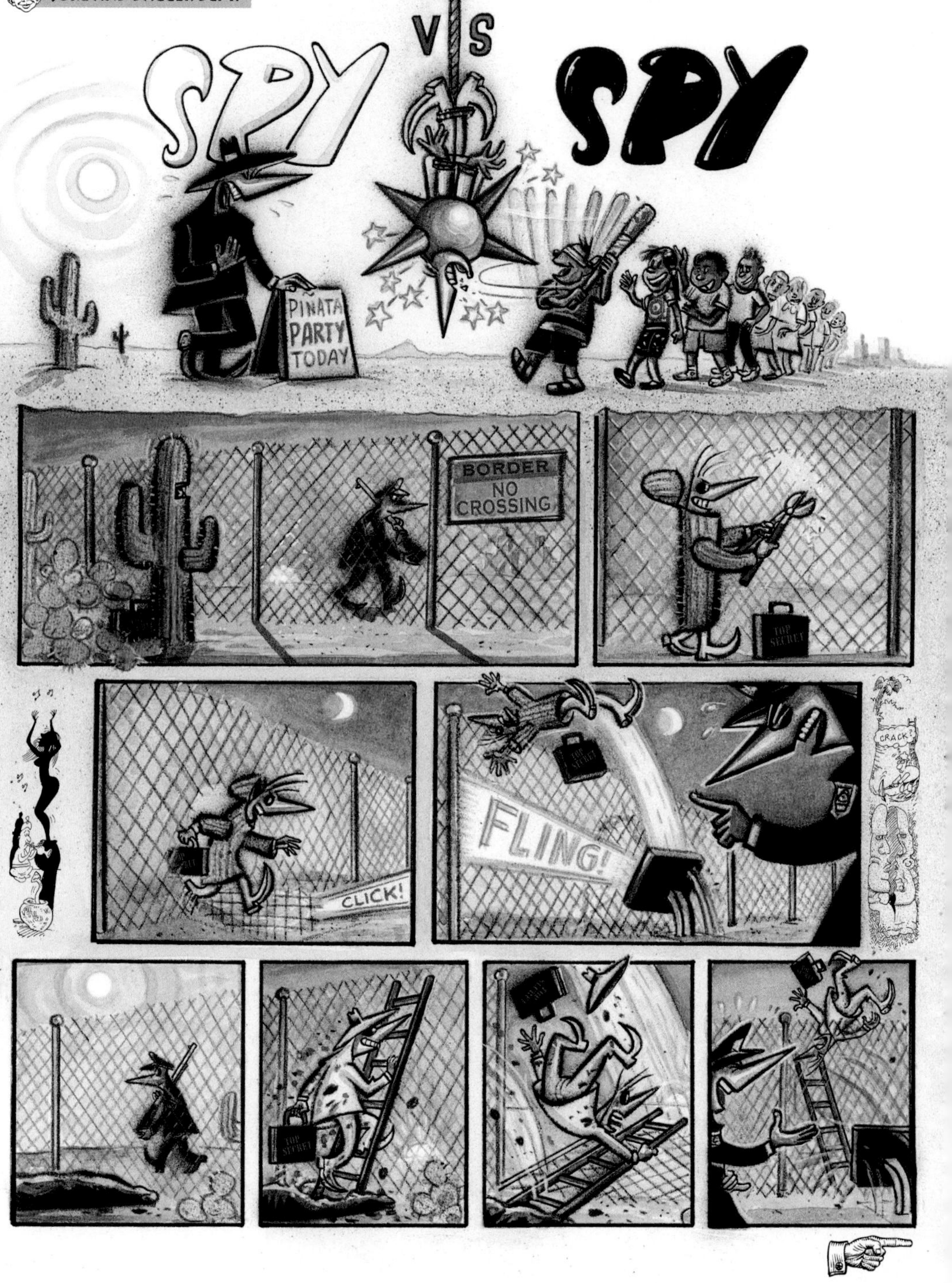
SPY VS SPY
PIÑATA PARTY TODAY
BORDER
NO CROSSING
TOP SECRET
CLICK!
FLING!
CRACK!
TOP SECRET

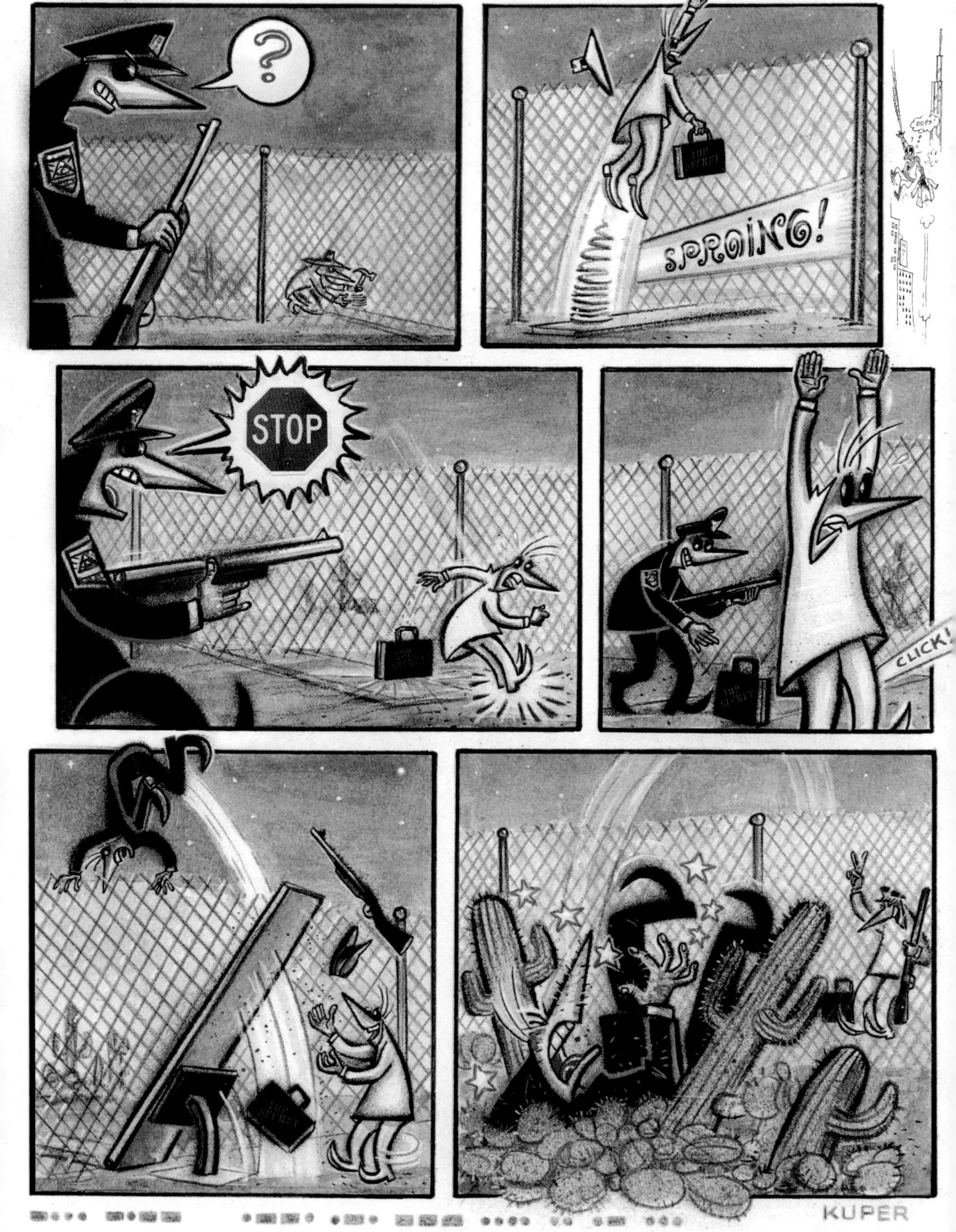
?
SPROING!
STOP
CLICK!
KUPER

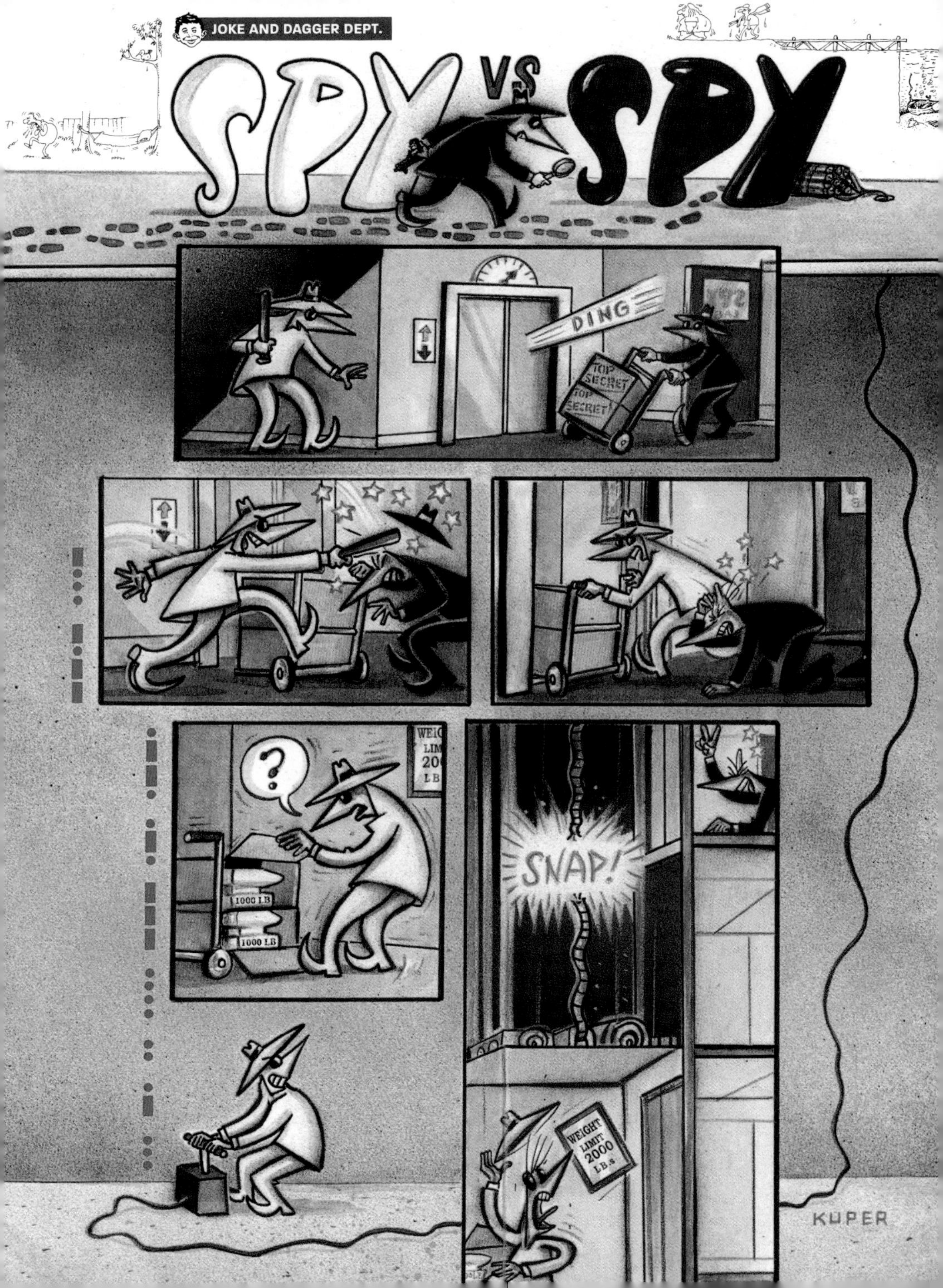
JOKE AND DAGGER DEPT.
SPY vs SPY
DING
TOP SECRET
TOP SECRET
?
1000 LB
1000 LB
SNAP!
WEIGHT LIMIT 2000 LB.s
KUPER

JOKE AND DAGGER DEPT.

SPY vs SPY

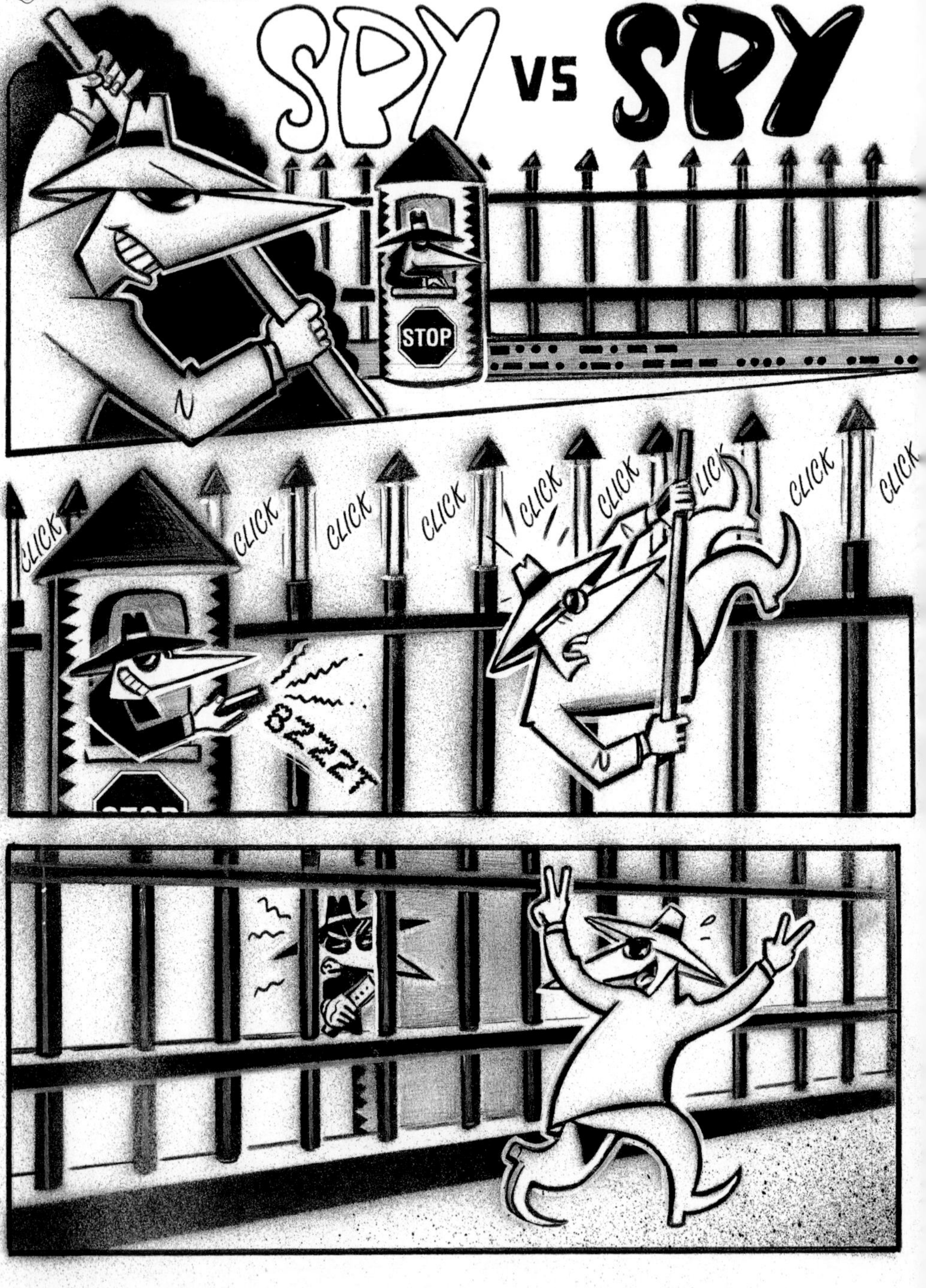
STOP
CLICK
CLICK
CLICK
CLICK
CLICK
CLICK
LICK
CLICK
CLICK
BZZZT

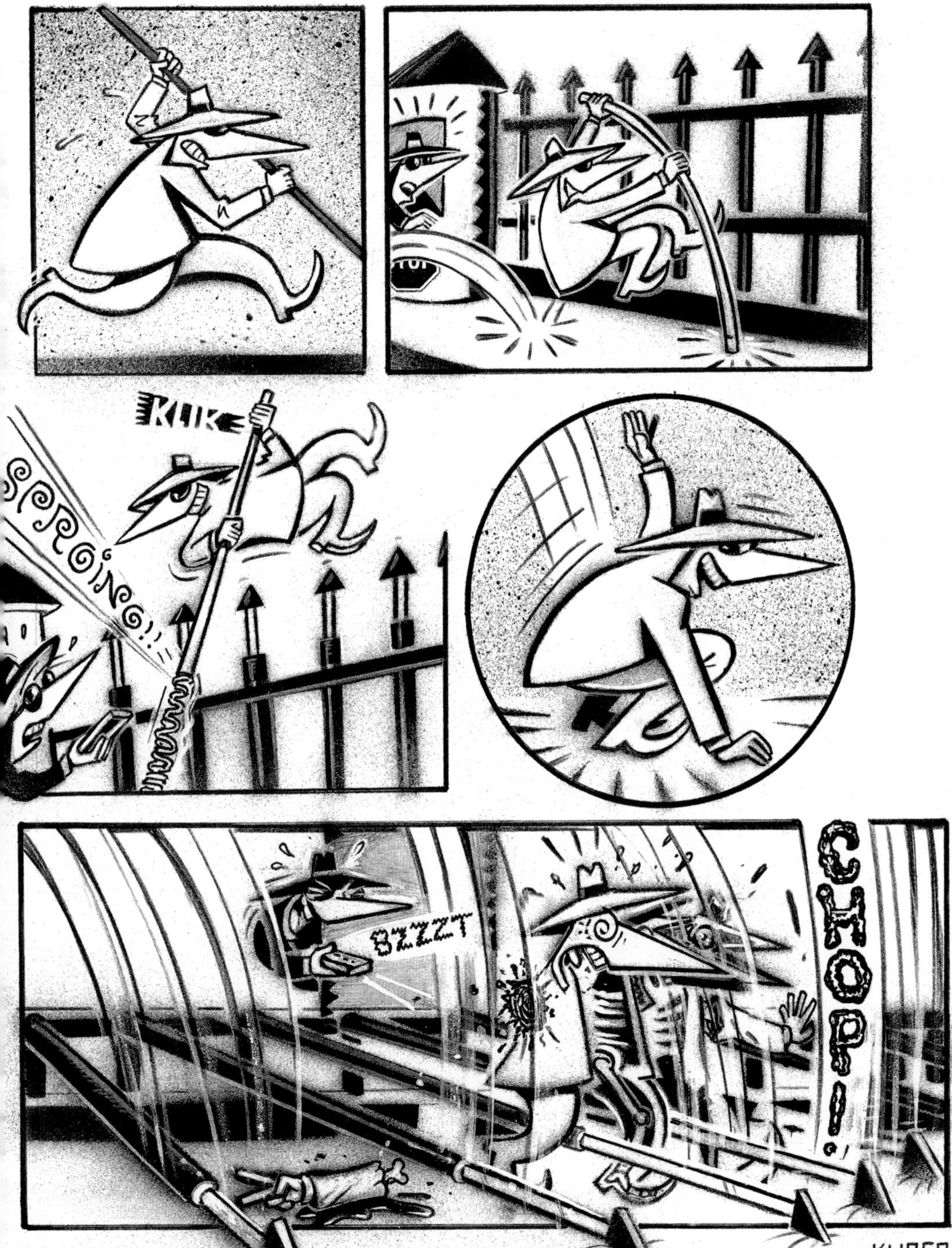
KLIK
SPROING!!
CHOP!!

KUPER

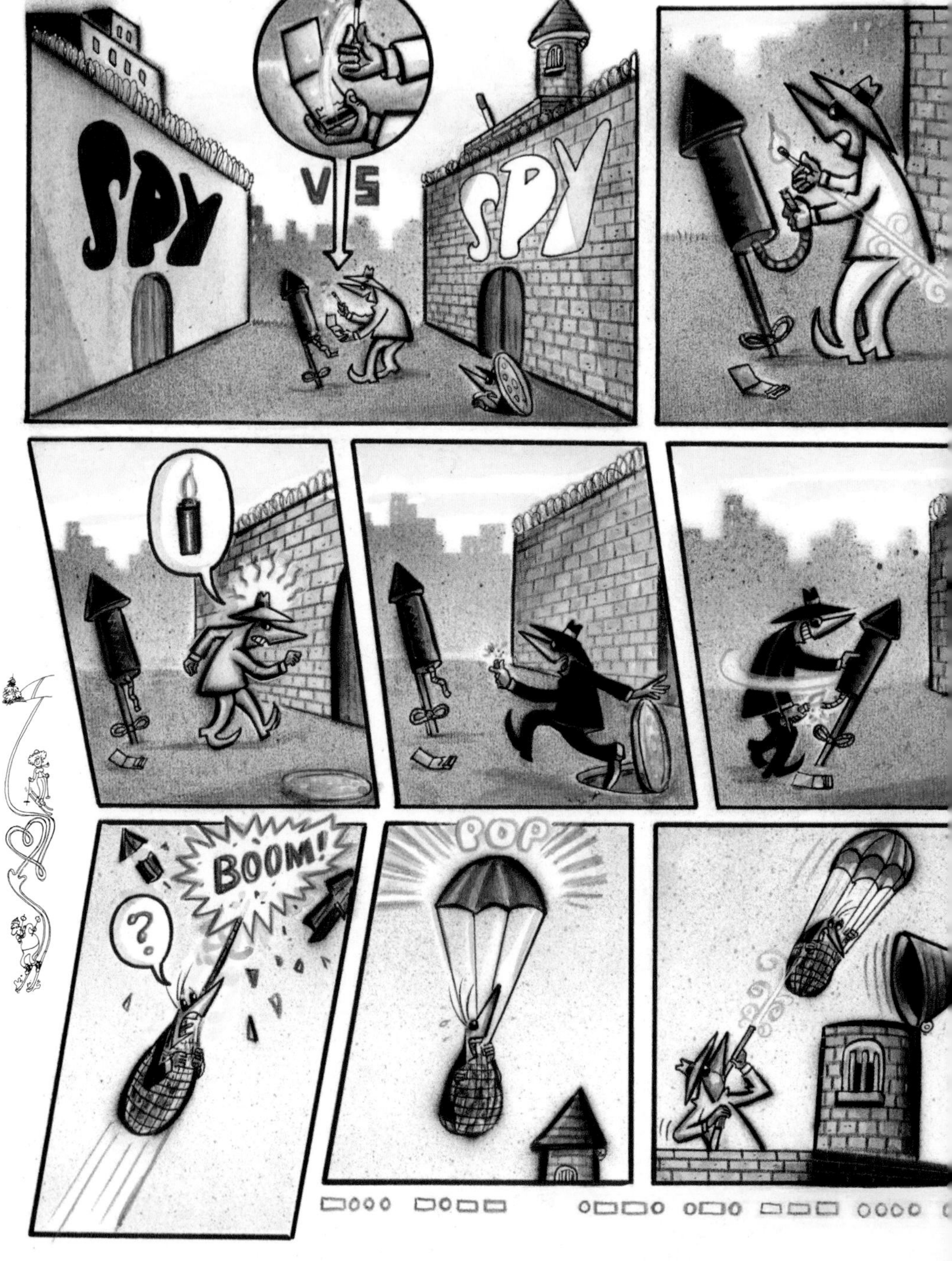
SPY
VS
SPY
BOOM!
?
POP

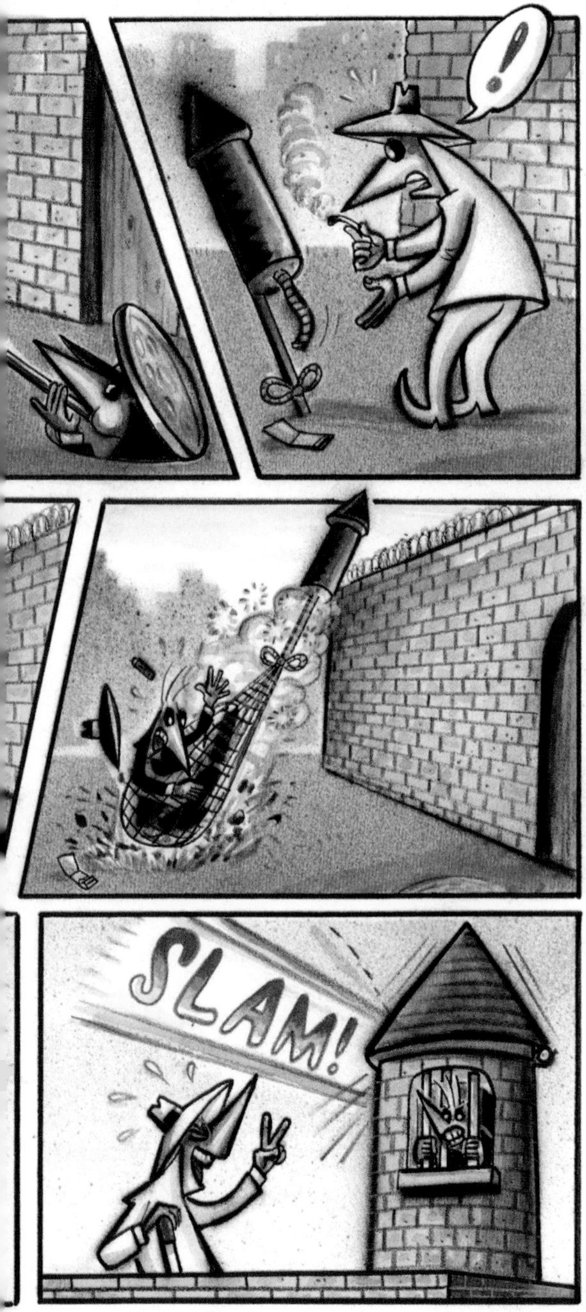
!
SLAM!

KUPER

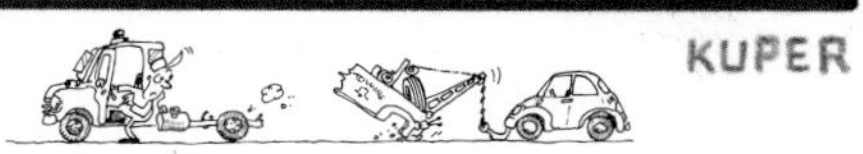

SPY vs SPY

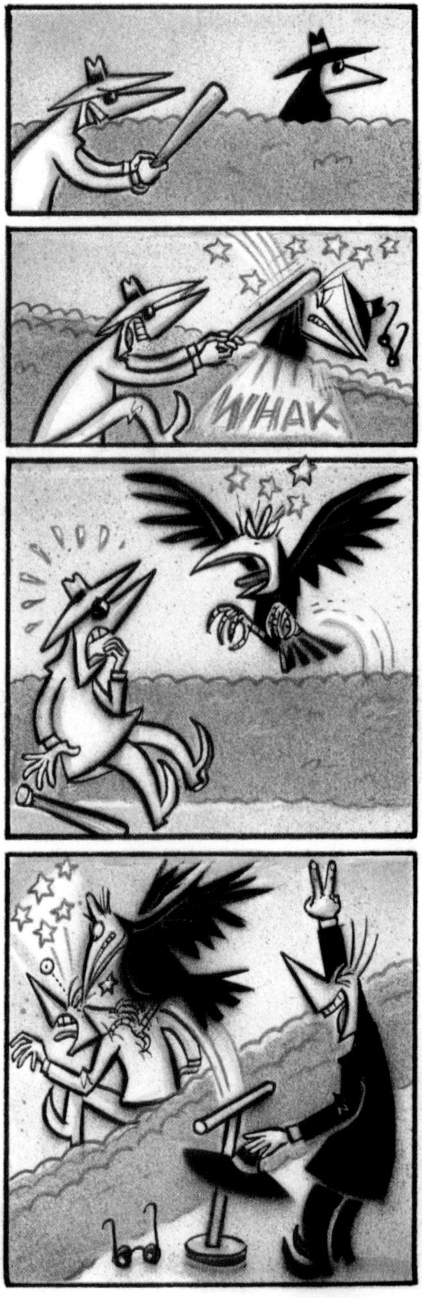
WHAK

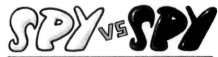

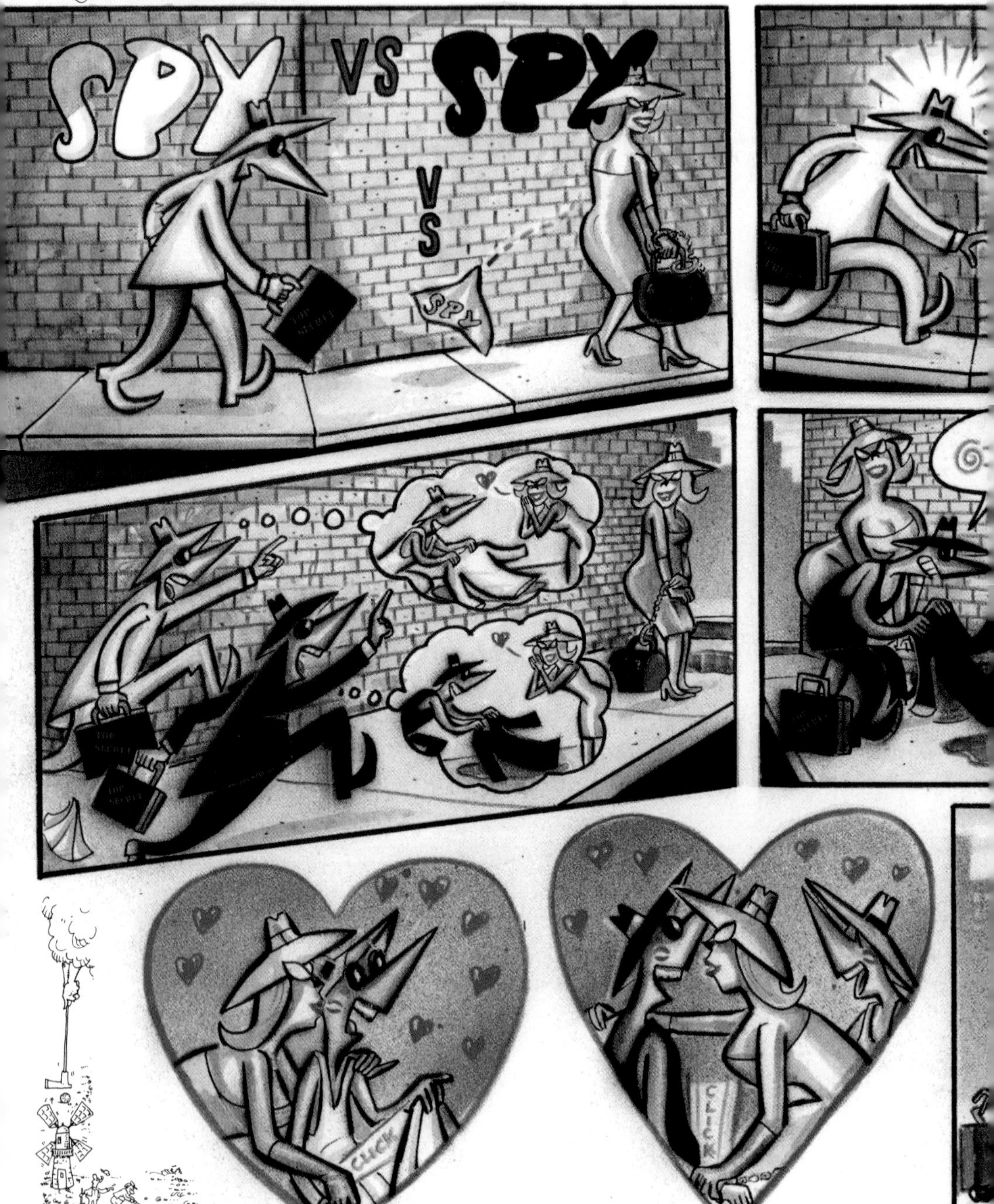
SPY VS SPY
VS
TOP SECRET
SPY
TOP SECRET
TOP SECRET
TOP SECRET
CLICK
CLICK

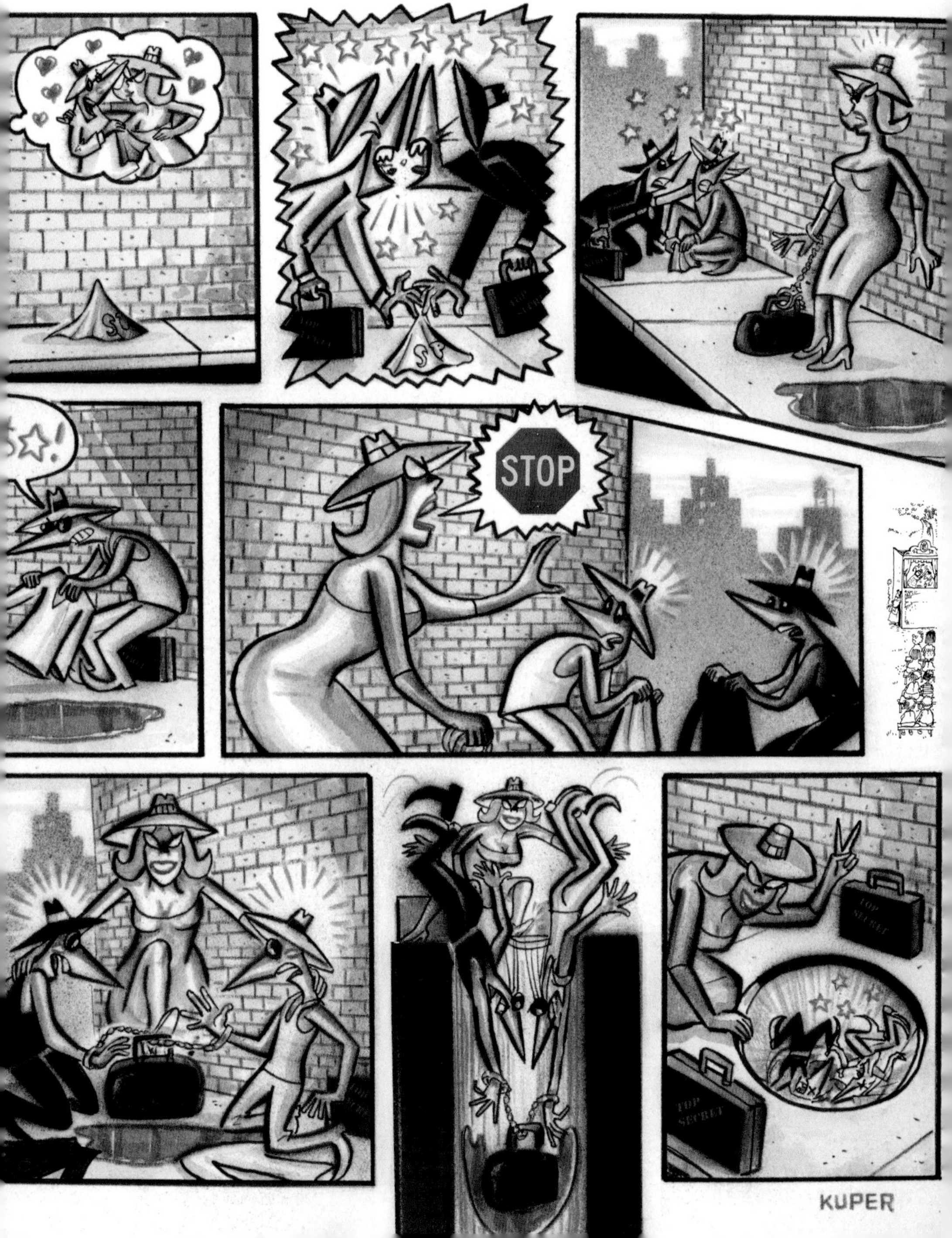
STOP
TOP SECRET
TOP SECRET
KUPER

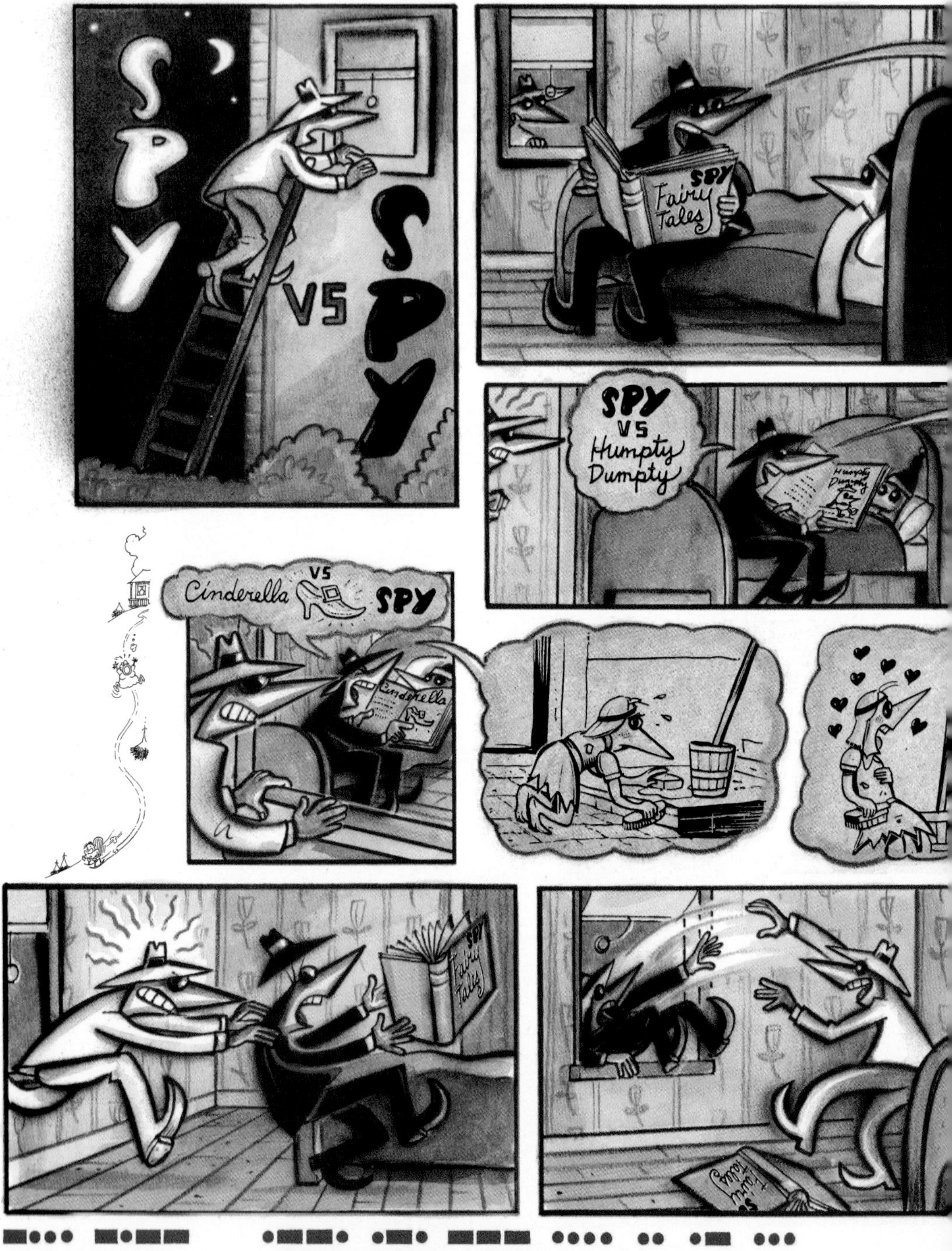
SPY VS SPY
SPY Fairy Tales
SPY VS Humpty Dumpty
Cinderella VS SPY
Cinderella
SPY Fairy Tales
Fairy Tales

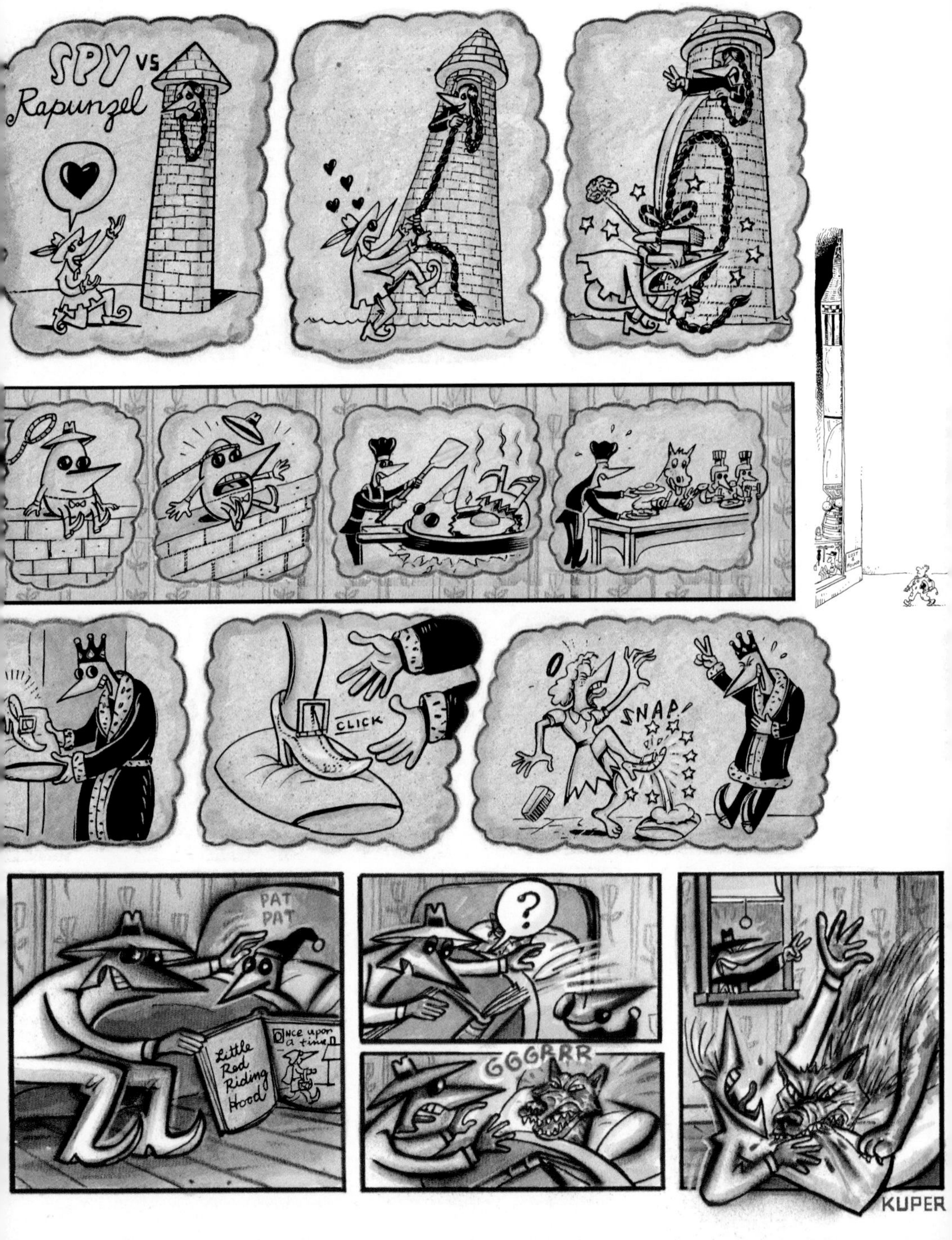
SPY VS
Rapunzel
CLICK
SNAP!
PAT
PAT
Little Red Riding Hood
ONCE upon a time
?
GGGRRR
KUPER

JOKE AND BANANA DEPT.

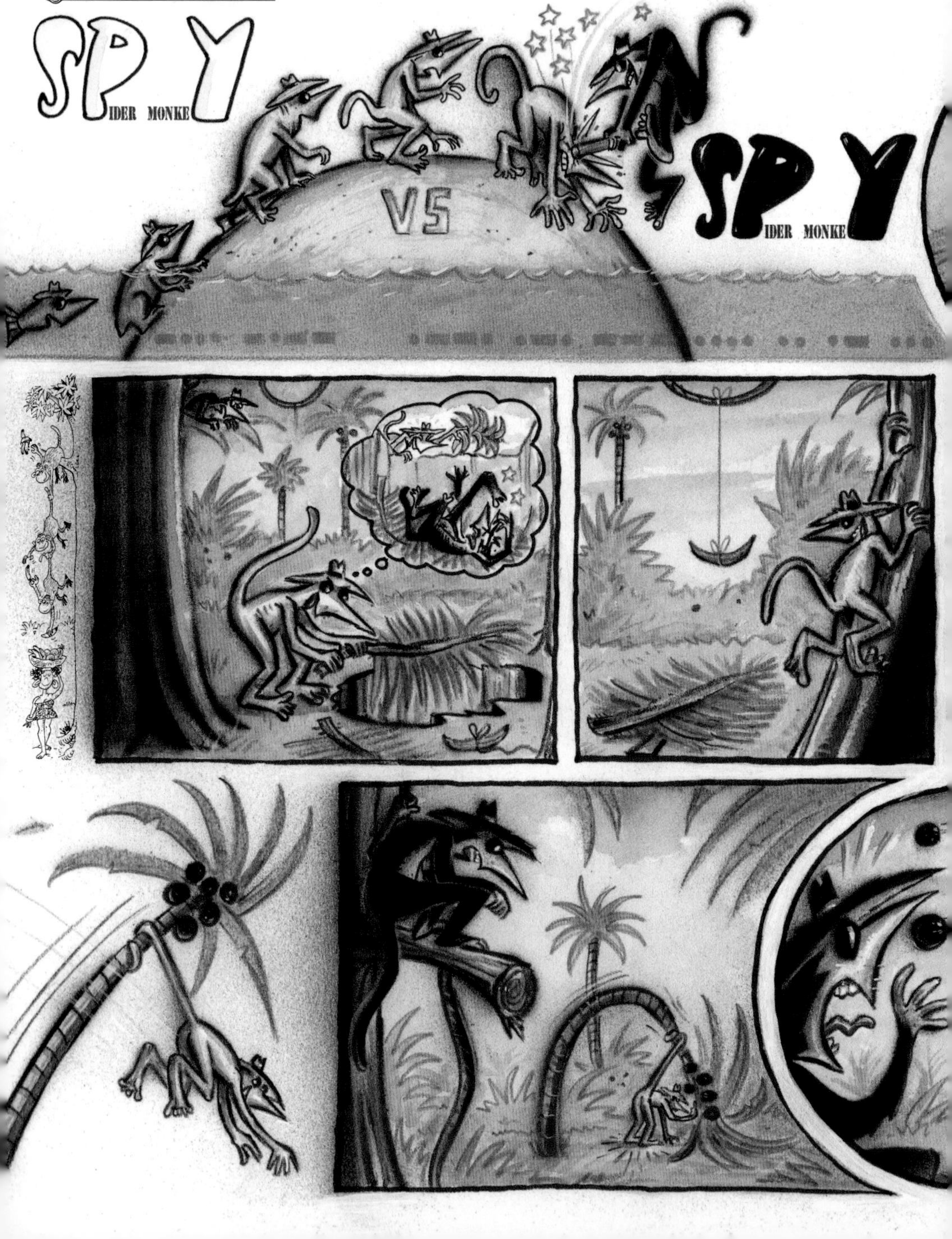
SPIDER MONKEY
VS
SPIDER MONKEY

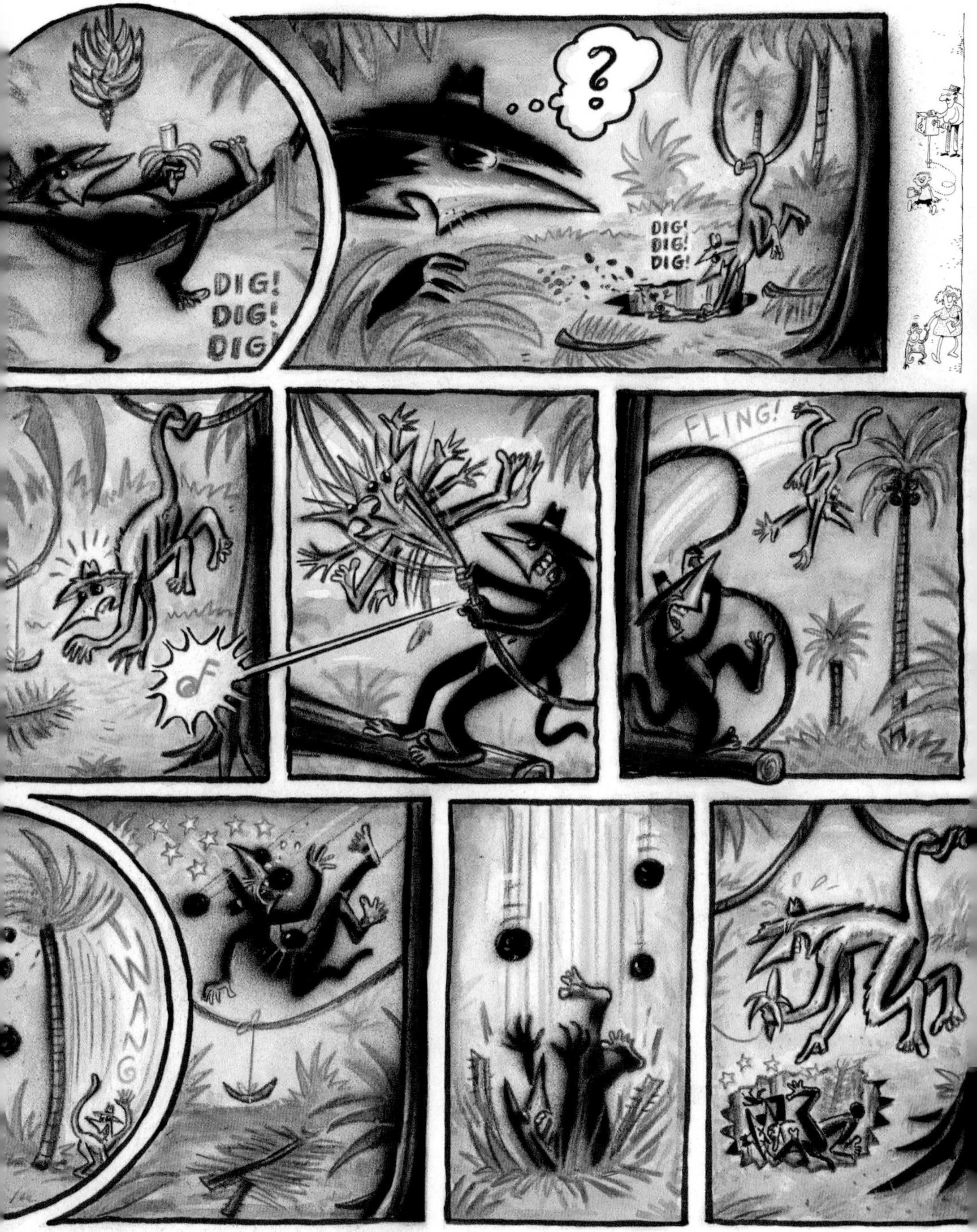
DIG!
DIG!
DIG!
?
DIG!
DIG!
DIG!
FLING!
WANG
KUPER

JOKE AND DAGGER DEPT.

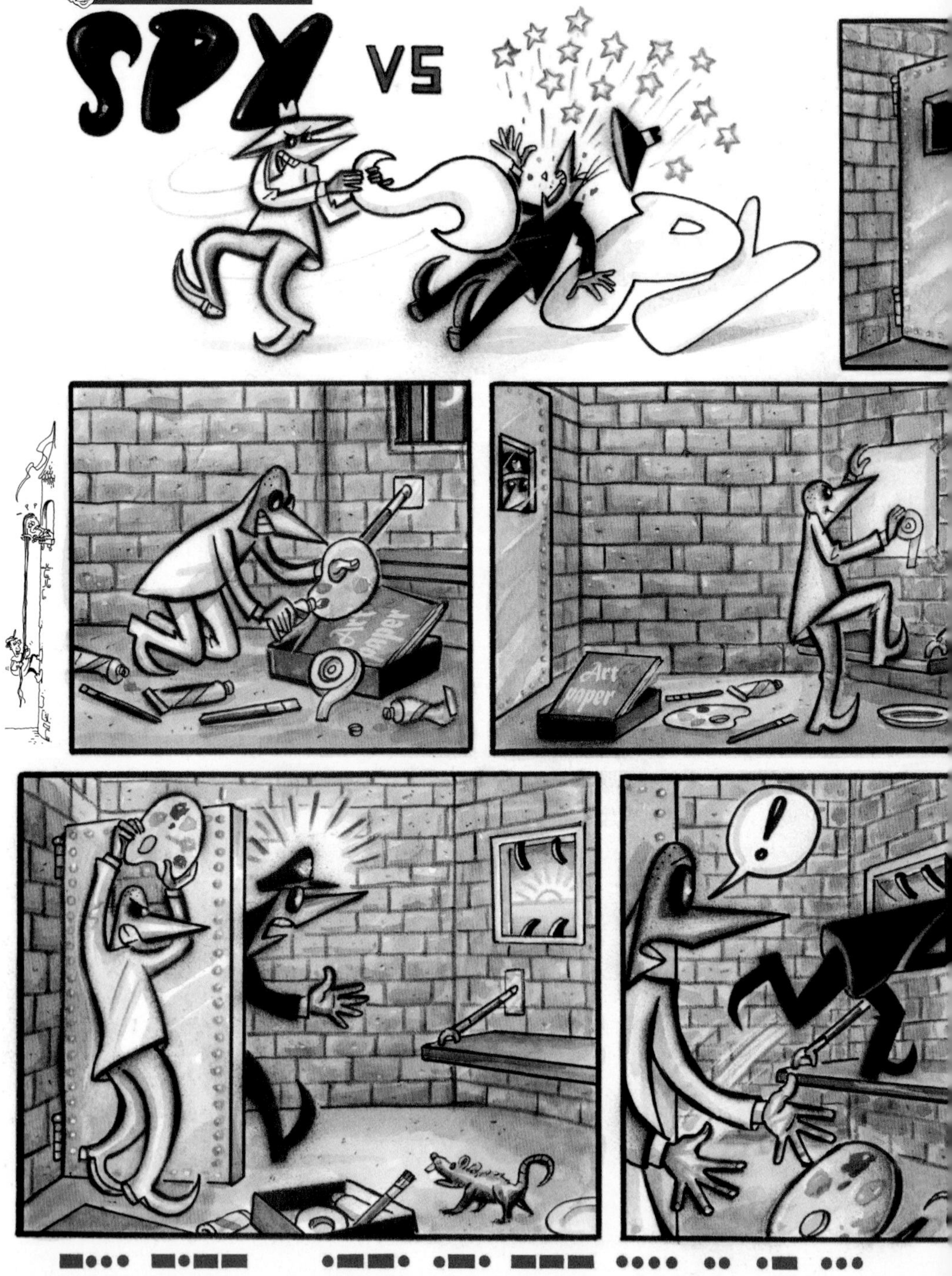
SPY VS SPY
Art paper
Art paper
!

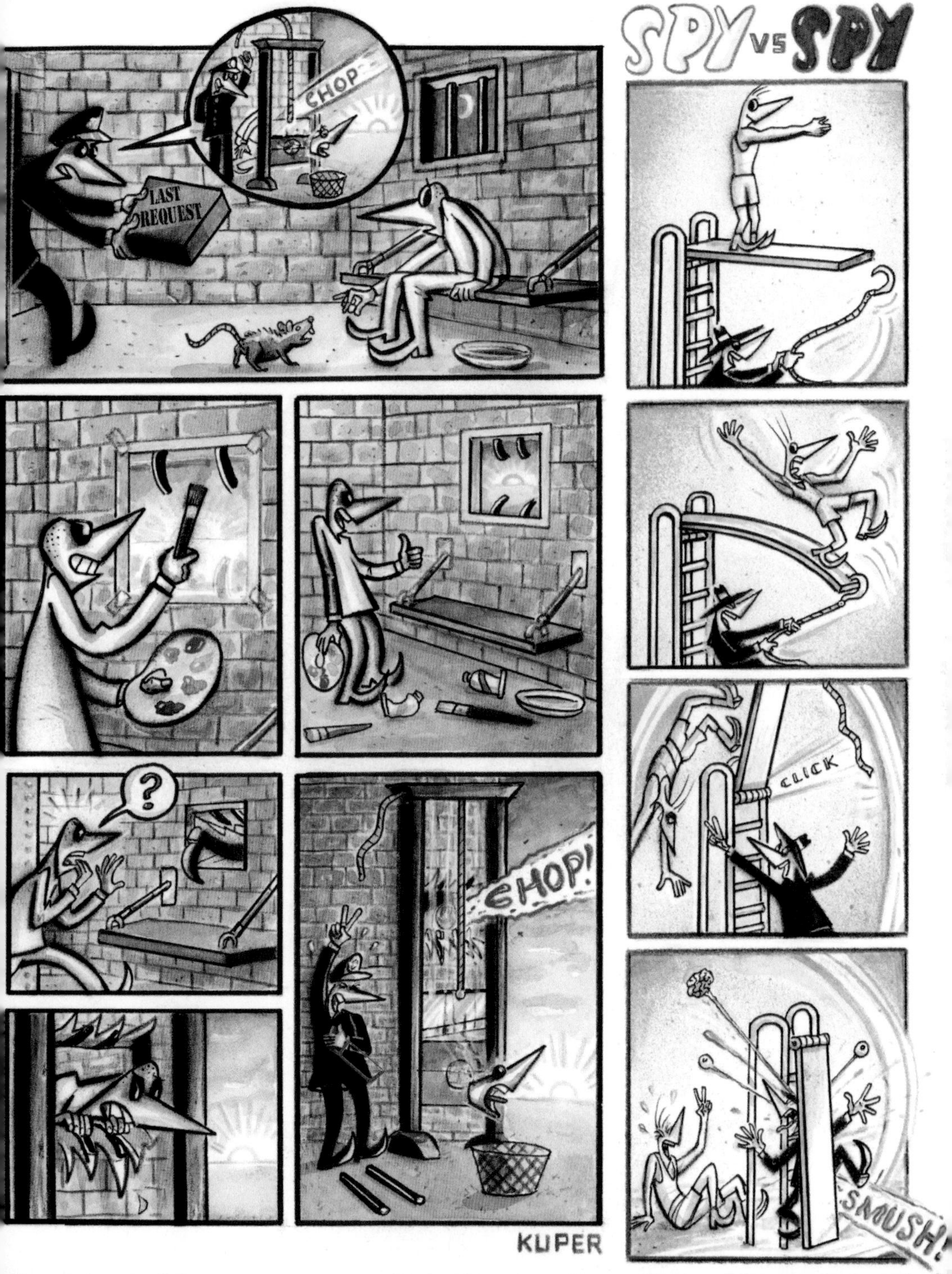
SPY vs SPY
CHOP
LAST REQUEST
?
CHOP!
CLICK
SMUSH!
KUPER

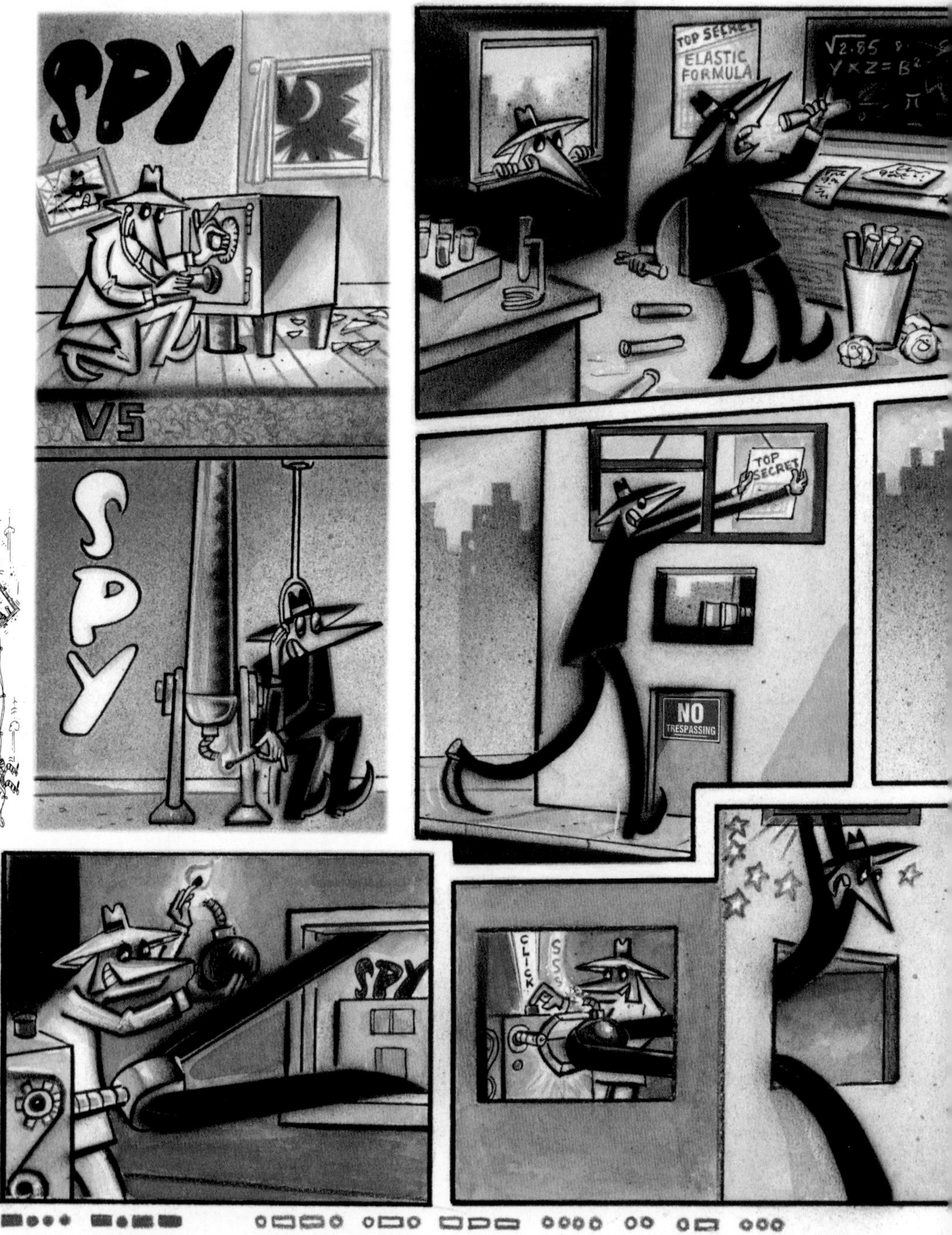
SPY
VS
SPY
TOP SECRET
ELASTIC FORMULA
√2.85
Y×Z=B²
TOP SECRET
NO TRESPASSING
CLICK
SSS
SPY

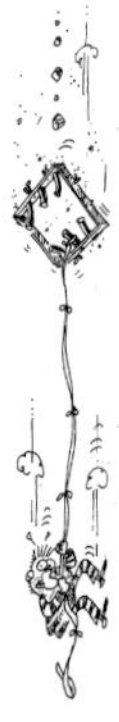

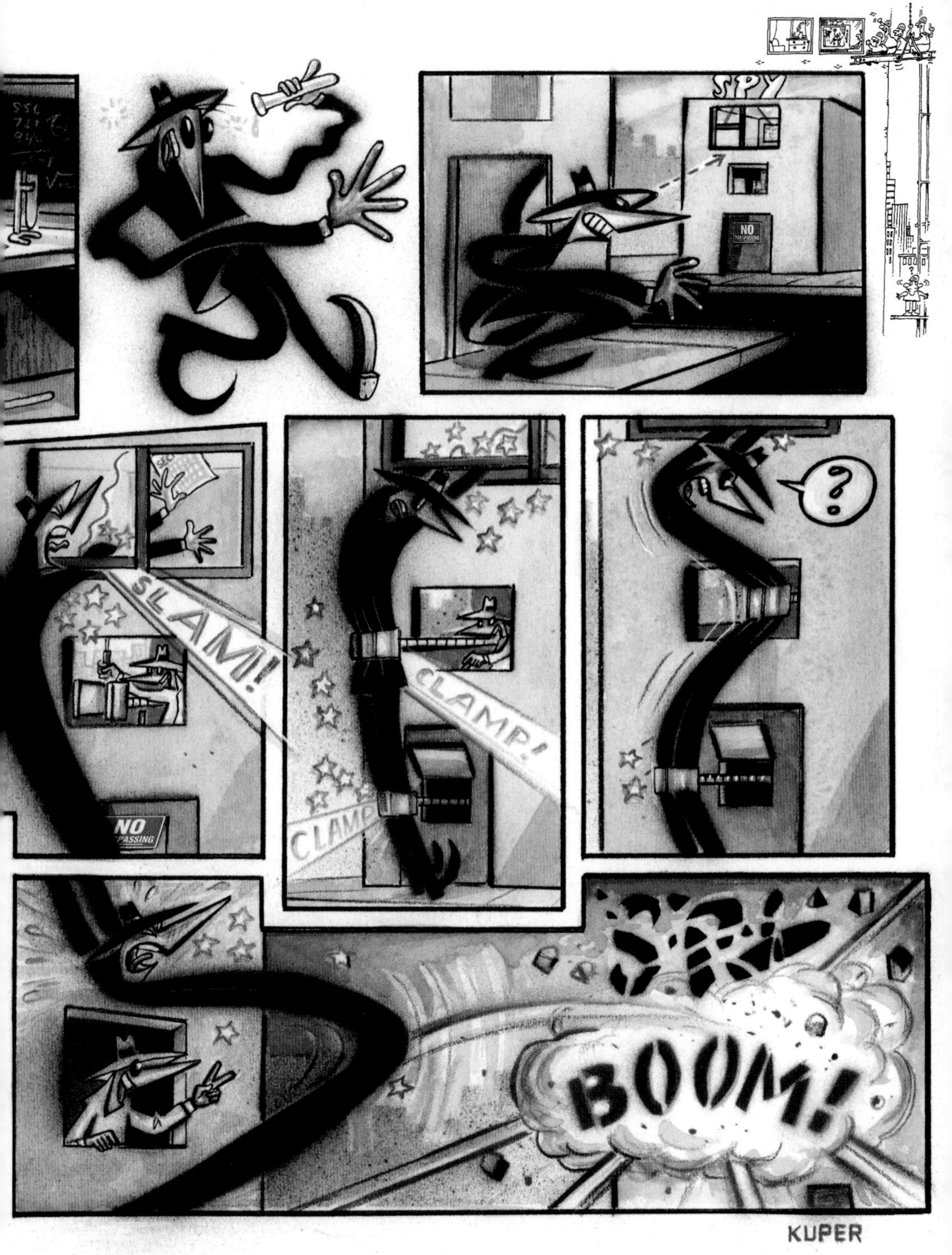
SPY
NO TRESPASSING
SLAM!
NO
CLAMP!
CLAMP!
CLAMP
?
BOOM!
KUPER

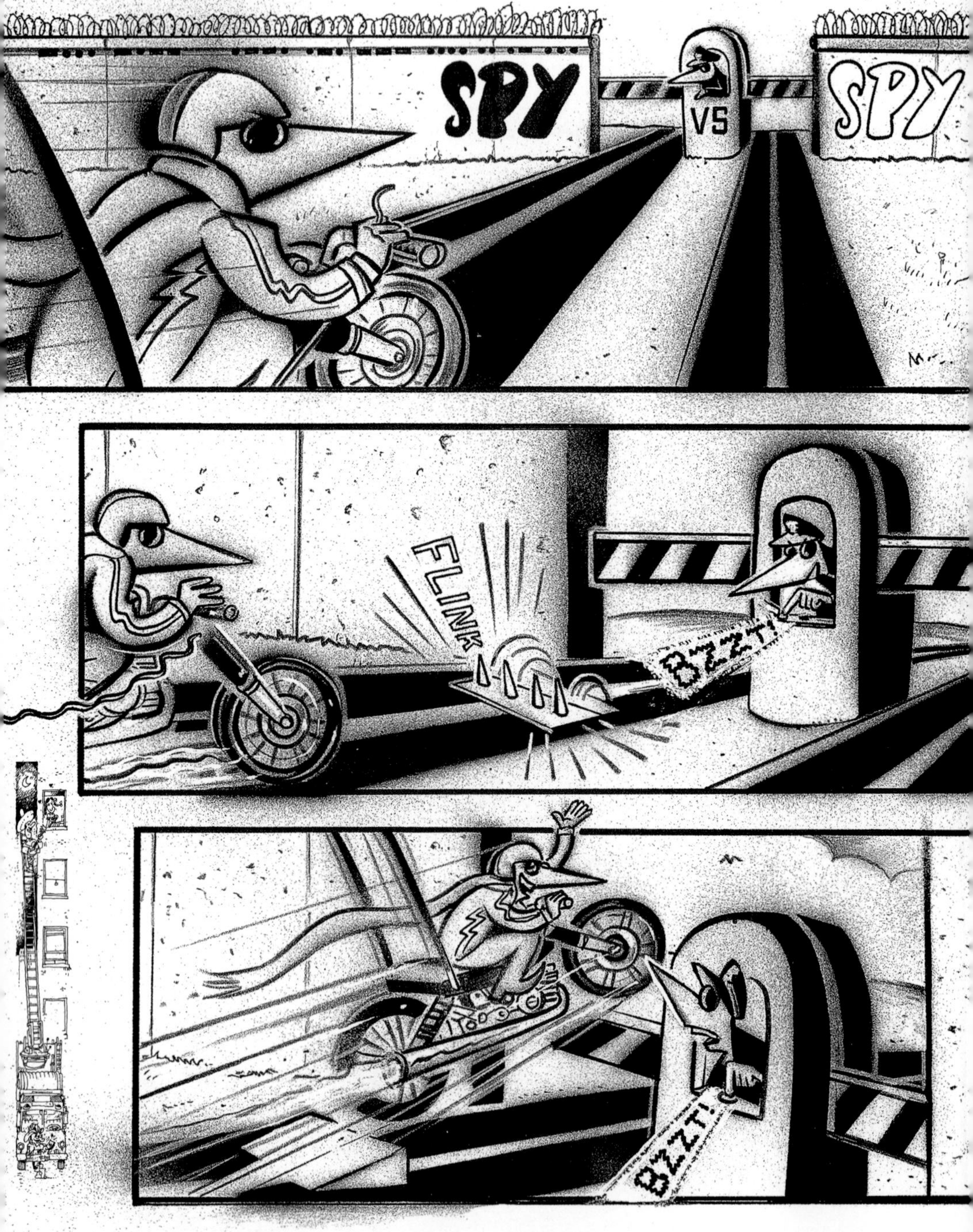
SPY
VS
SPY
FLINK
BZZT!
BZZT!

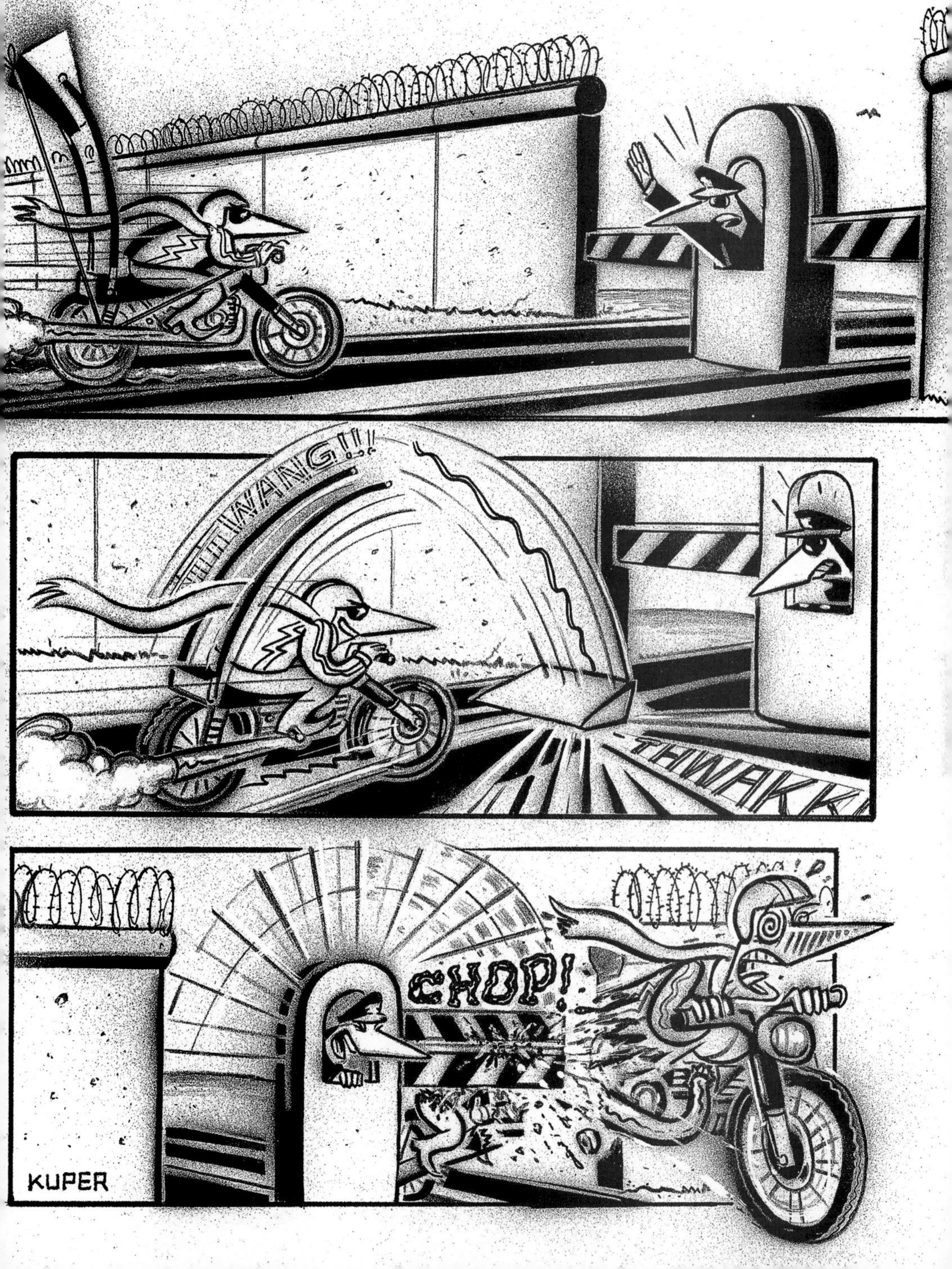
THWANG!!!
THWAKK
CHOP!
KUPER

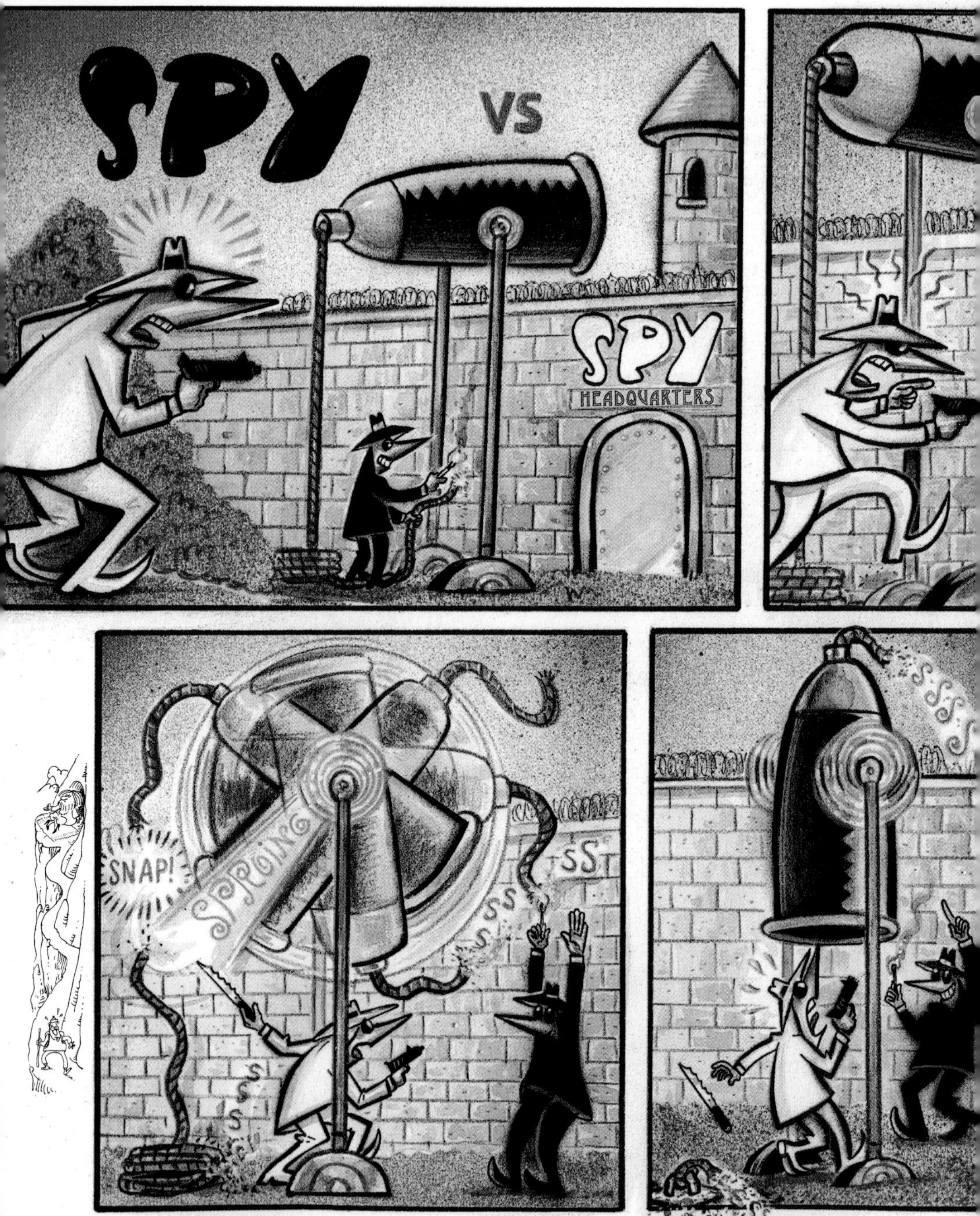
SPY VS
SPY
HEADQUARTERS
SNAP!
SPROING
SS

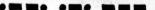

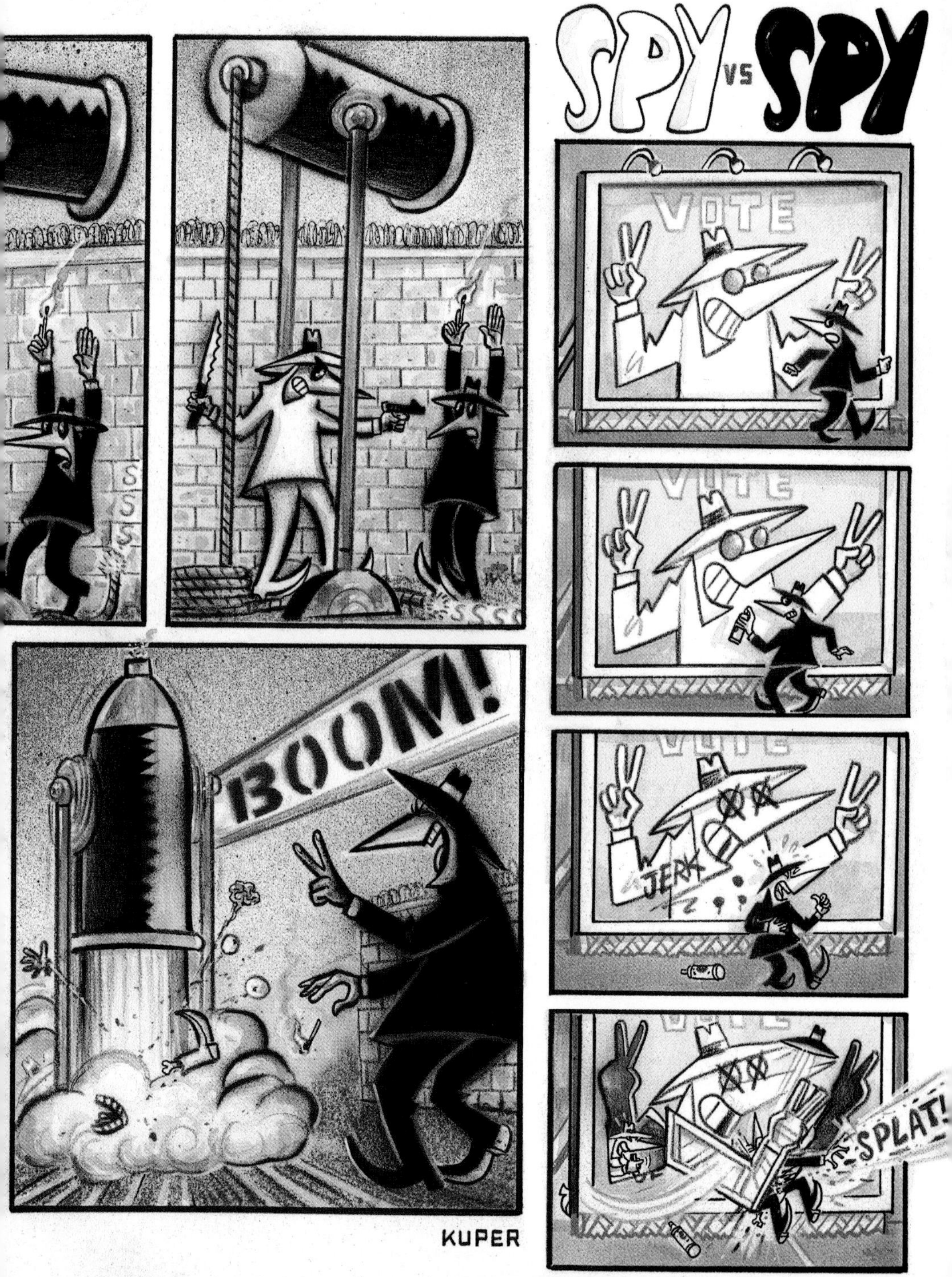
SPY vs SPY
SSS
SSSS
BOOM!
VOTE
VOTE
VOTE
JERK
VOTE
SPLAT!
KUPER

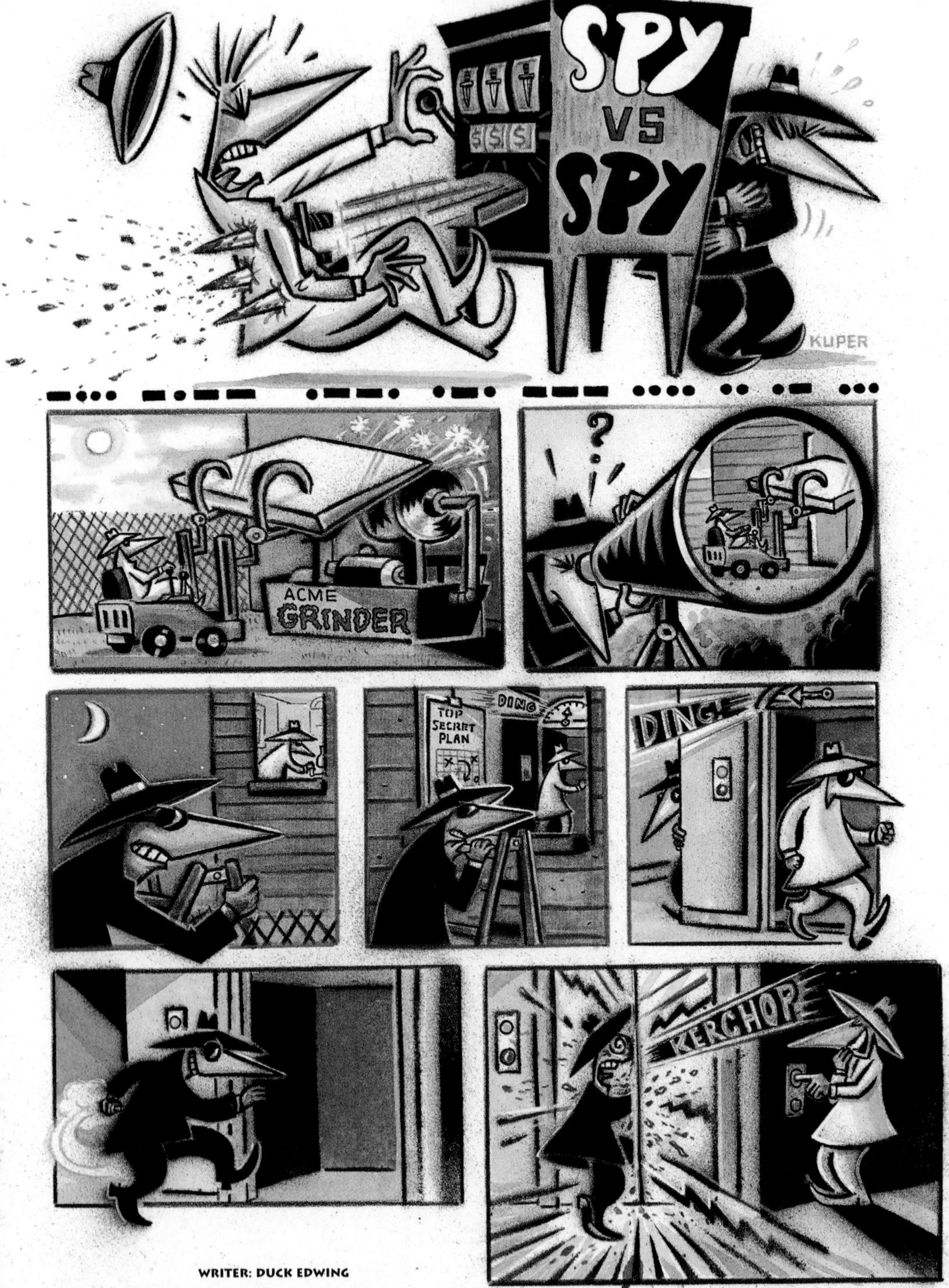
SPY
VS
SPY
KUPER
ACME
GRINDER
?
TOP
SECRET
PLAN
DING
DING
KERCHOP

WRITER: DUCK EDWING

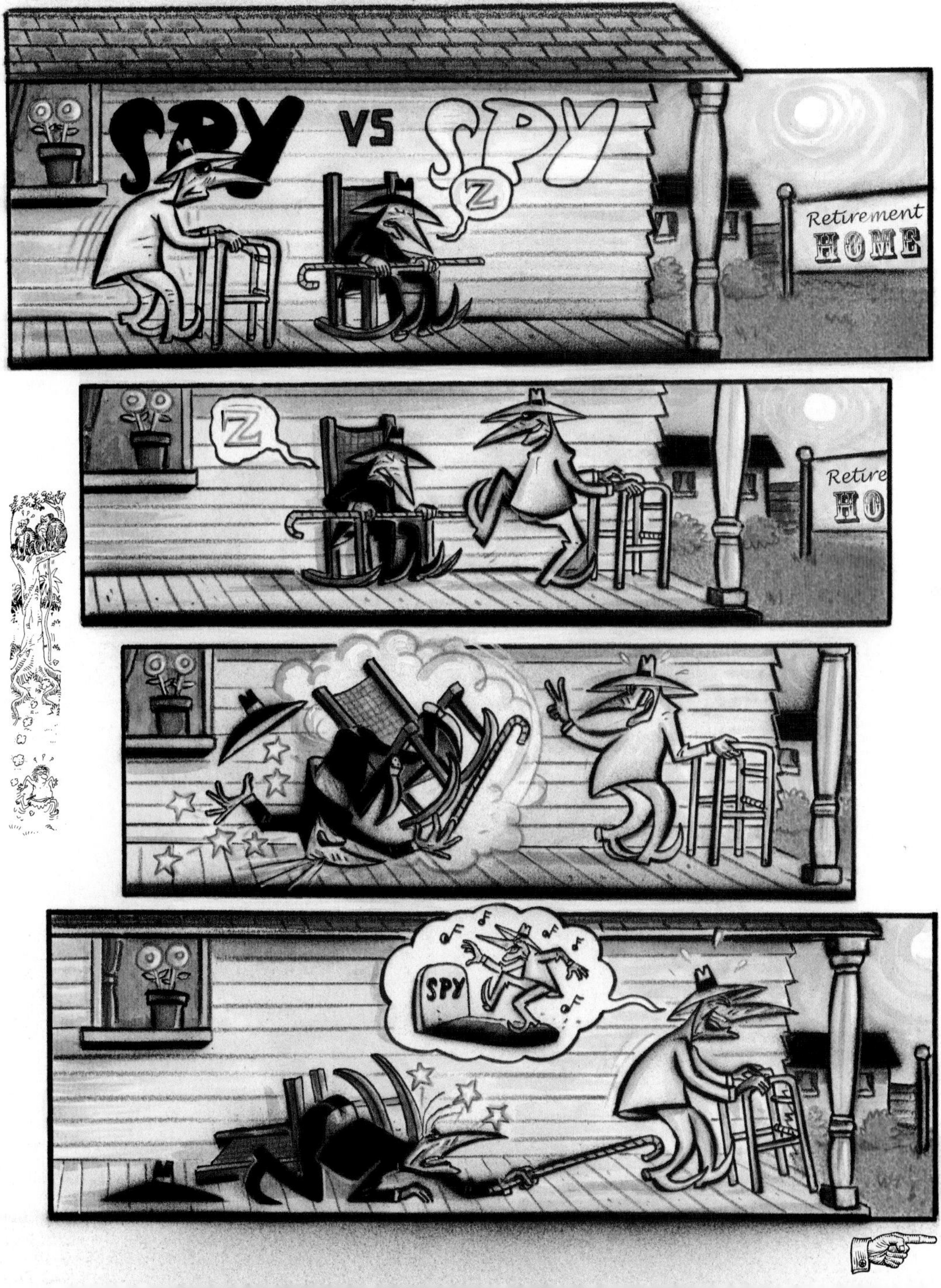
SPY VS SPY
Z
Retirement
HOME
Z
SPY

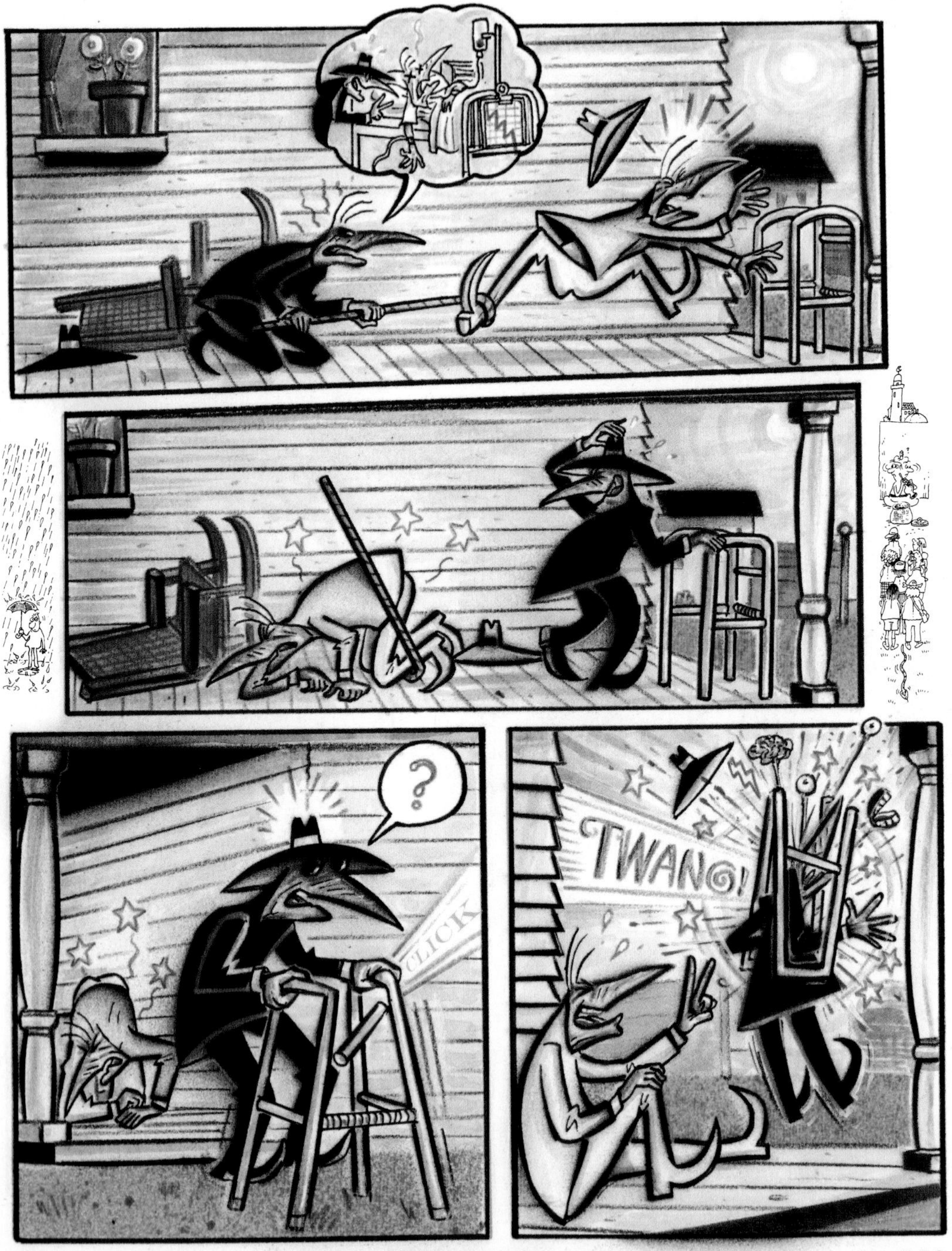
?
CLICK
TWANG!
KUPER

JOKE AND DAGGER DEPT.

SPY VS SPY

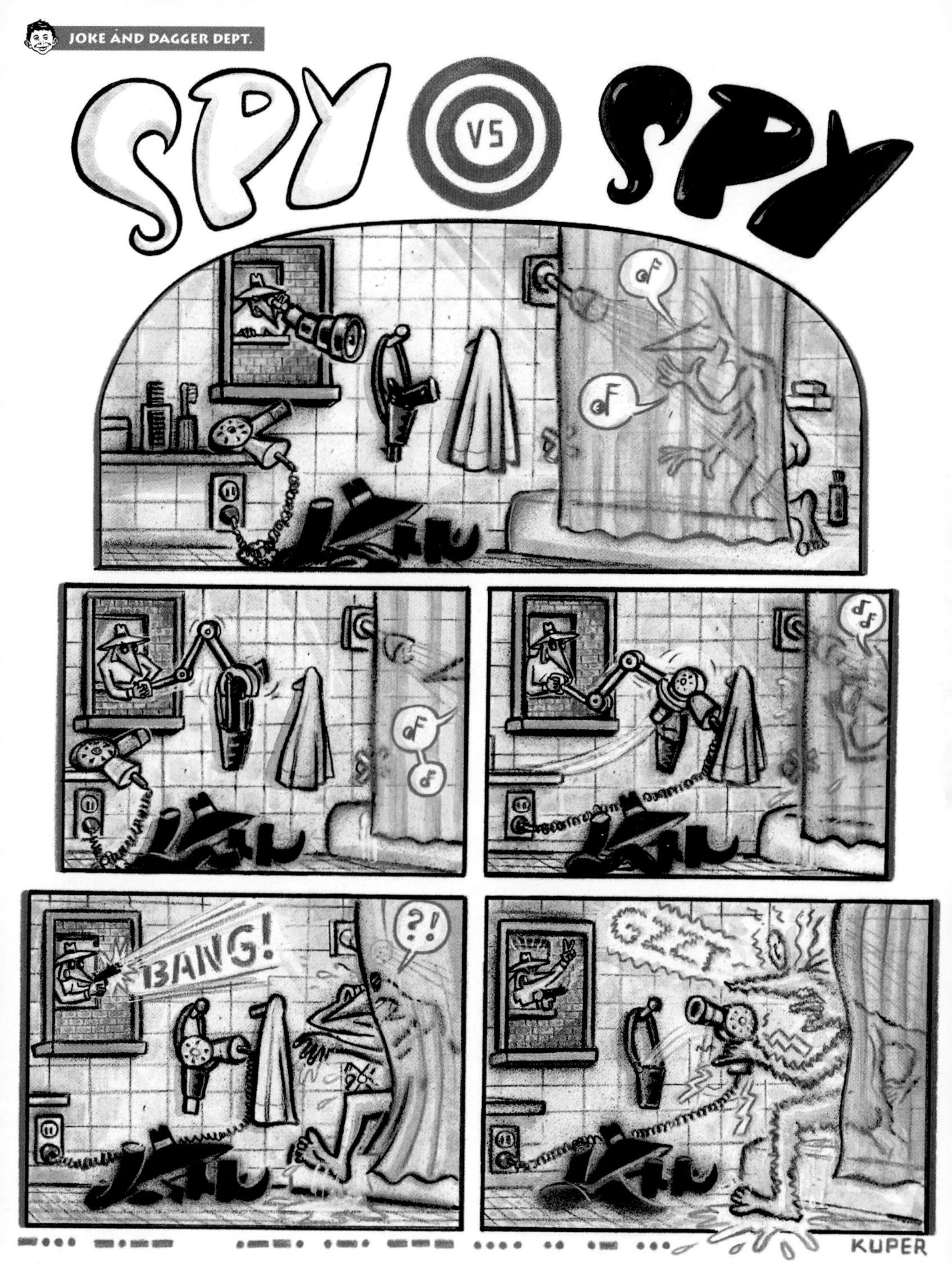
BANG!
?!
KUPER

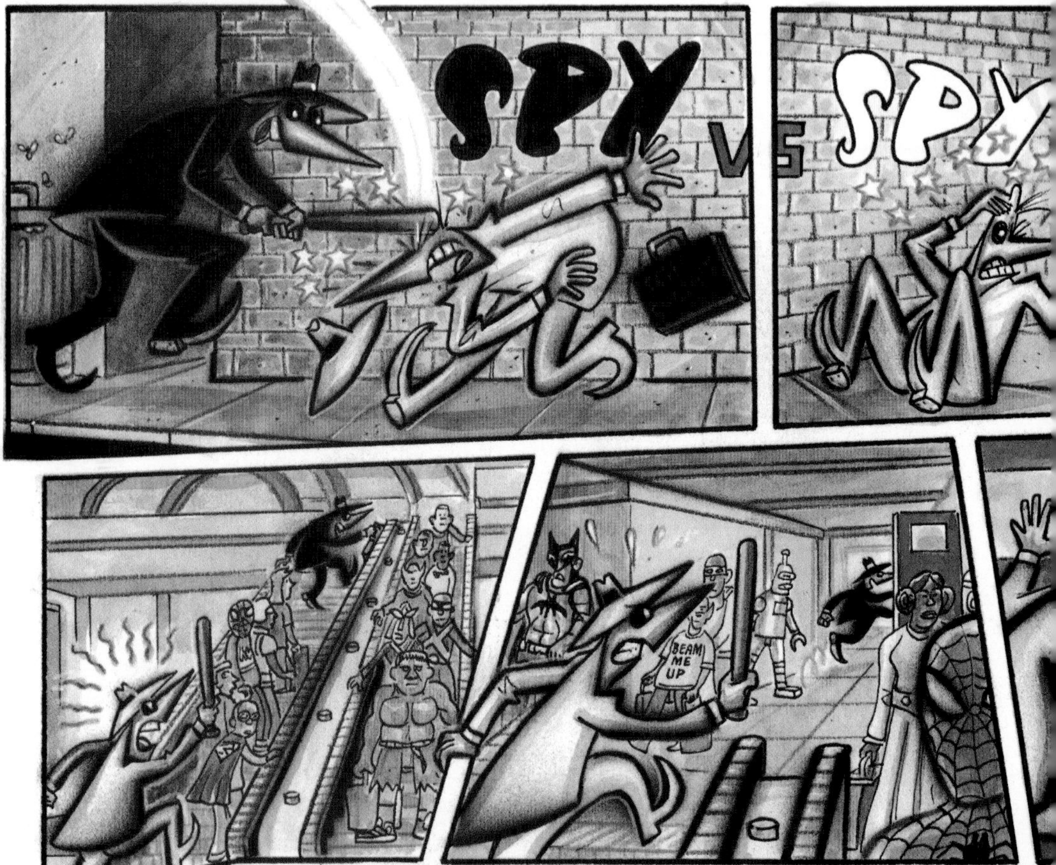
SPY
VS
SPY
BEAM ME UP

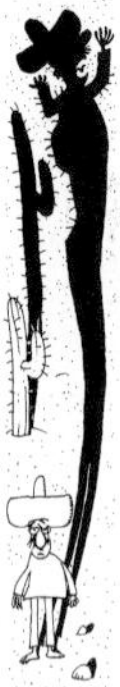

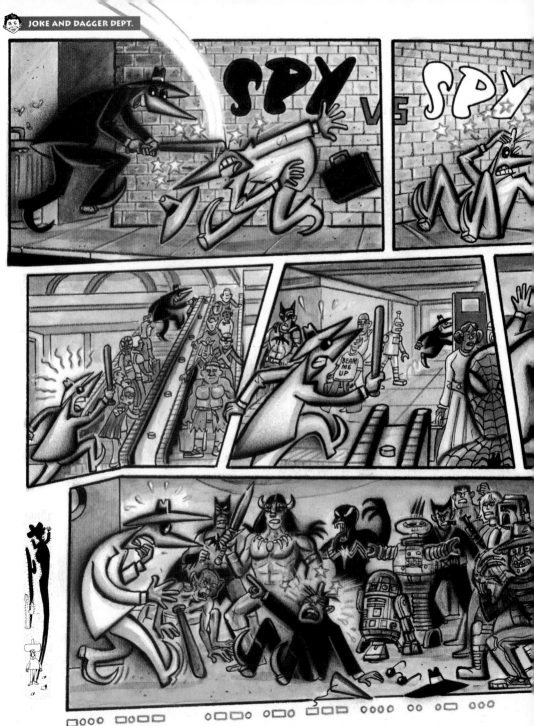

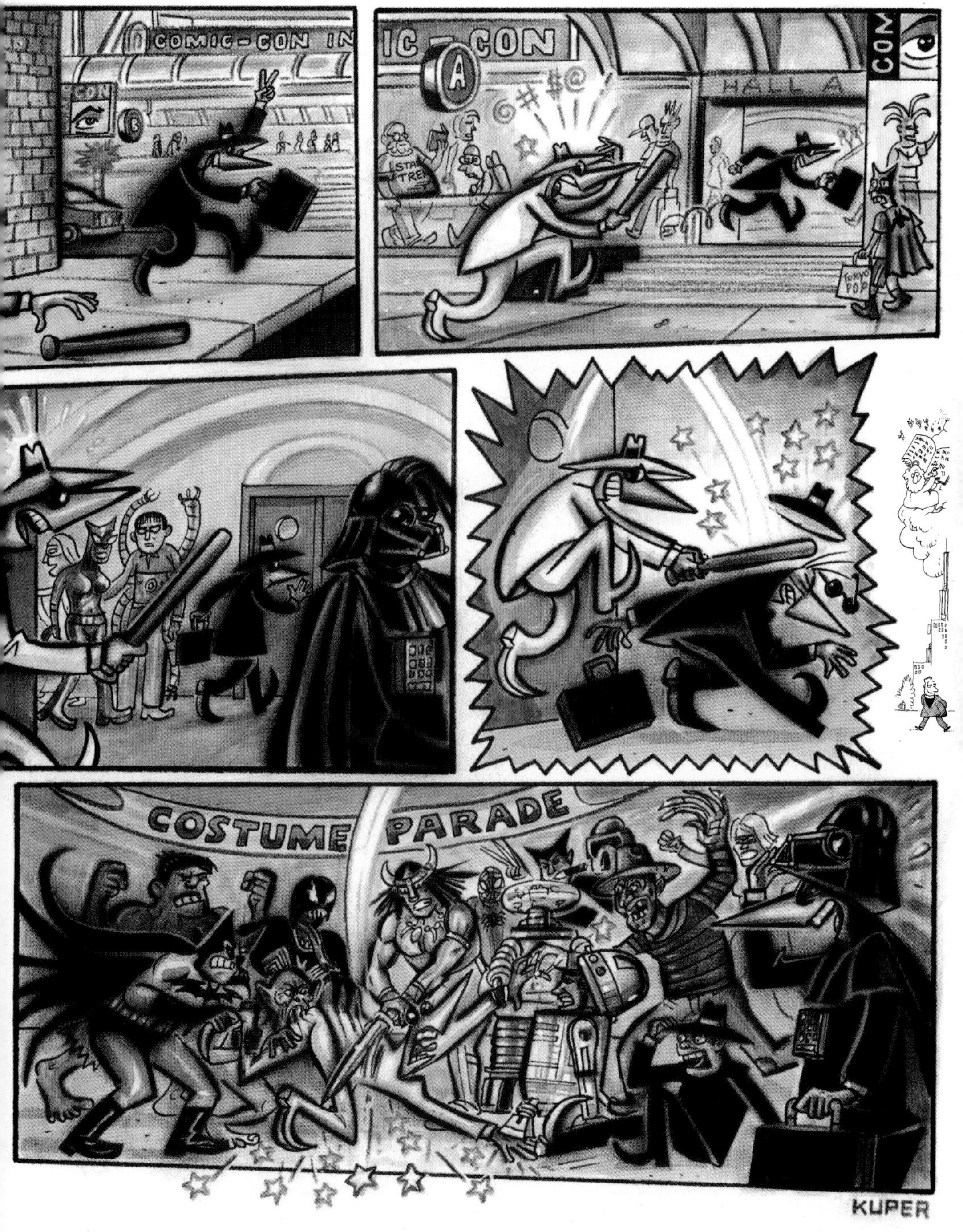

COMIC-CON IN
CON
B
IC - CON
A
HALL A
COM
STAR TREK
TOKYO POP
COSTUME PARADE
KUPER

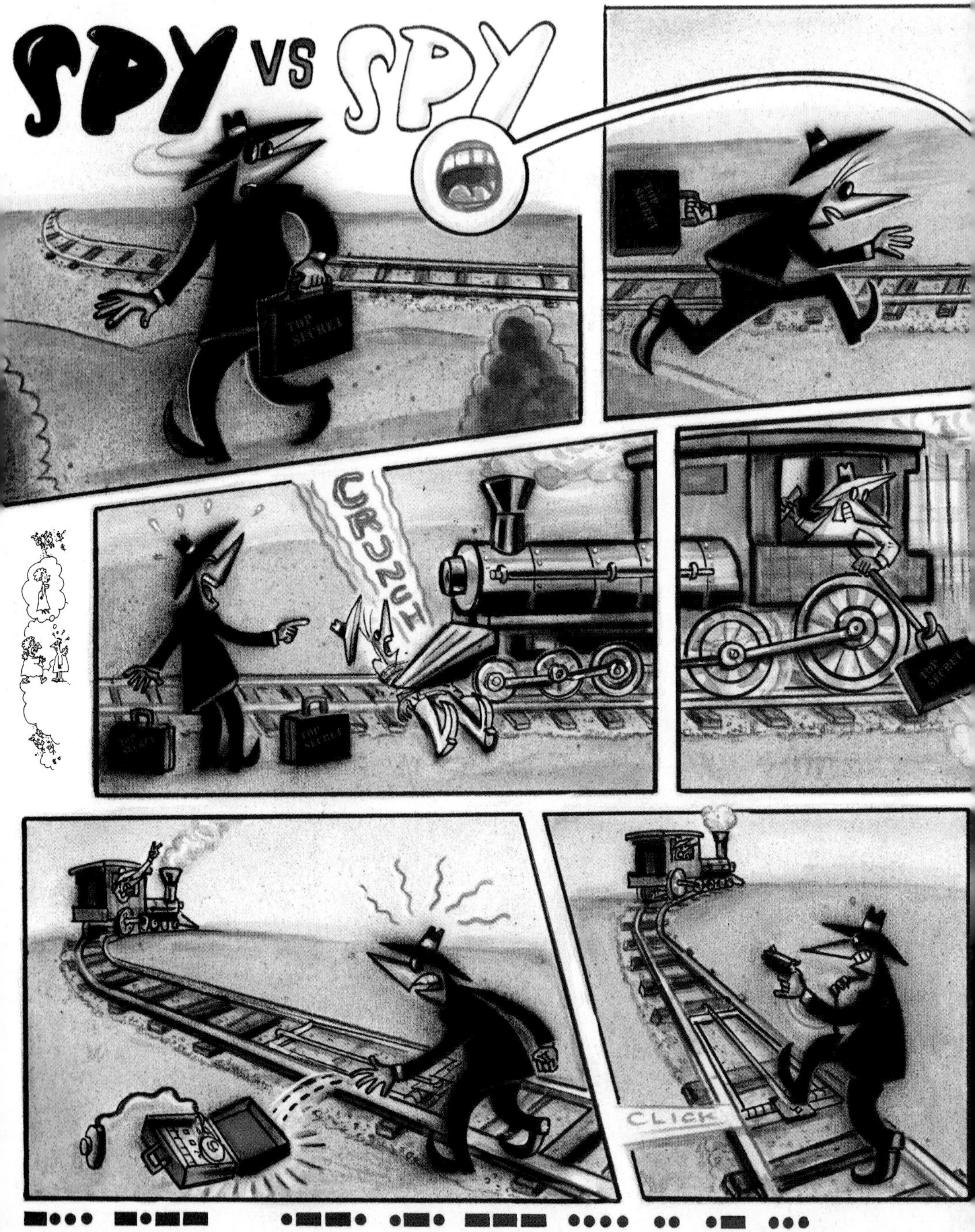
SPY VS SPY
TOP SECRET
TOP SECRET
CRUNCH
TOP SECRET
CLICK

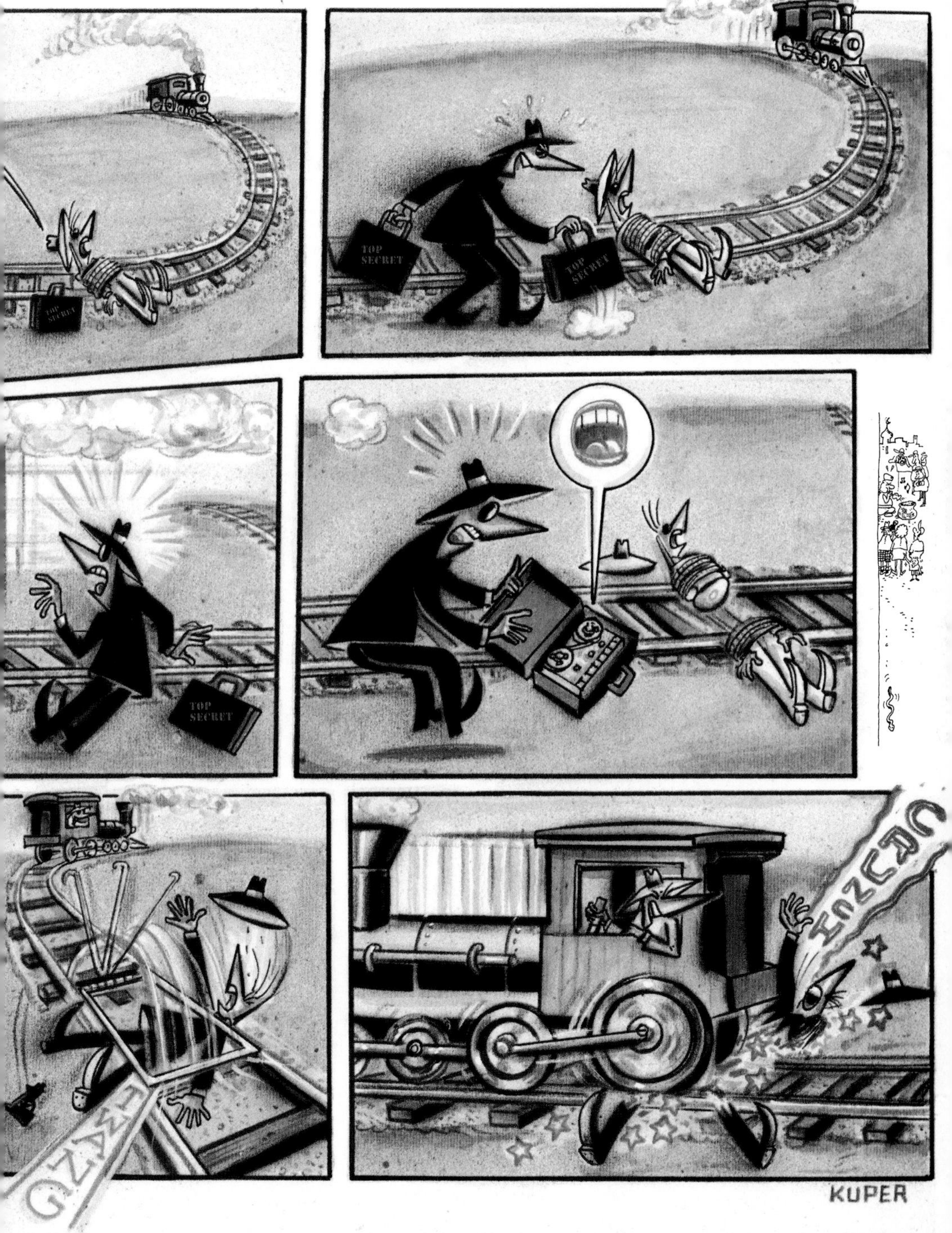
TOP SECRET
TOP SECRET
TOP SECRET
TOP SECRET
KUPER

SPY VS SPY

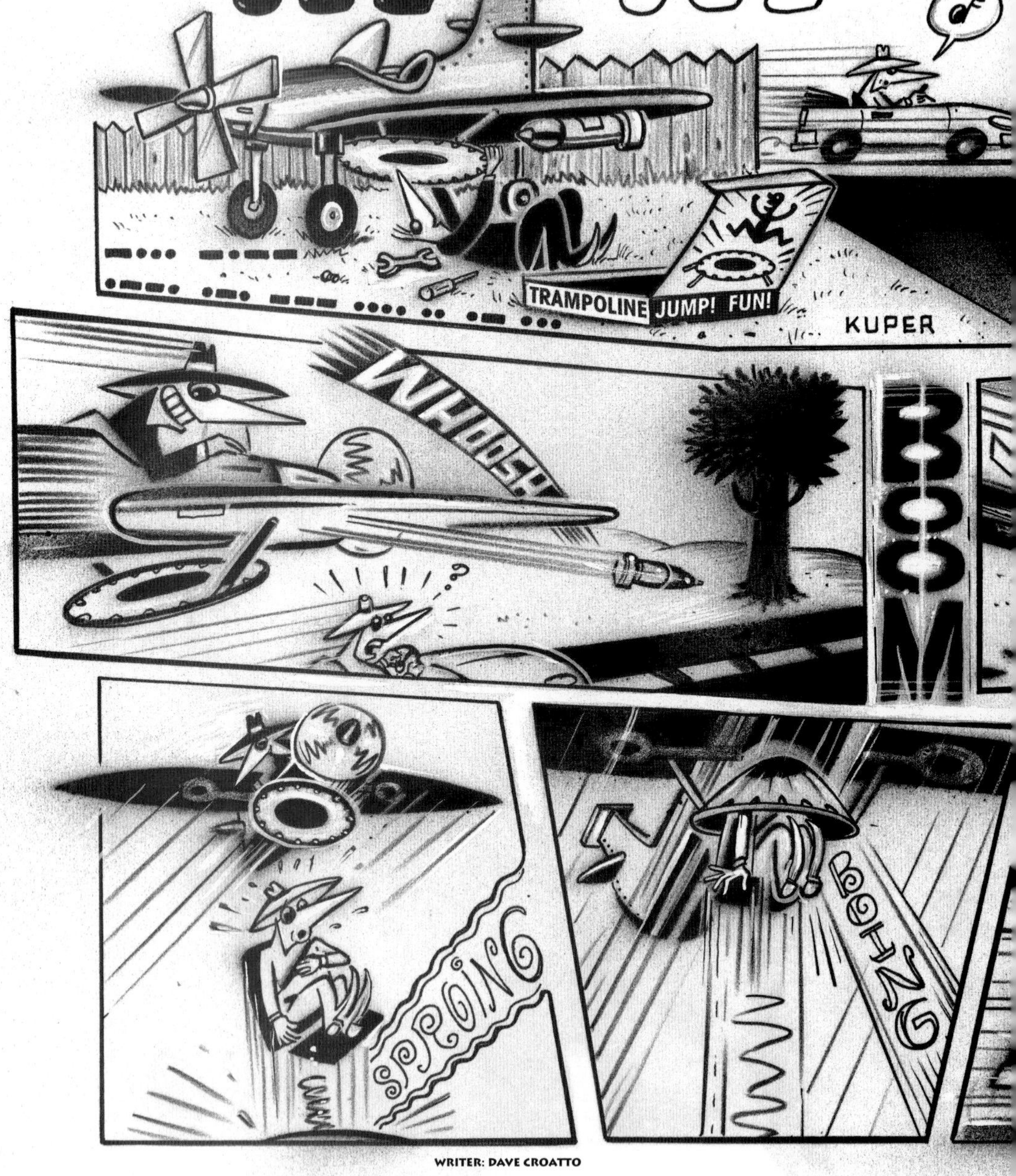
TRAMPOLINE JUMP! FUN!
KUPER
WHOOSH
BOOM
SPRONG
BOING

WRITER: DAVE CROATTO

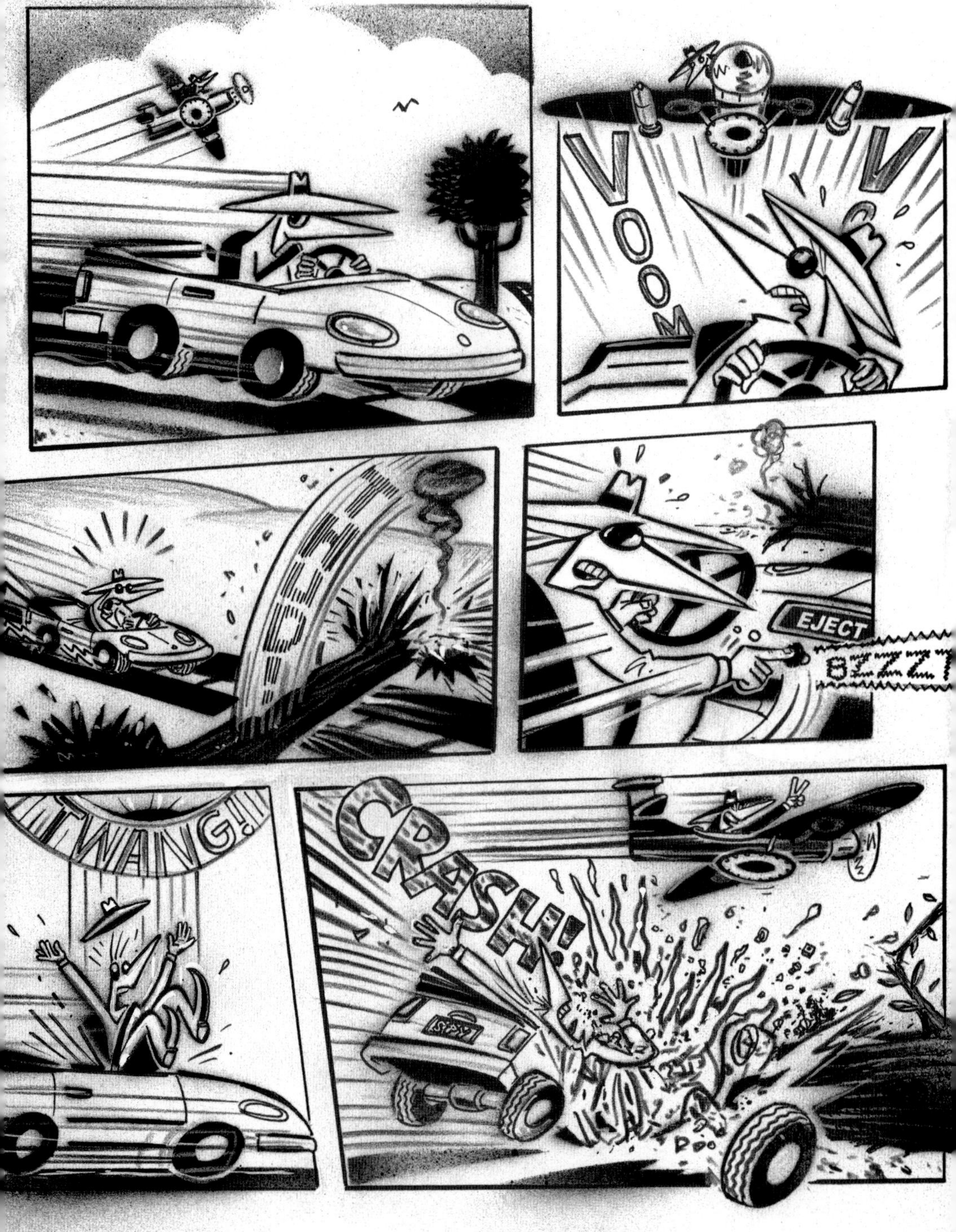

VROOOM
CHUNK
EJECT
BZZZT
TWANG!
CRASH!
SPY

SPY VS SPY VS SPY

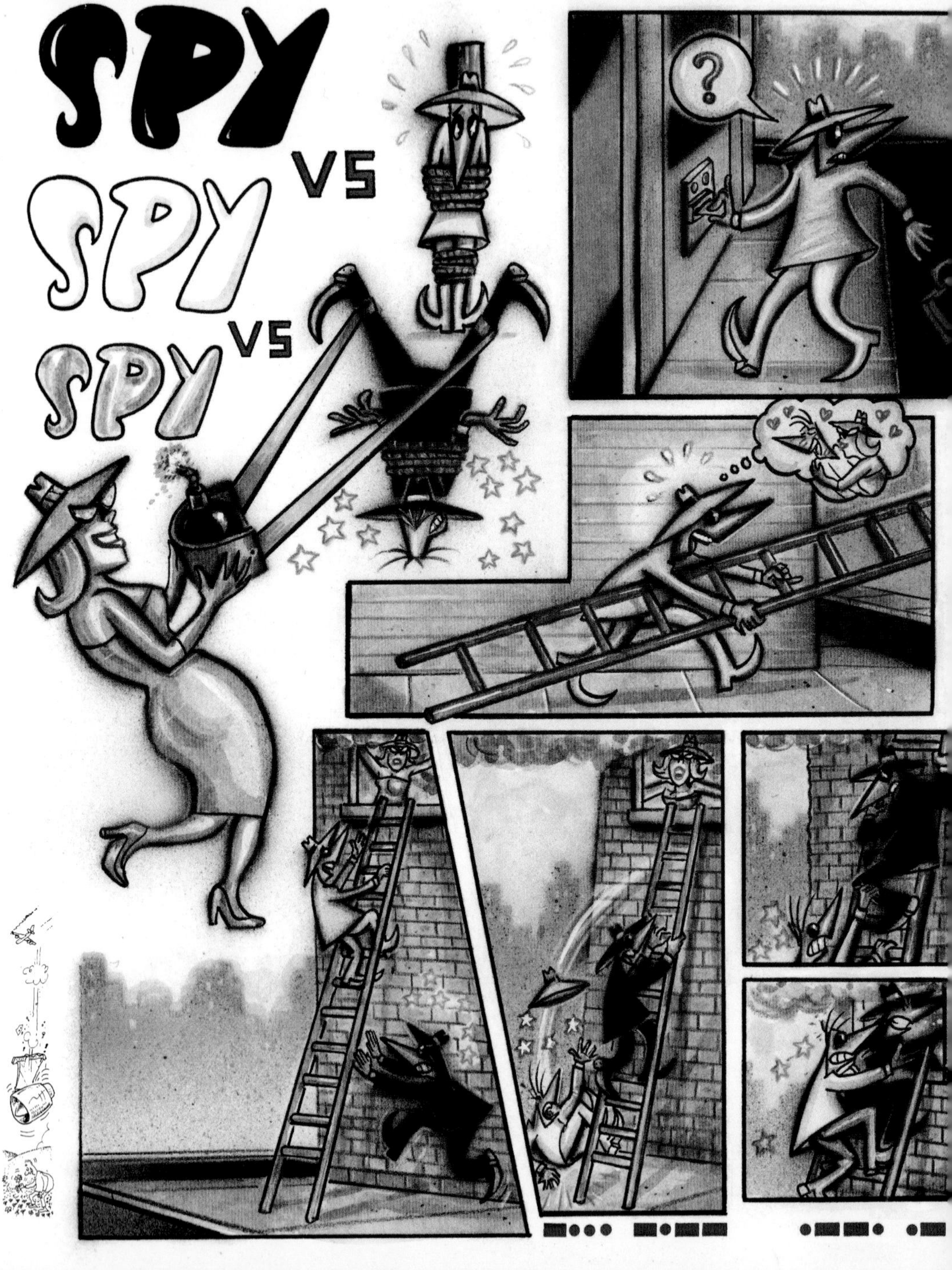

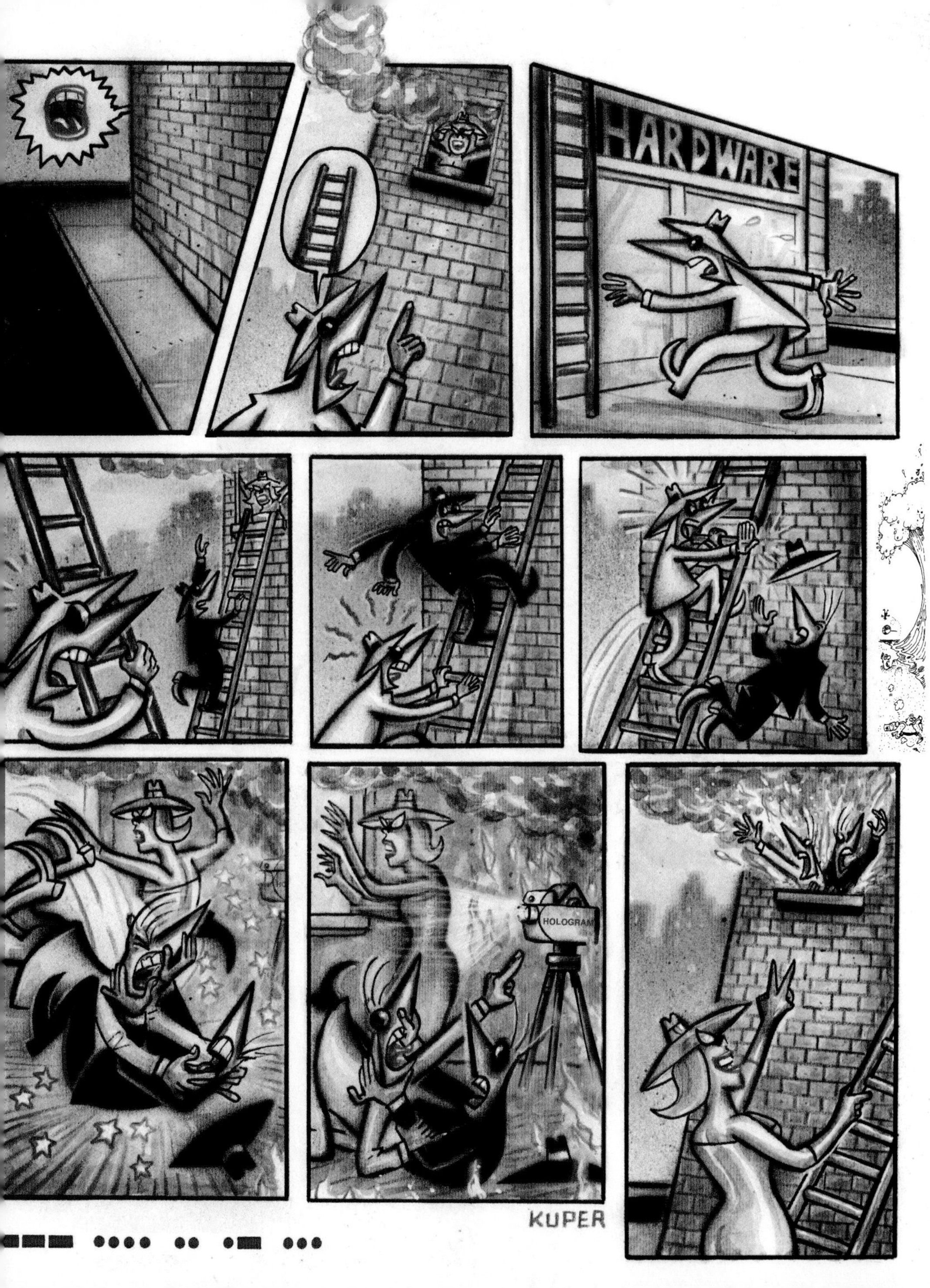

HARDWARE
HOLOGRAM
KUPER

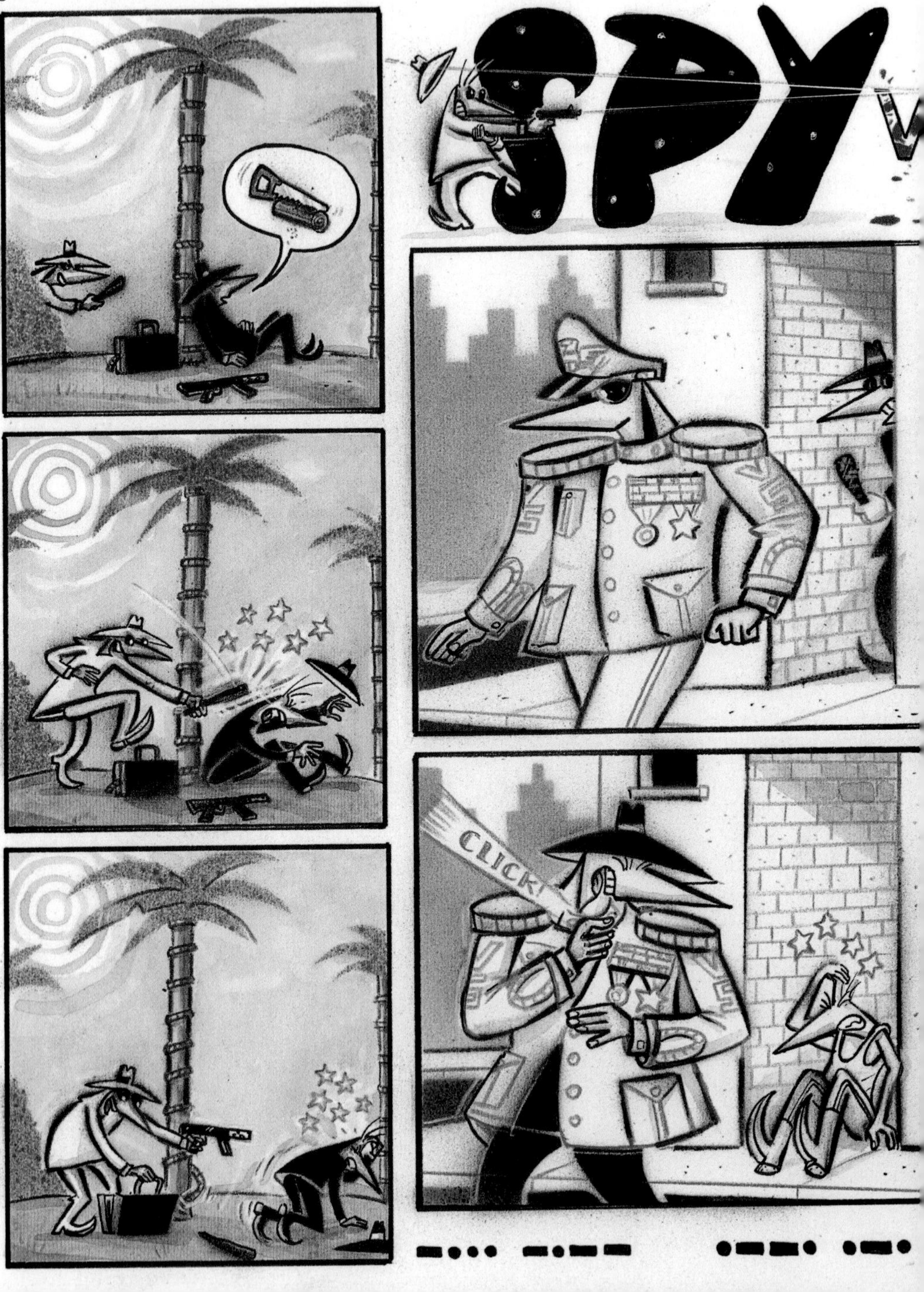
SPY
CLICK!

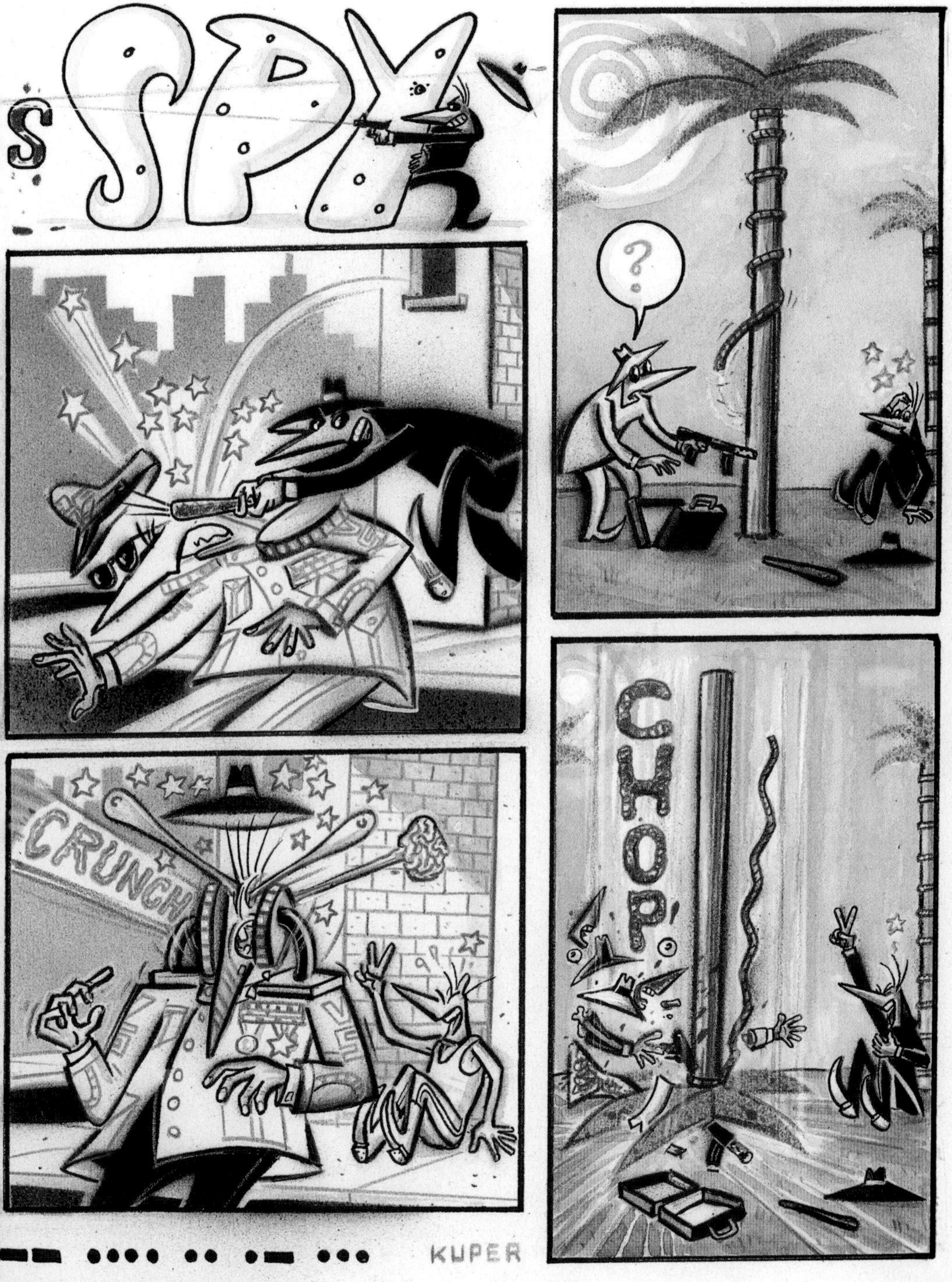
SPY
?
CRUNCH
CHOP
KUPER

JOKE AND DAGGER DEPT.

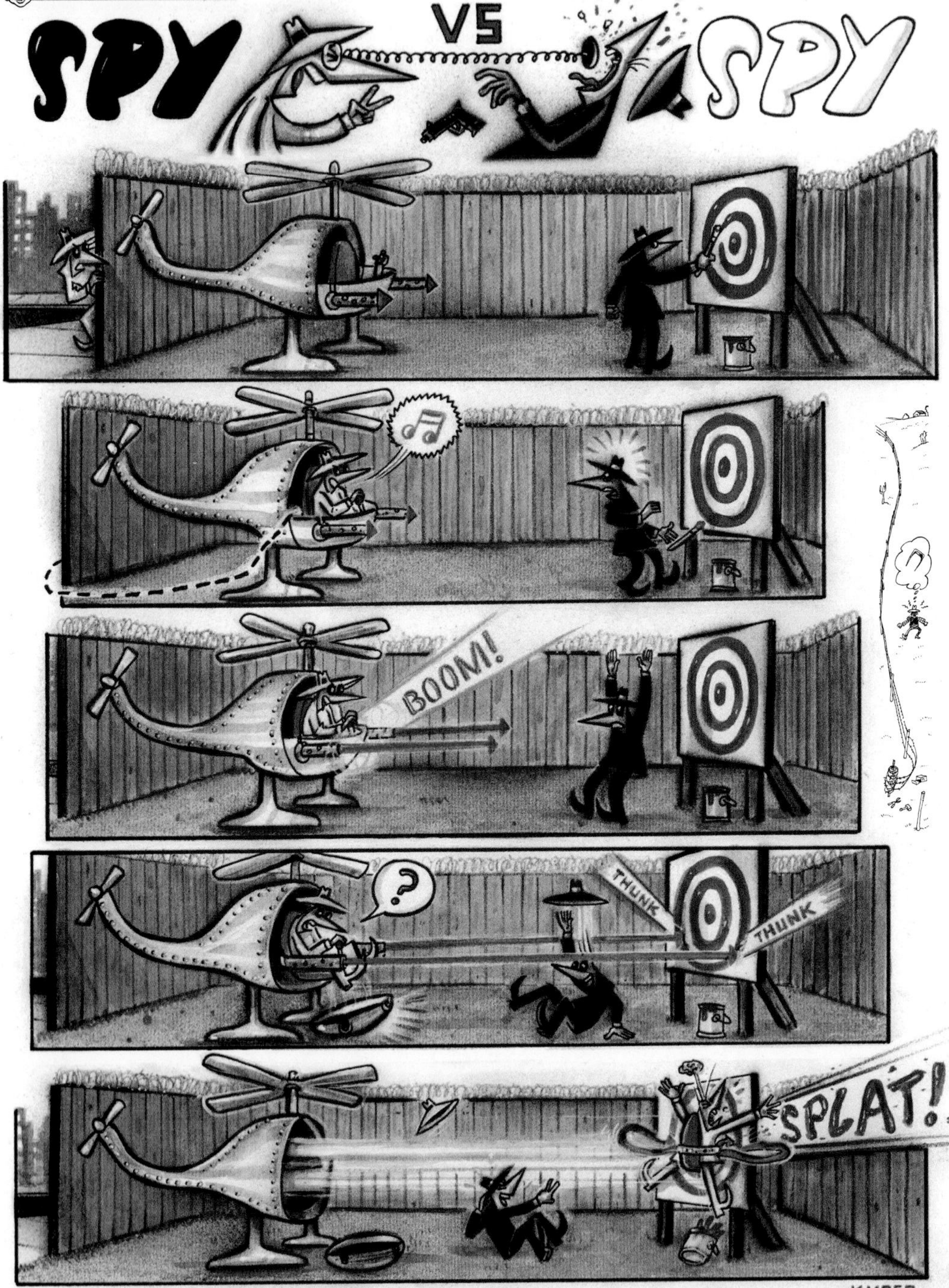
SPY VS SPY
BOOM!
?
THUNK
THUNK
SPLAT!
KUPER

More Misadventures from the
Diabolical Duo of Double Cross and Deceit!

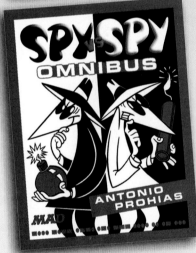

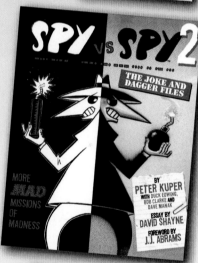

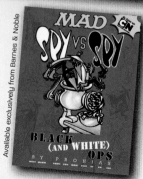

Available exclusively from Barnes & Noble

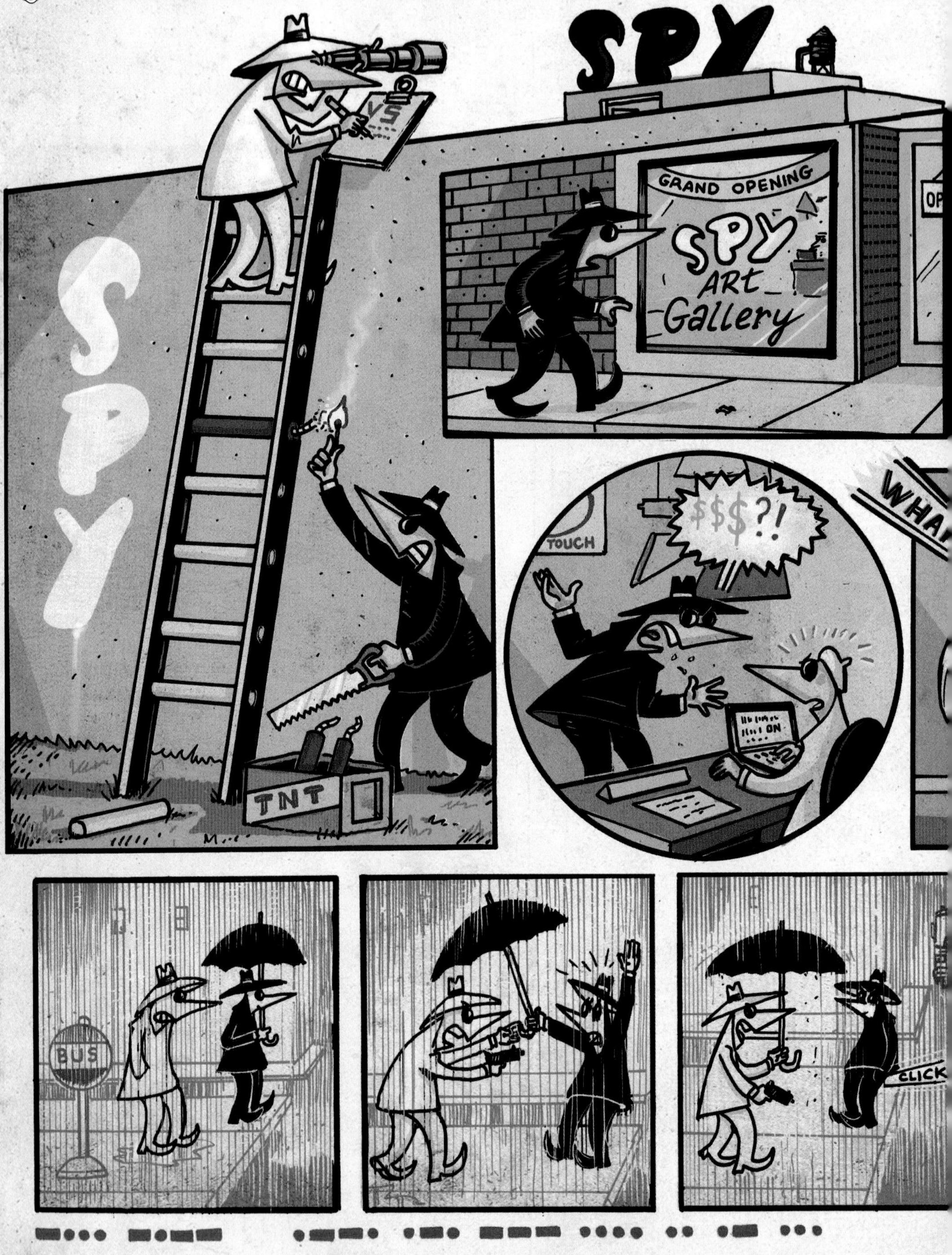
SPY
VS
SPY
GRAND OPENING
SPY
ART
Gallery
TNT
$$$?!
TOUCH
ON
BUS
CLICK

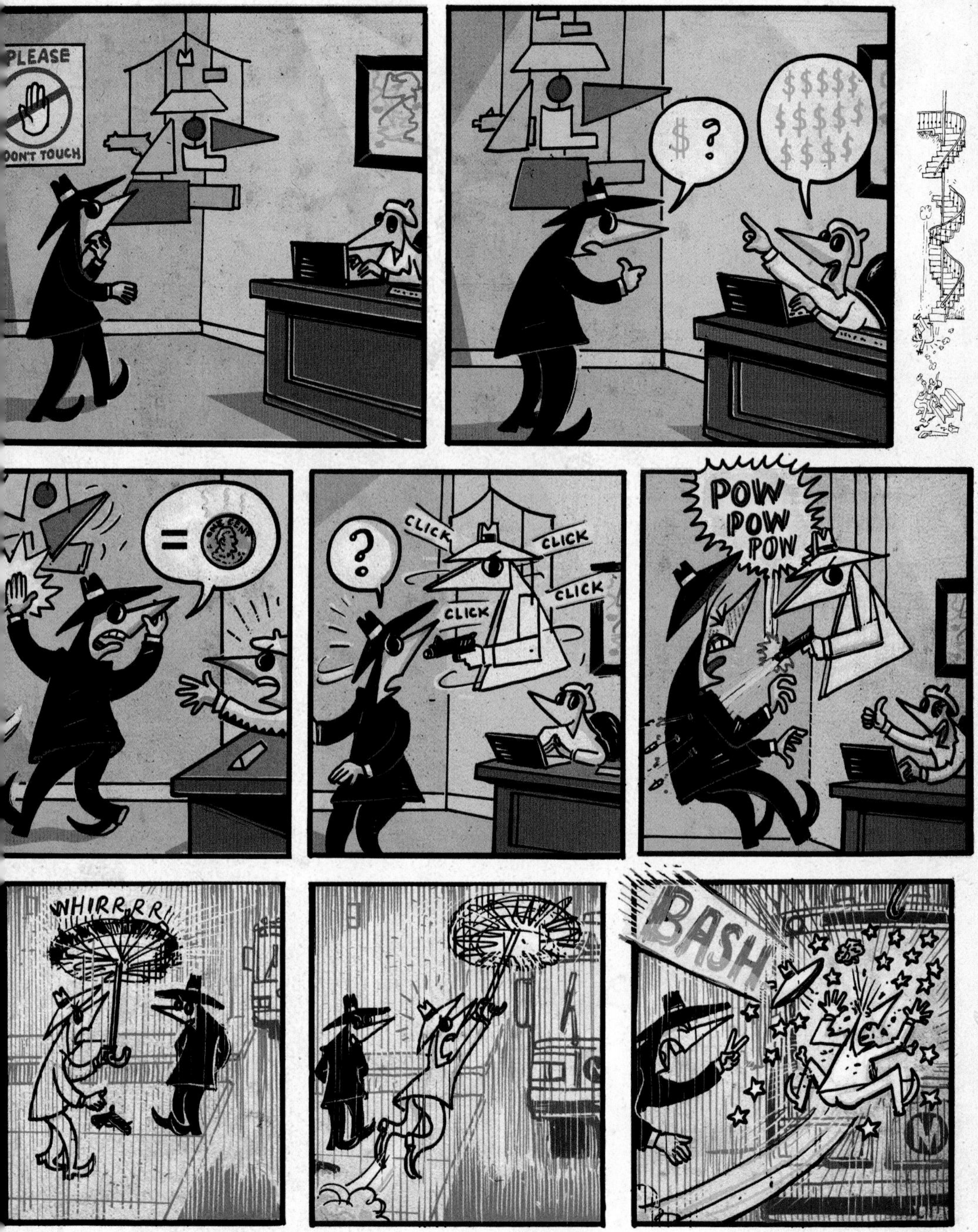
PLEASE
ON'T TOUCH
$?
$$$$$
$$$$$
$$$$
=
?
CLICK
CLICK
CLICK
CLICK
POW
POW
POW
WHIRRRRR!
BASH

KUPER

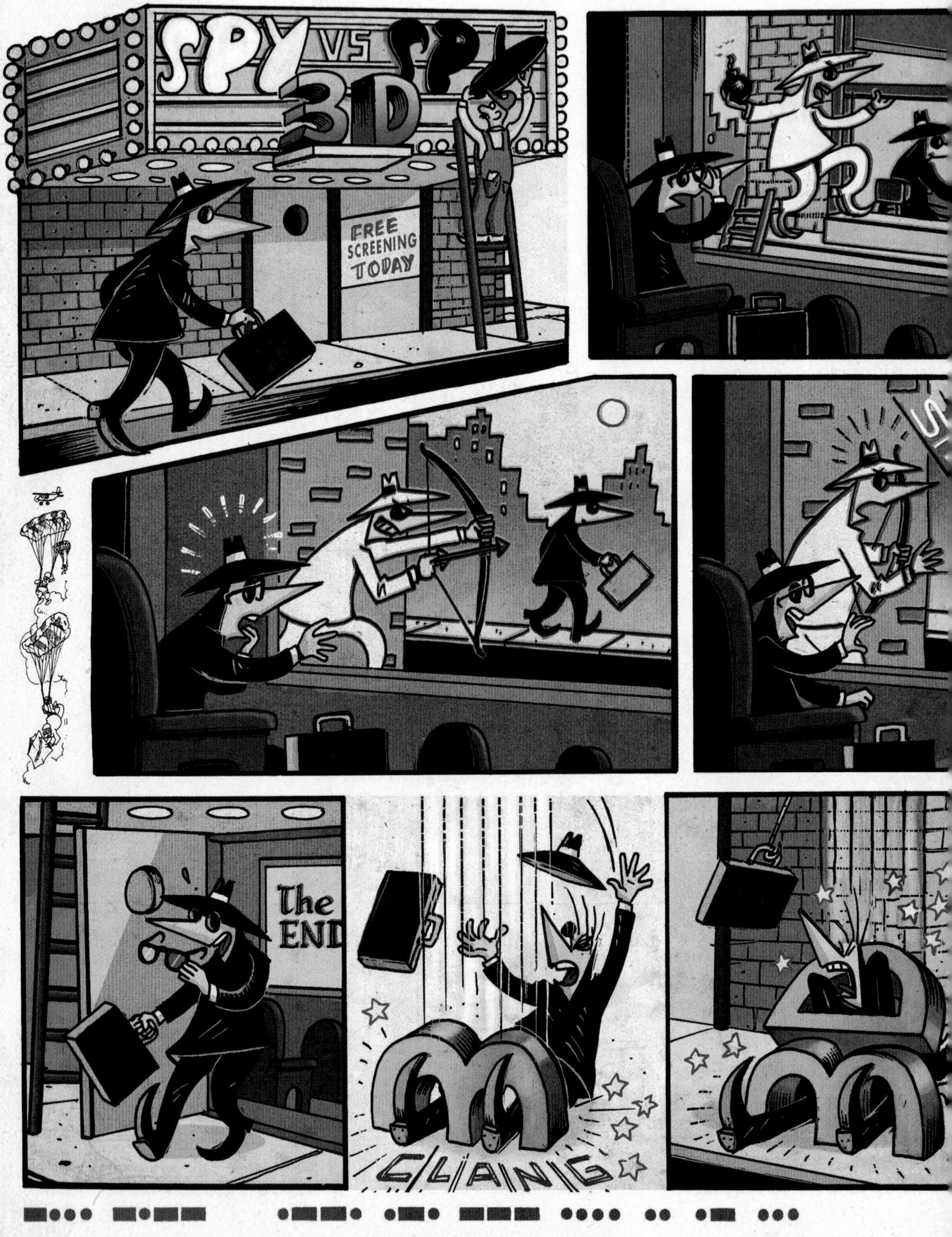
SPY VS SPY
3D
FREE SCREENING TODAY
The END
CLANG

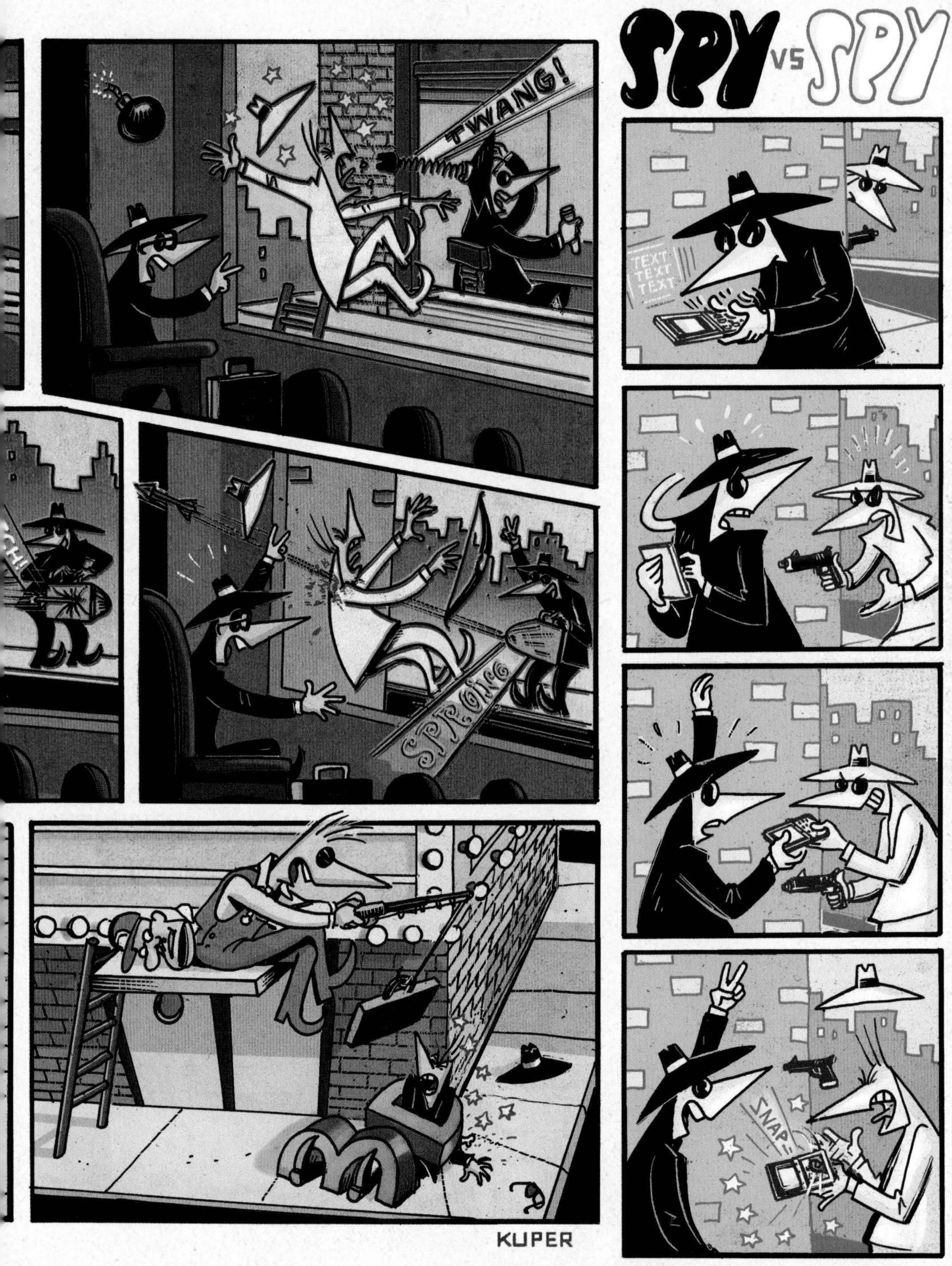
SPY vs SPY
TWANG!
TEXT TEXT TEXT
SPROING
SNAP
KUPER

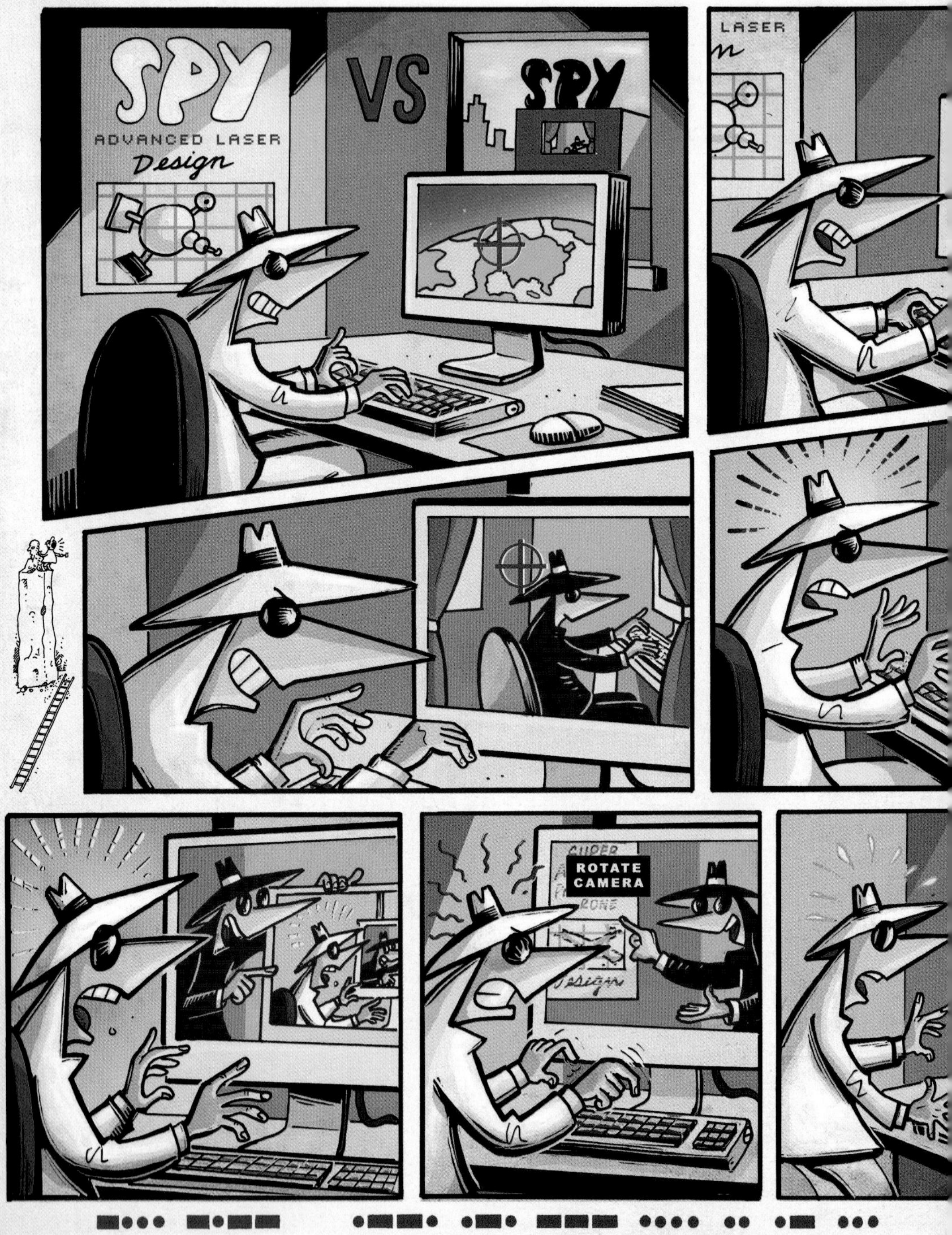
SPY
VS
SPY
ADVANCED LASER
Design
LASER
ROTATE CAMERA

SPY vs SPY

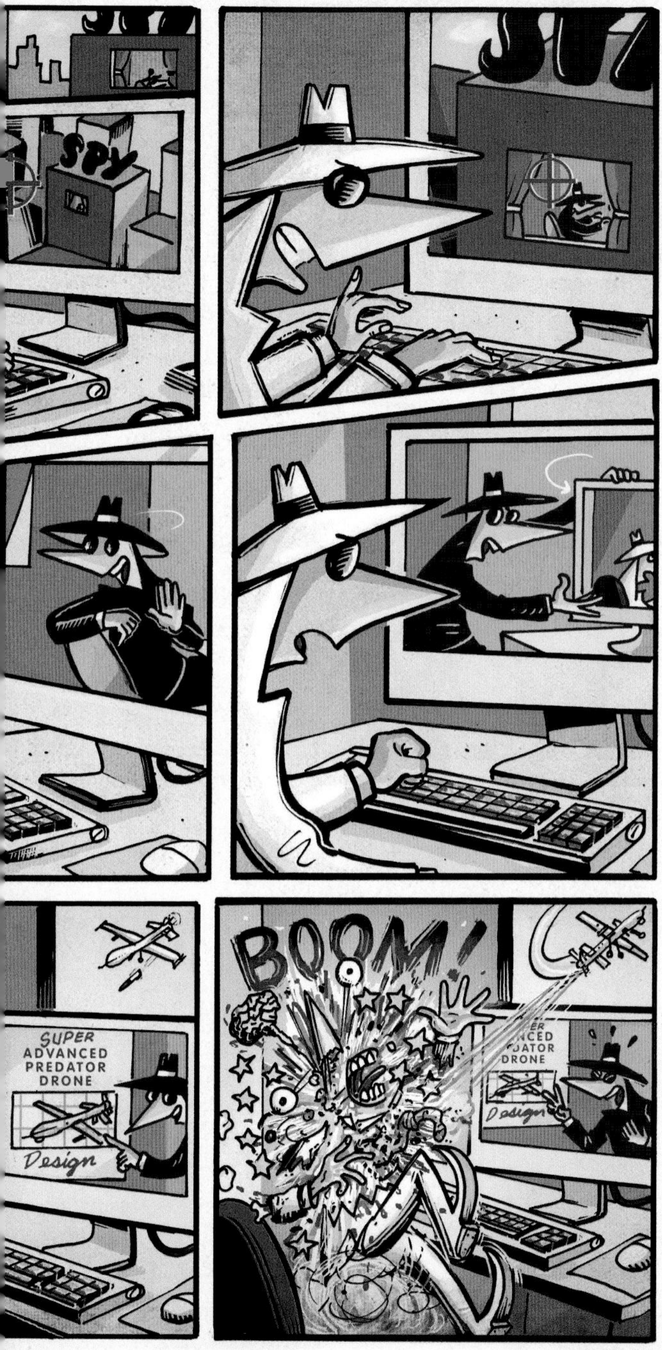

SPY
SUPER
ADVANCED
PREDATOR
DRONE
Design
BOOM!
KUPER

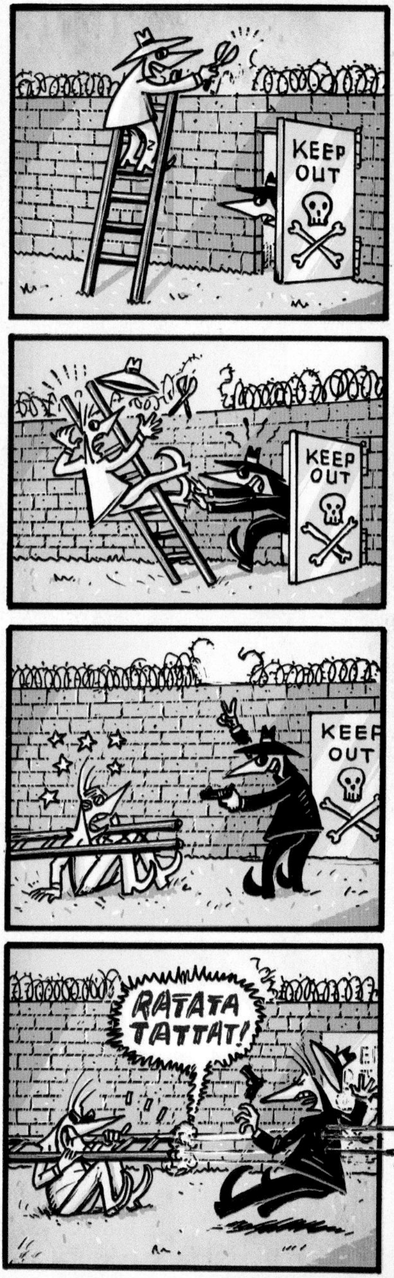

KEEP
OUT
RATATA
TATTAT!

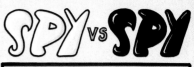

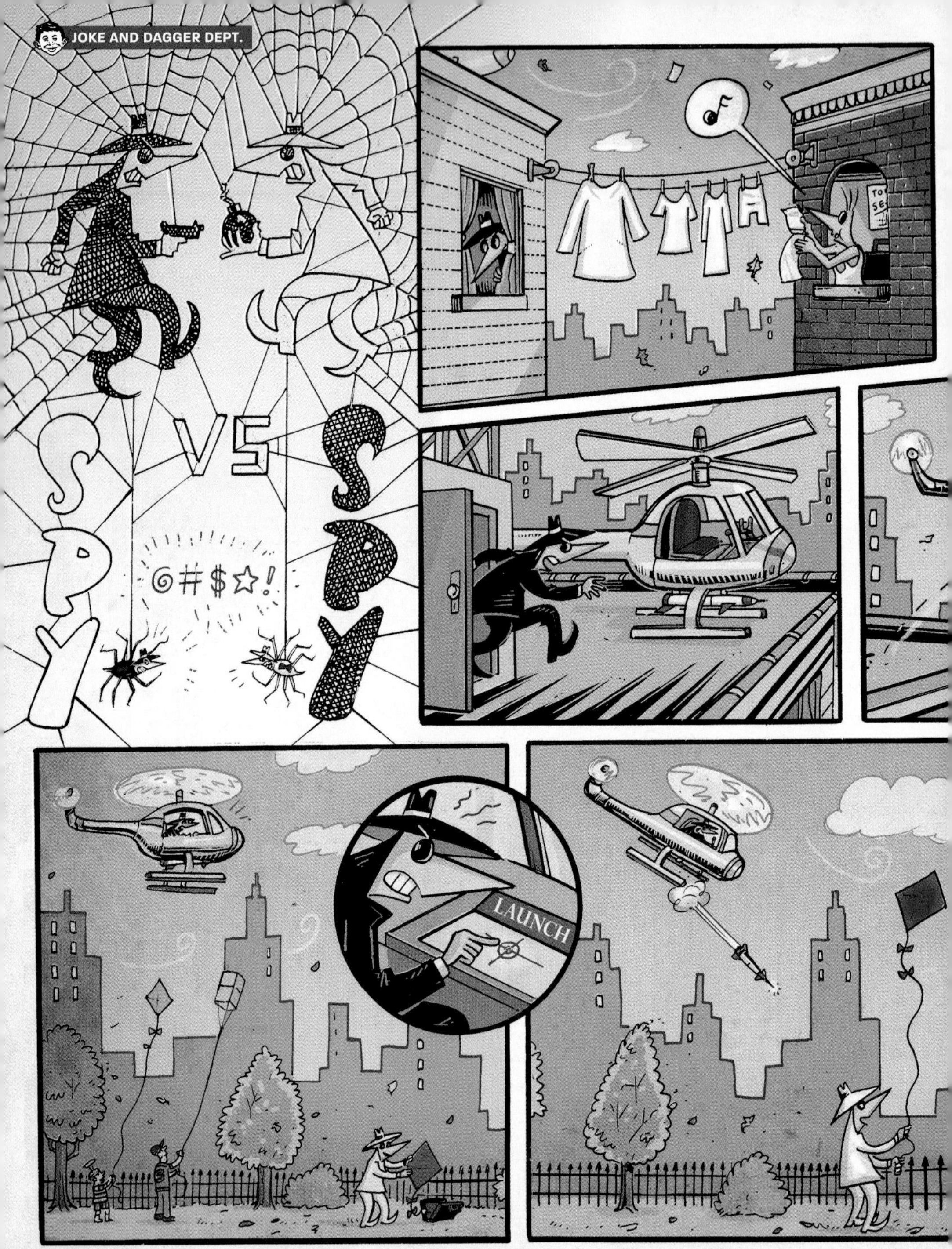
SPY VS SPY
@#$☆!
LAUNCH

SPY vs SPY

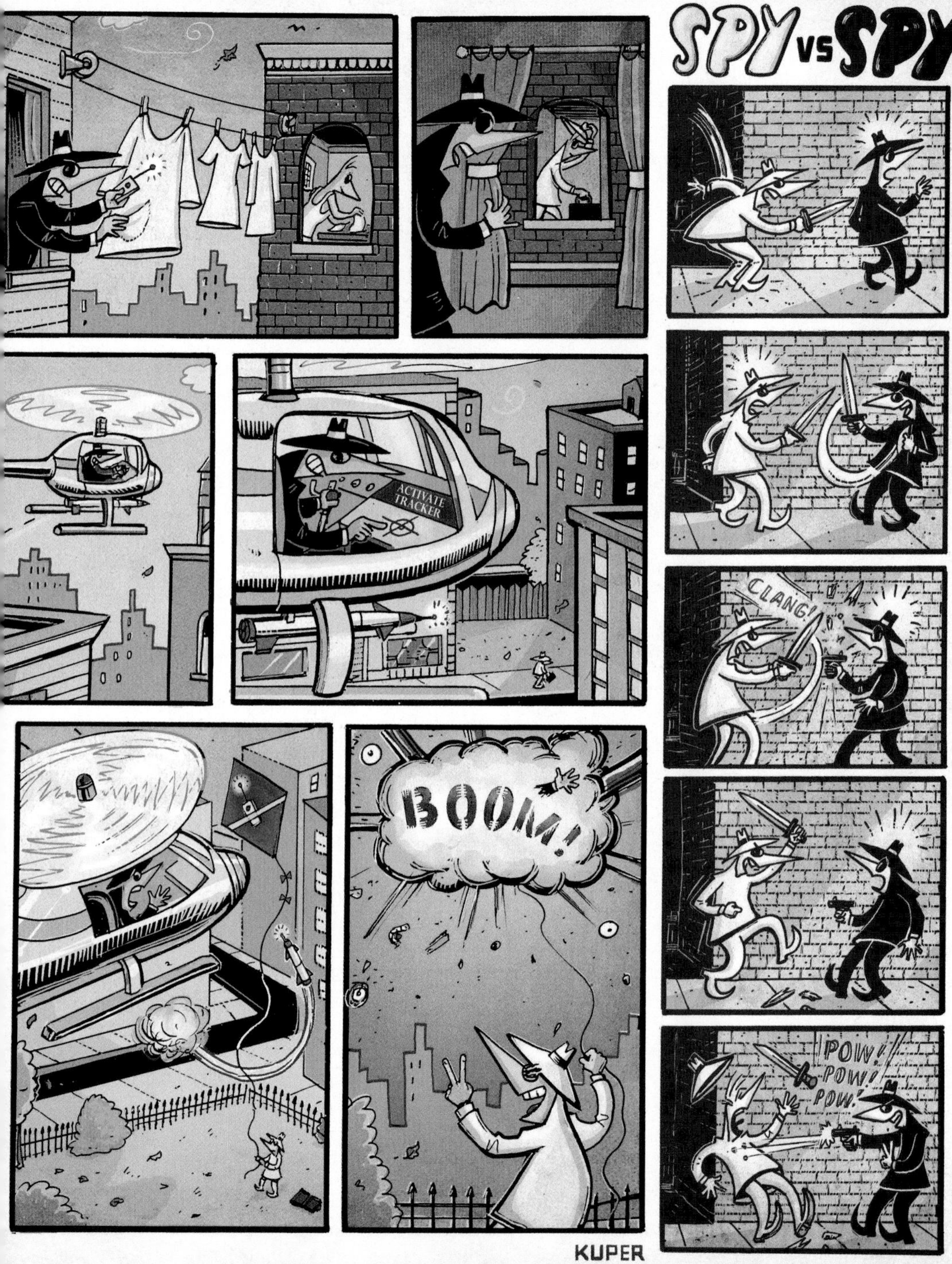
ACTIVATE TRACKER
BOOM!
CLANG!
POW! POW! POW!

KUPER

JOKE AND DAGGER DEPT.

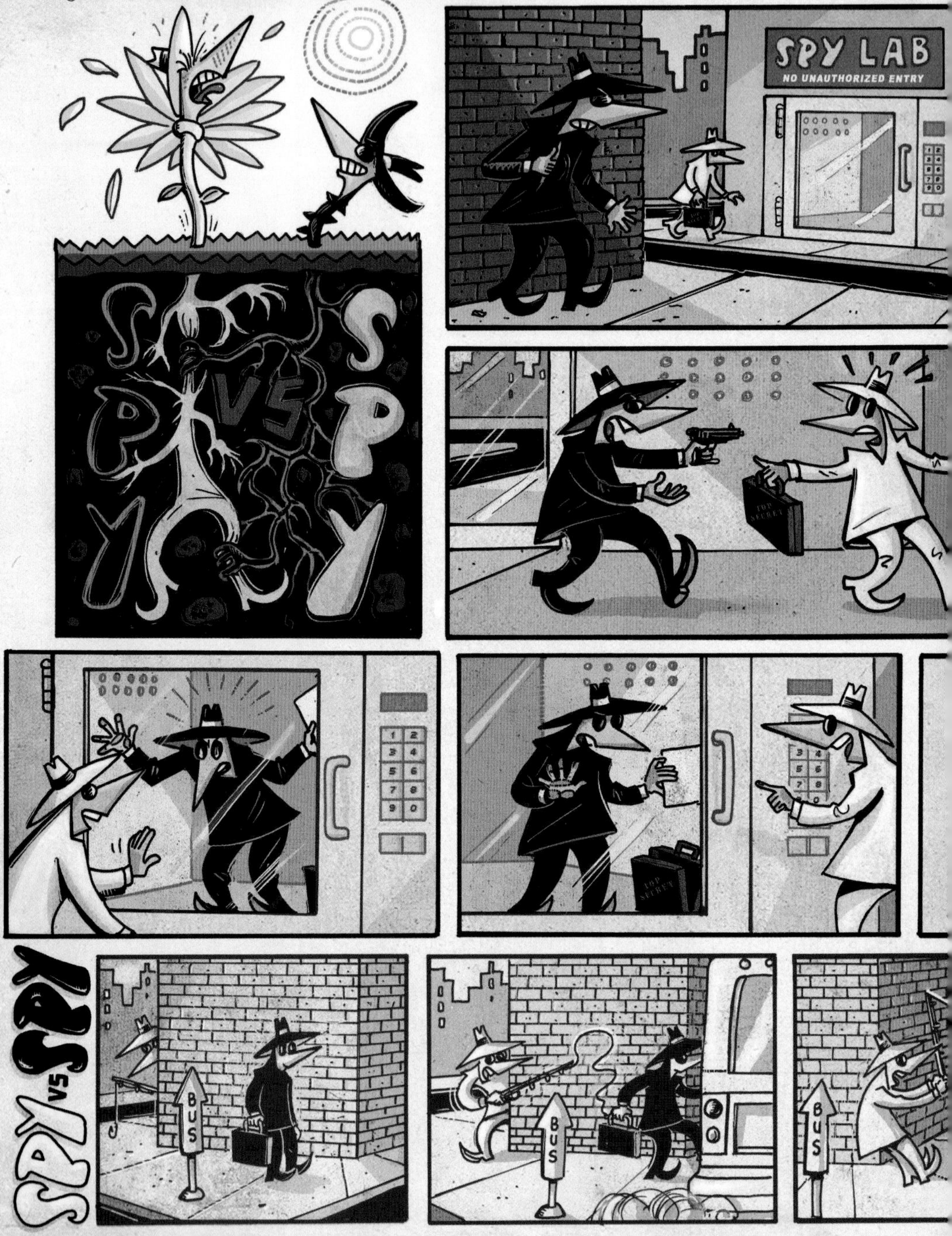
SPY VS SPY
SPY LAB
NO UNAUTHORIZED ENTRY
TOP SECRET
BUS
SPY VS SPY

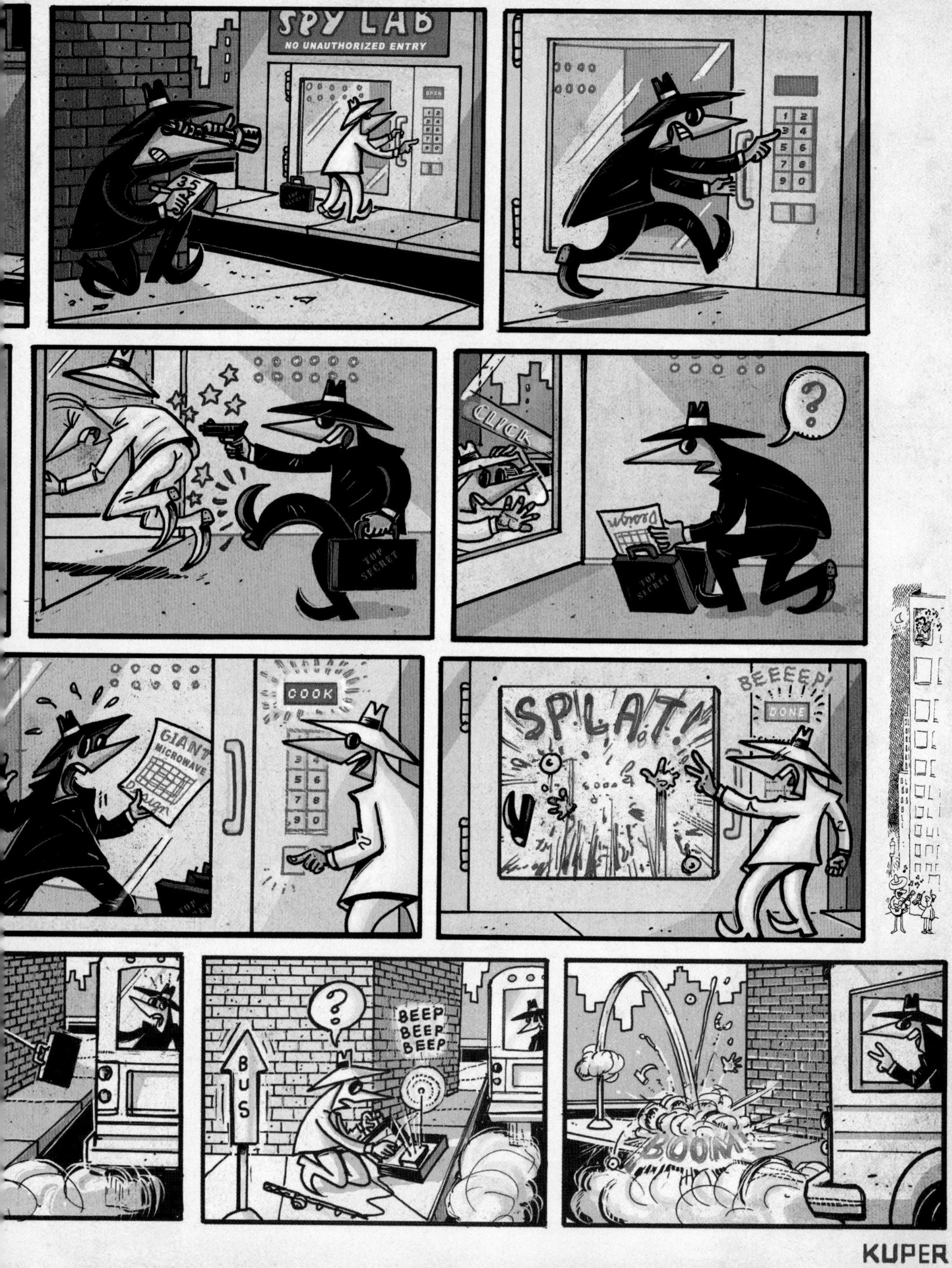
SPY LAB
NO UNAUTHORIZED ENTRY
OPEN
35
TOP SECRET
CLICK
?
GIANT MICROWAVE Design
COOK
BEEEEP!
DONE
SPLAT!
?
BEEP BEEP BEEP
BUS
BOOM

KUPER

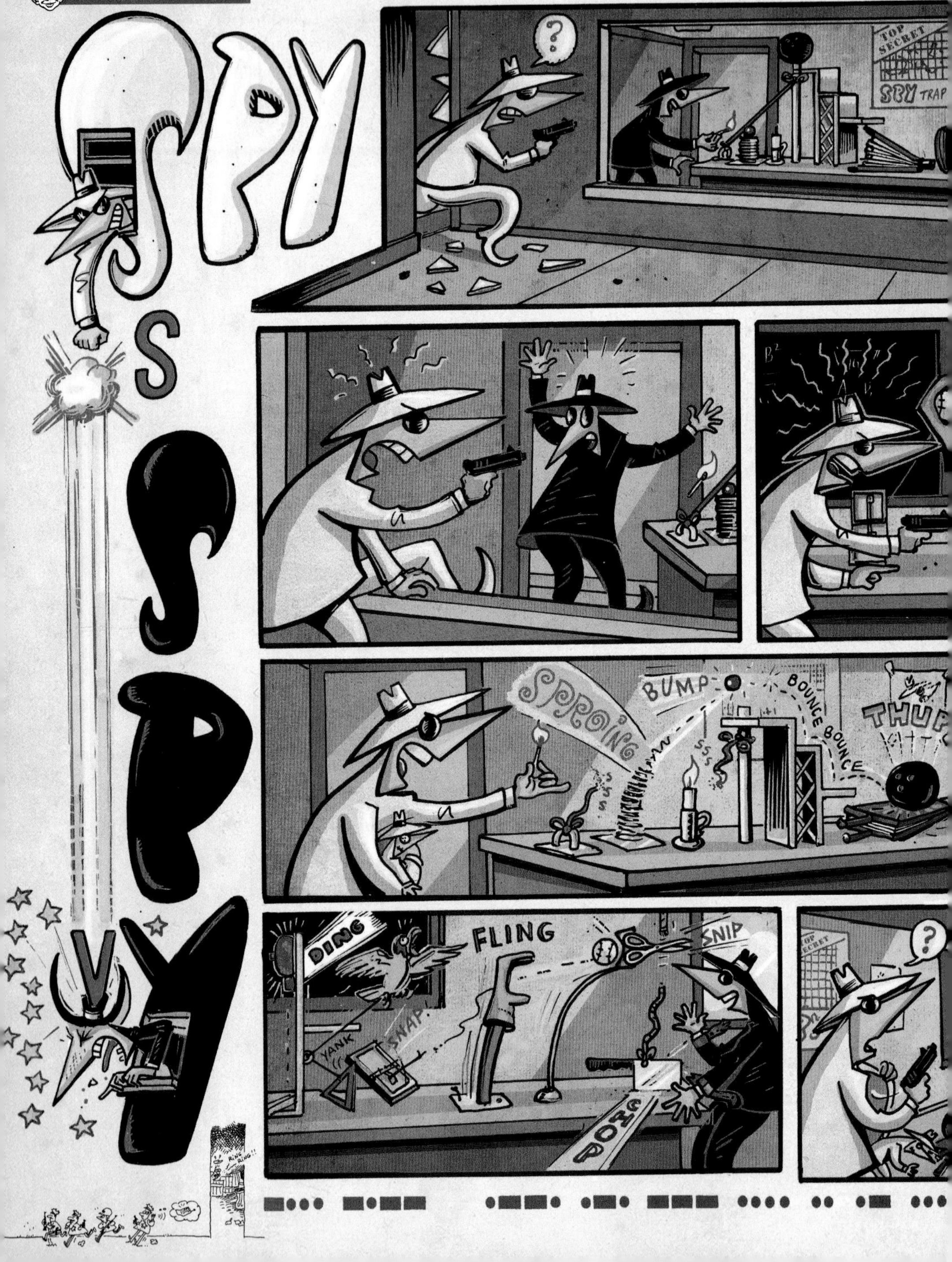
SPY vs SPY
?
TOP SECRET
SPY TRAP
SPROING
BUMP
BOUNCE
BOUNCE
BOUNCE
DING
FLING
SNIP
SNAP
YANK
TOP SECRET
?
RING RING!!

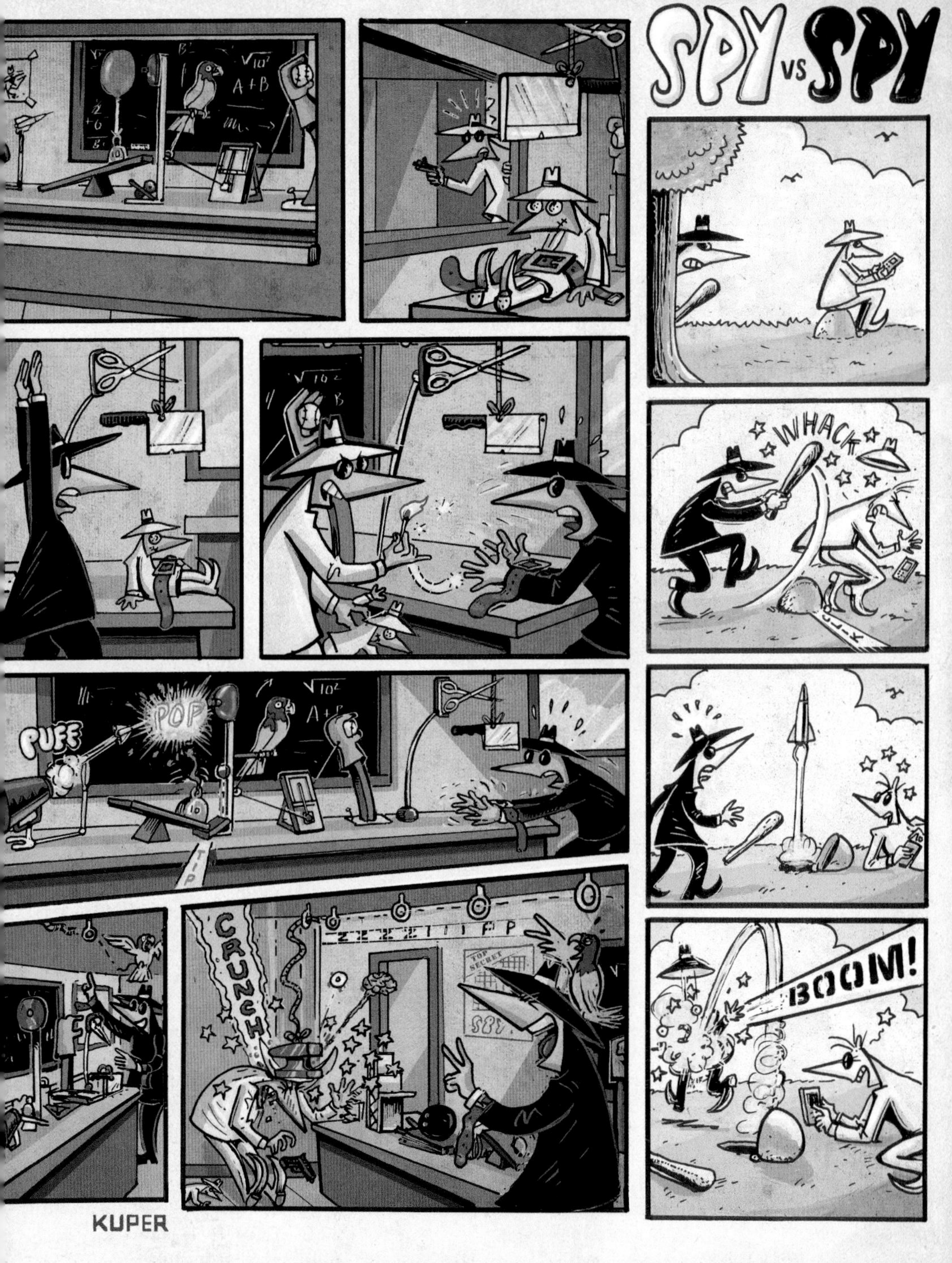
SPY vs SPY
WHACK
BOOM!
PUFF
POP
TOP SECRET
CRUNCH
KUPER

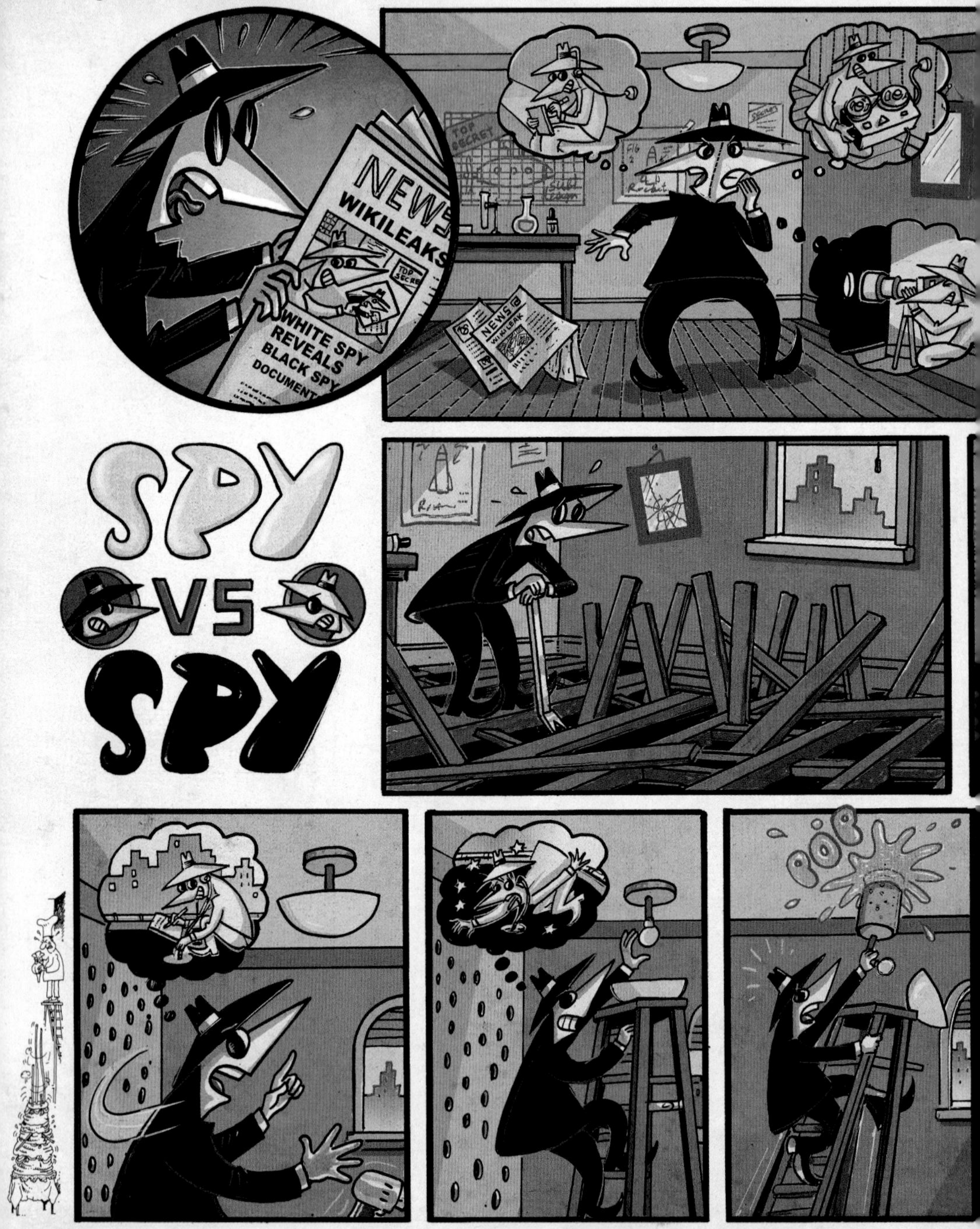
NEWS
WIKILEAKS
TOP SECRET
WHITE SPY REVEALS BLACK SPY DOCUMENT
TOP SECRET
NEWS
WIKILEAK
SPY VS SPY
POP

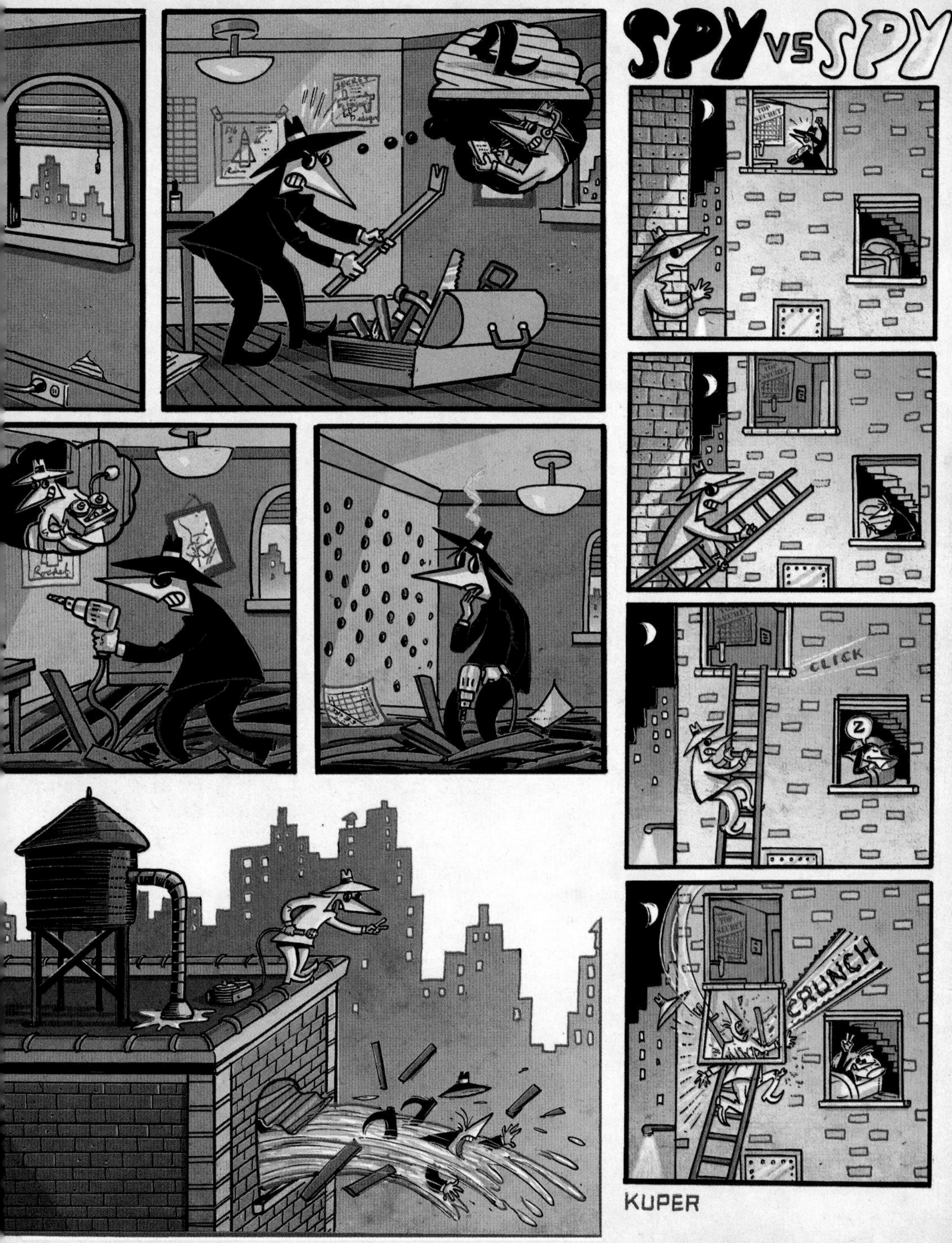
SPY vs SPY
TOP SECRET
CLICK
Z
CRUNCH
KUPER

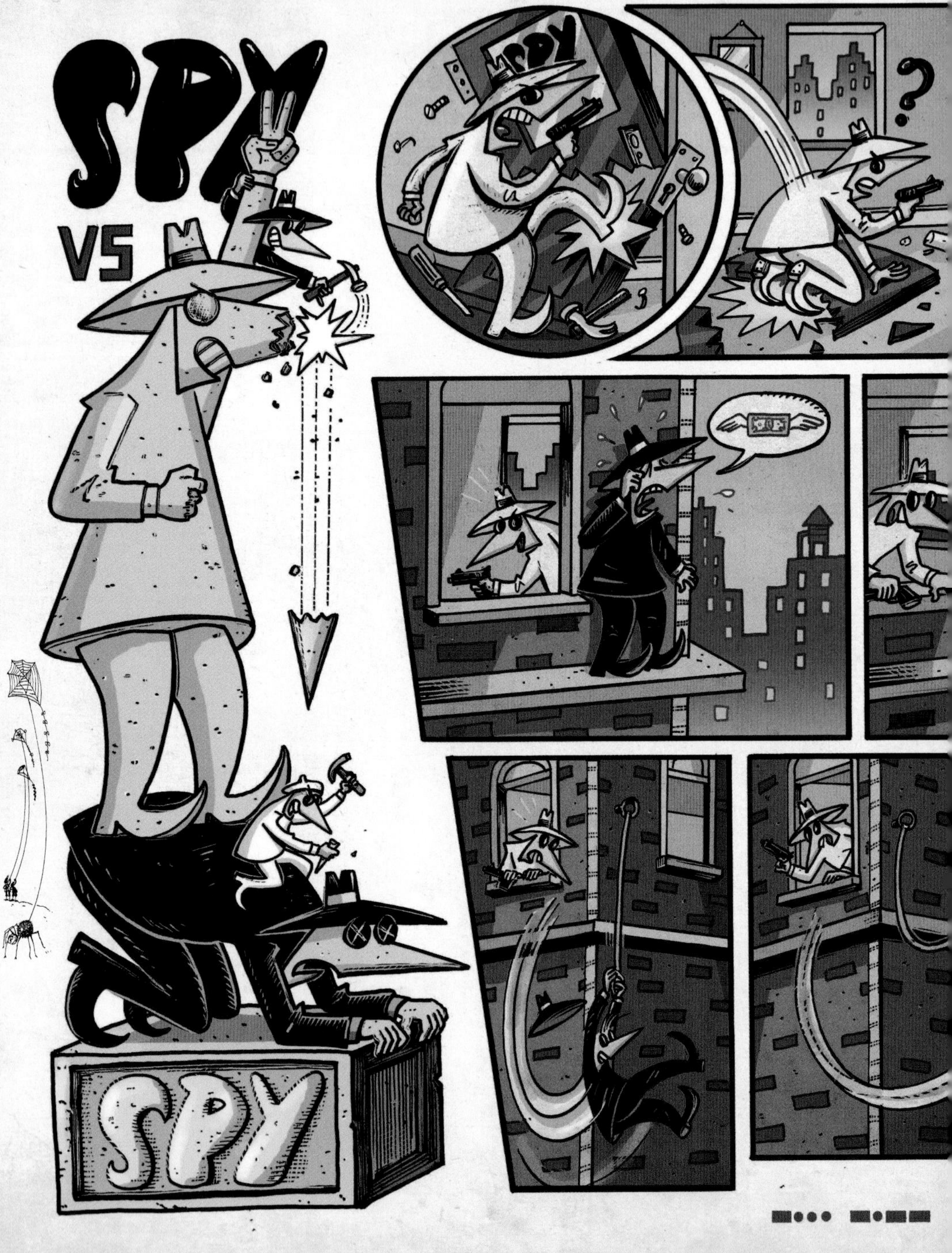
SPY
VS
SPY
SPY
SPY
?

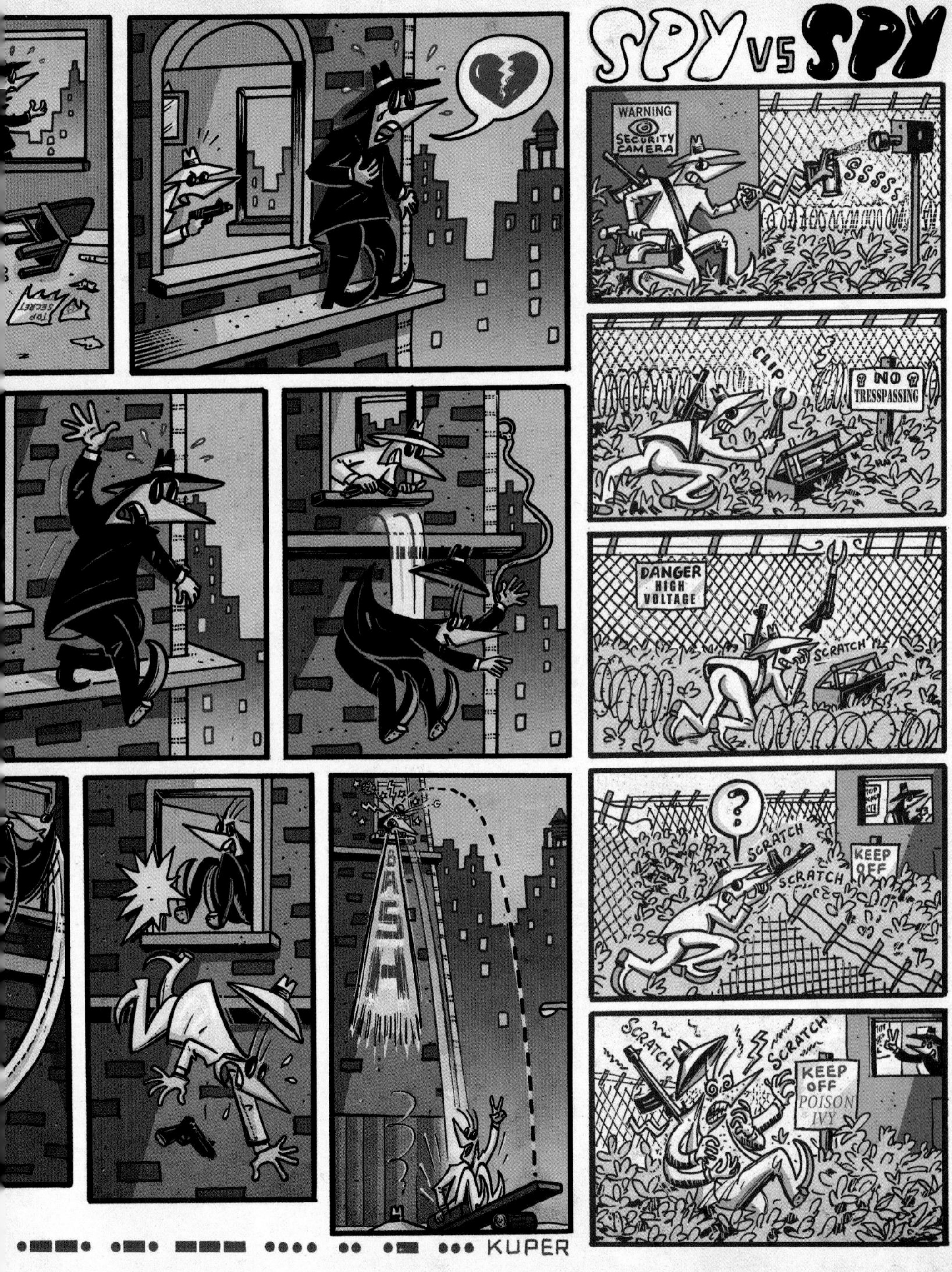

TOP SECRET
SPY vs SPY
WARNING SECURITY CAMERA
SSSSS
CLIP
NO TRESSPASSING
DANGER HIGH VOLTAGE
SCRATCH
BASH
?
SCRATCH
KEEP OFF
SCRATCH
SCRATCH
SCRATCH
KEEP OFF POISON IVY
KUPER

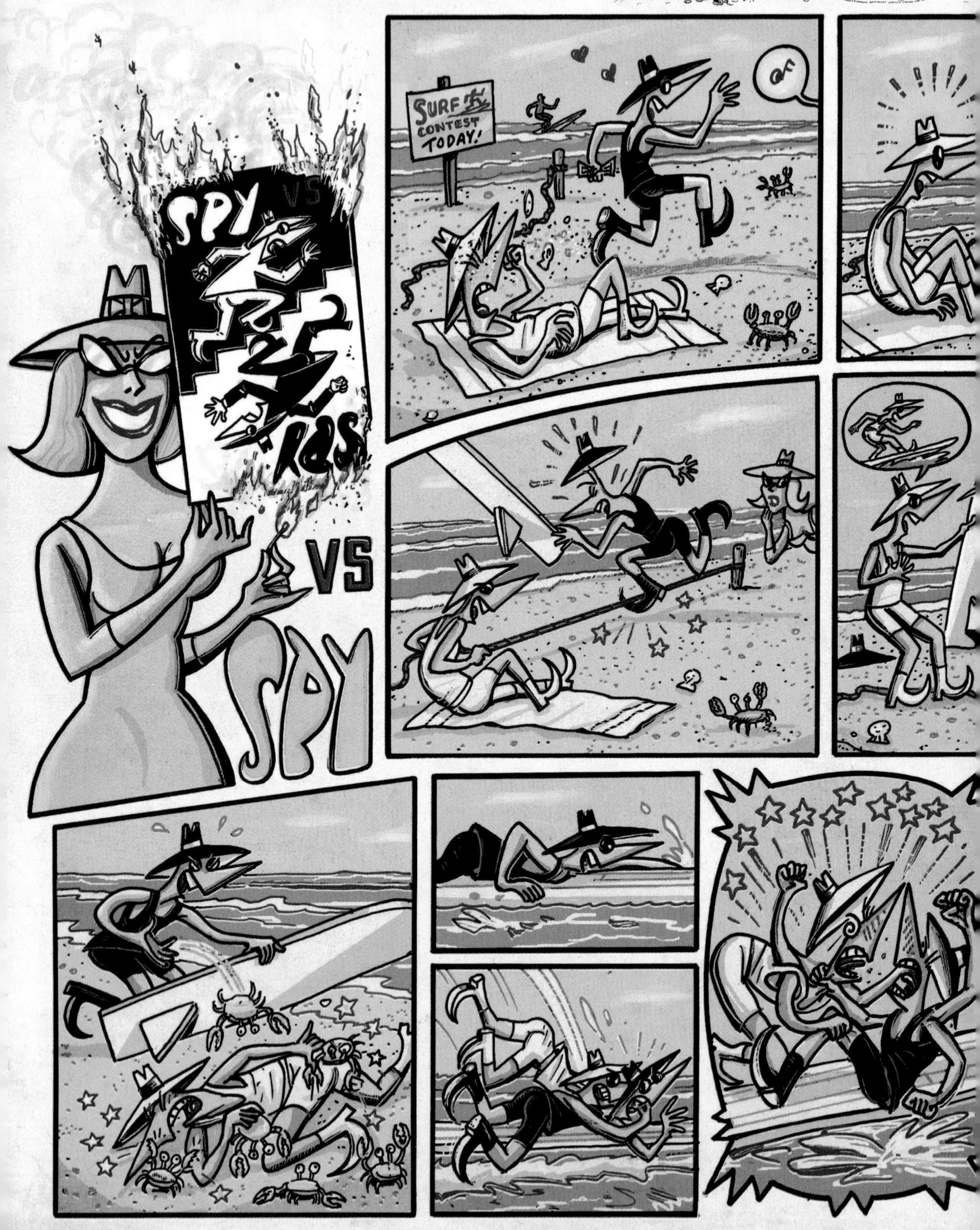
SPY VS SPY
SURF CONTEST TODAY!

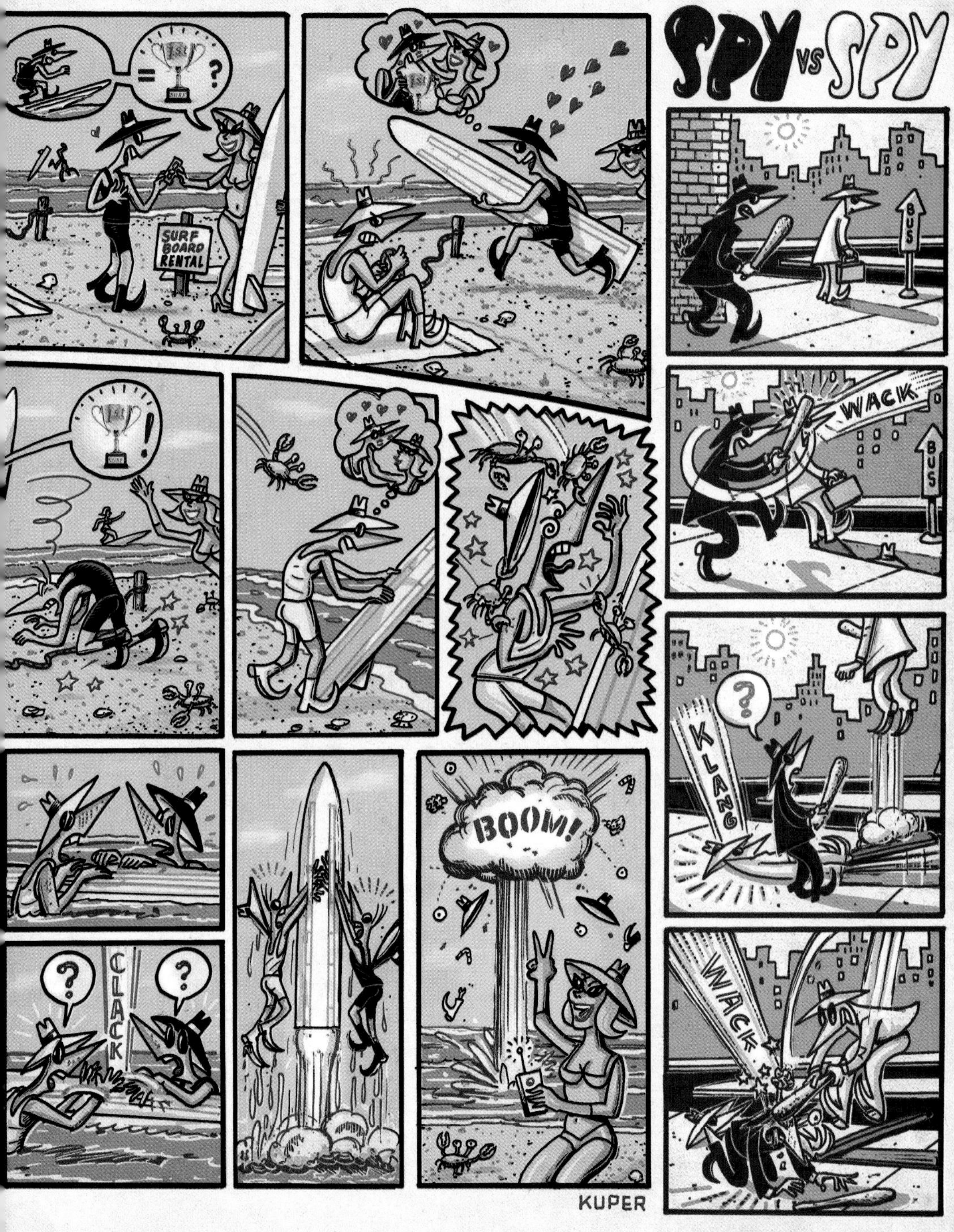
SPY vs SPY
1st
SURF
=
?
SURF BOARD RENTAL
1st
1st
SURF
!
BUS
WACK
BUS
?
KLANG
BOOM!
?
?
CLACK
WACK
KUPER

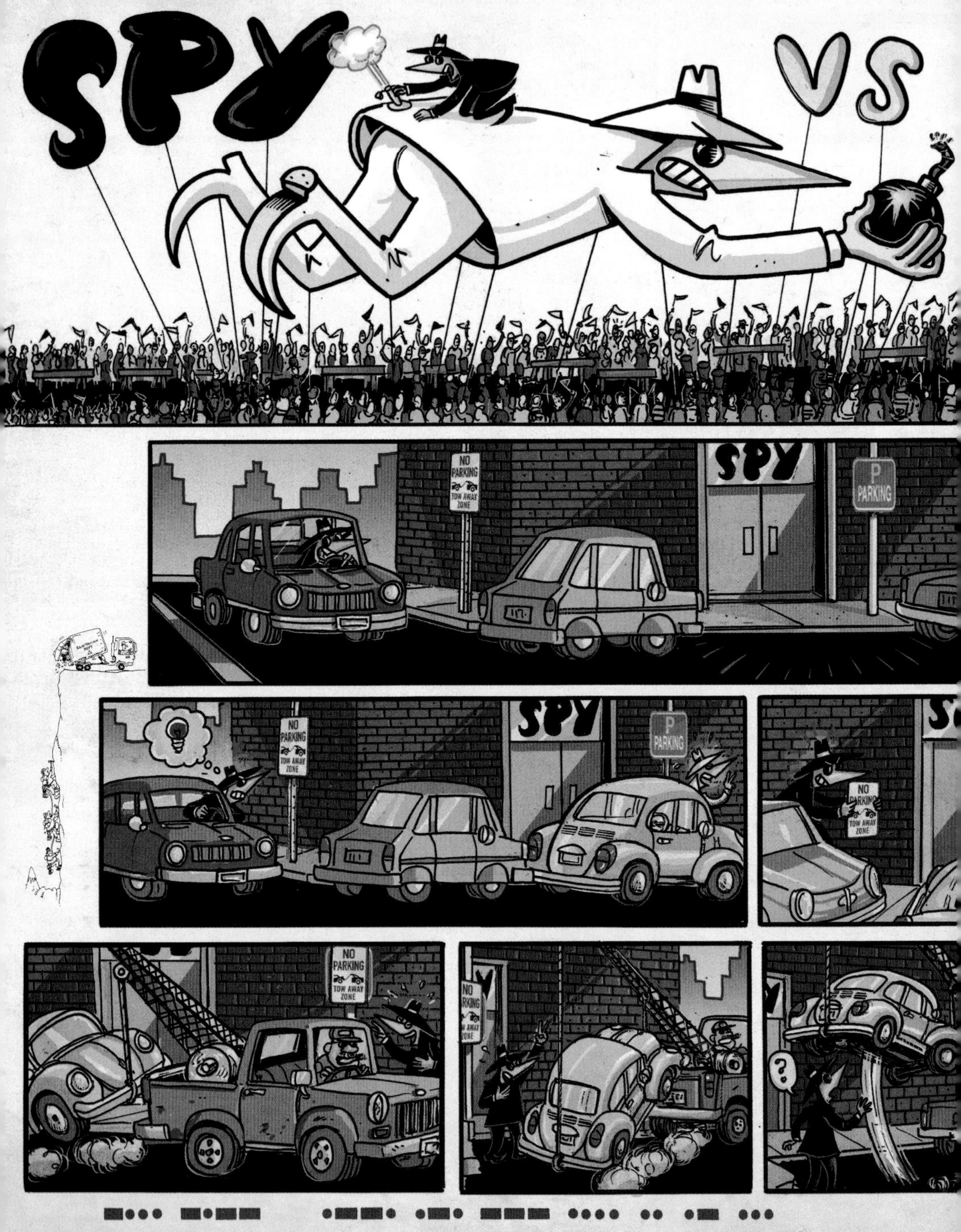
SPY
VS
NO PARKING
TOW AWAY ZONE
SPY
P
PARKING
?

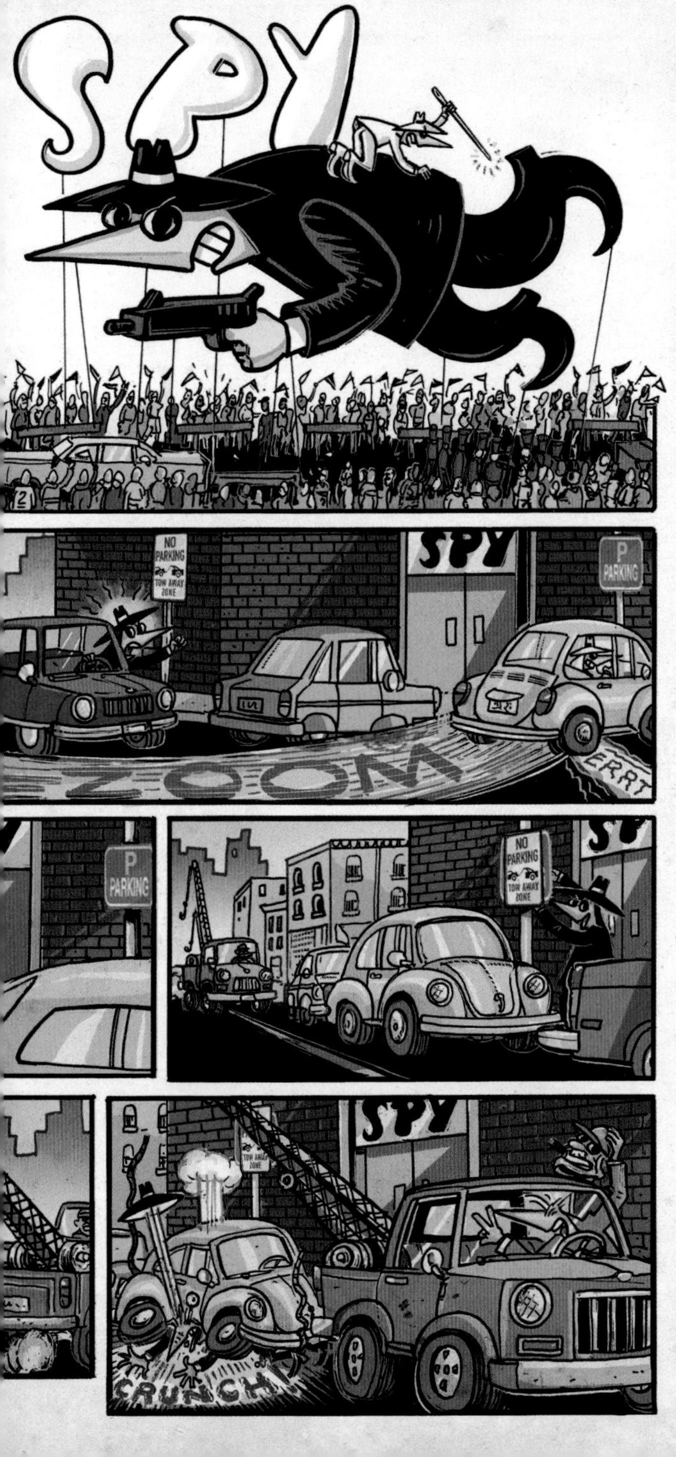
SPY
NO PARKING
TOW AWAY ZONE
SPY
P PARKING
ZOOM
ERRT
P PARKING
NO PARKING
TOW AWAY ZONE
SPY
SPY
TOW AWAY ZONE
CRUNCH!

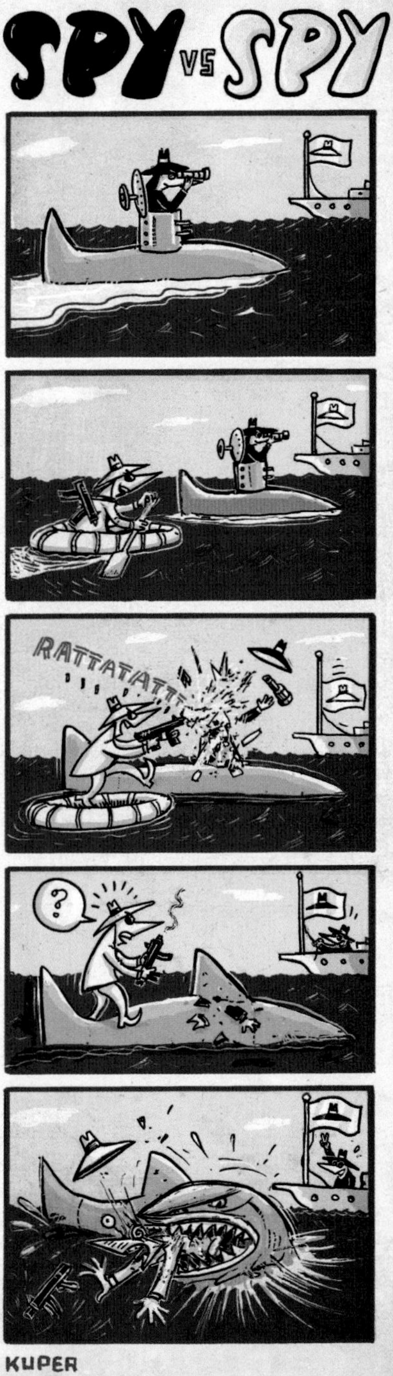
SPY vs SPY
RATTATATT
?
KUPER

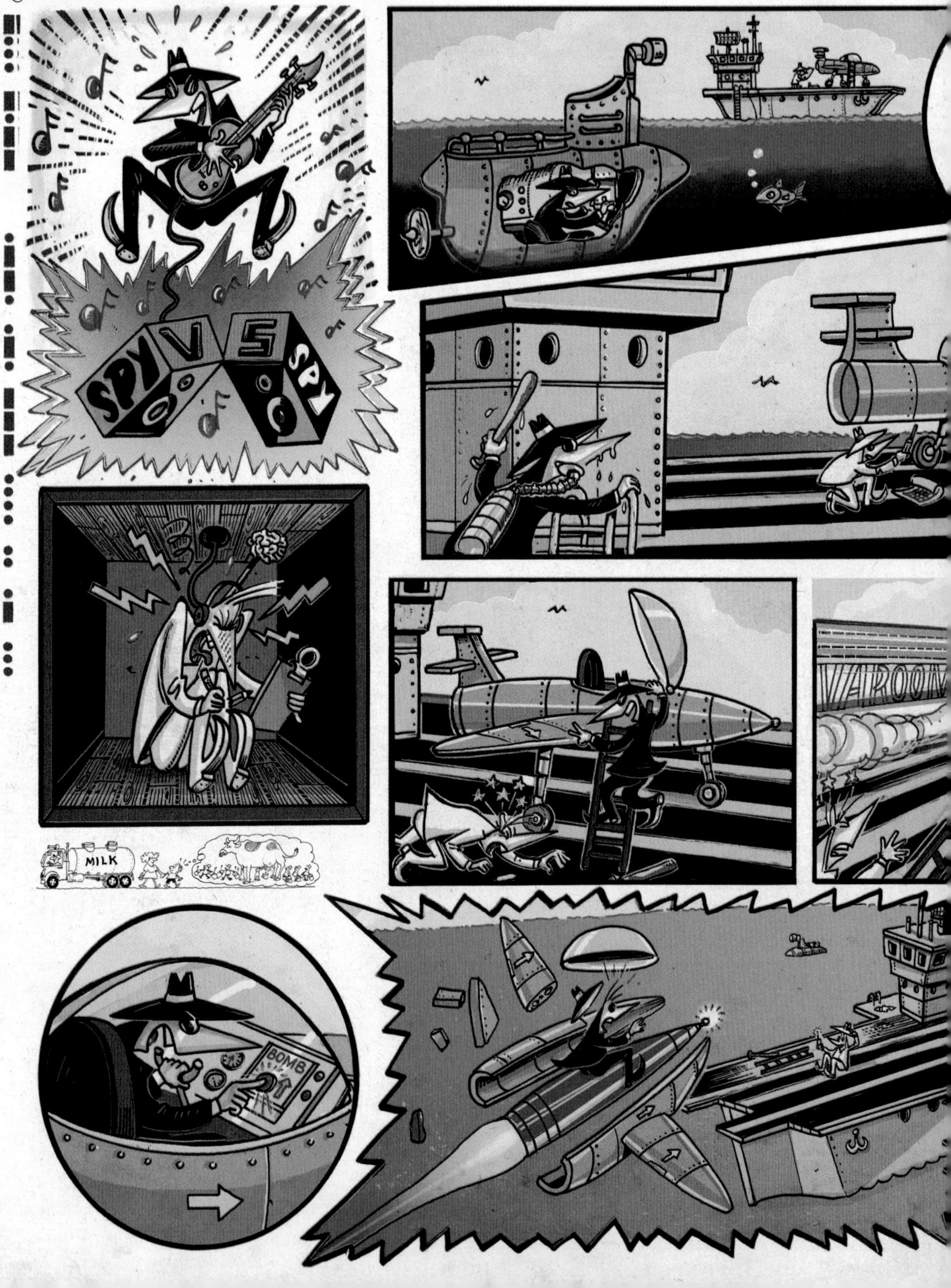
SPY VS SPY
MILK
VAROO
BOMB

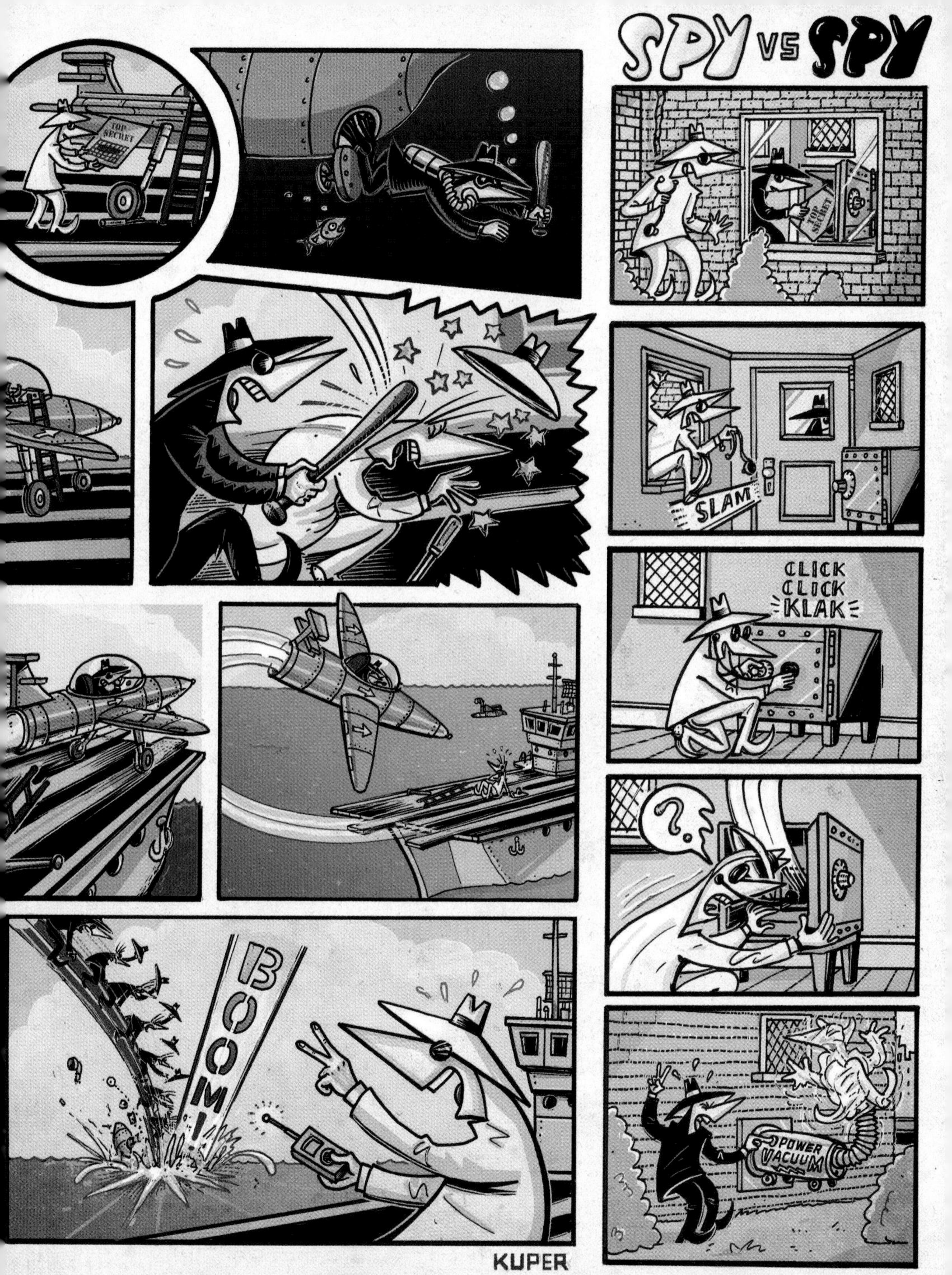
SPY VS SPY
TOP SECRET
TOP SECRET
SLAM
CLICK
CLICK
KLAK
?
BOOM!
POWER
VACUUM
KUPER

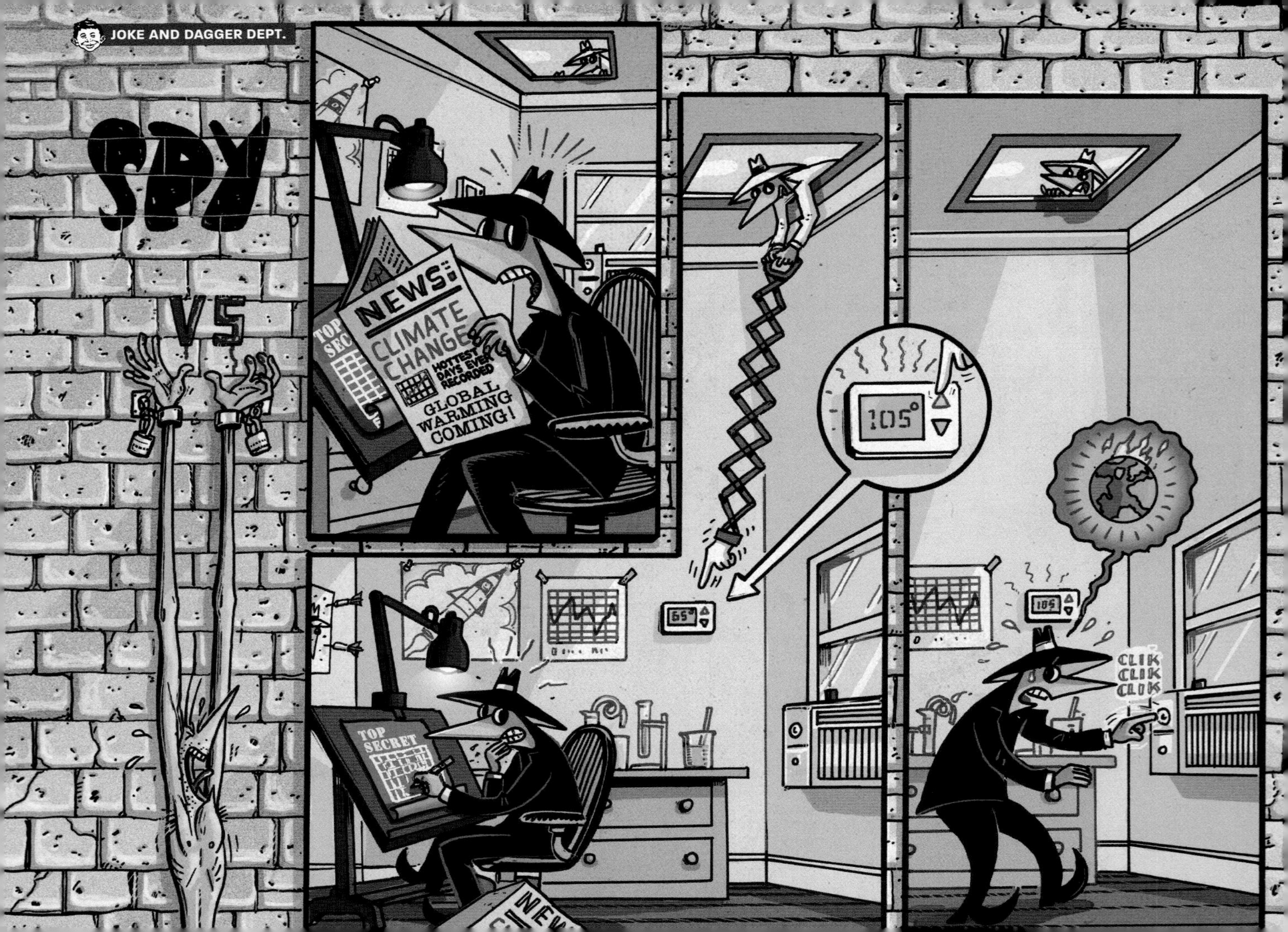
JOKE AND DAGGER DEPT.
SPY VS
NEWS
CLIMATE CHANGE
HOTTEST DAYS EVER RECORDED
GLOBAL WARMING COMING!
TOP SECRET
105°
65°
CLIK
CLIK
CLIK

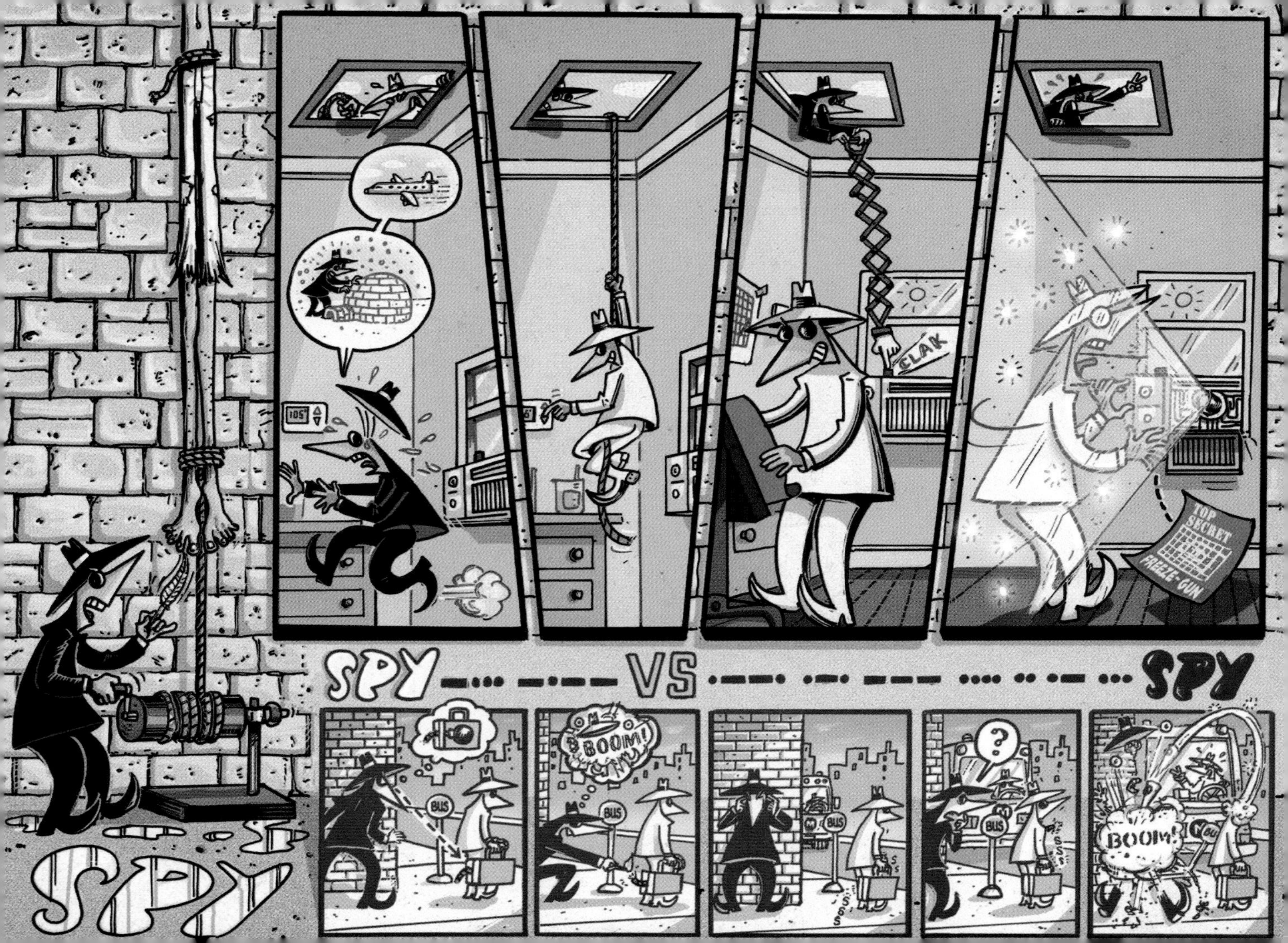

SPY
105°
CLAK
TOP SECRET
FREEZE-GUN
SPY VS SPY
BUS
BOOM!
?
BOOM!

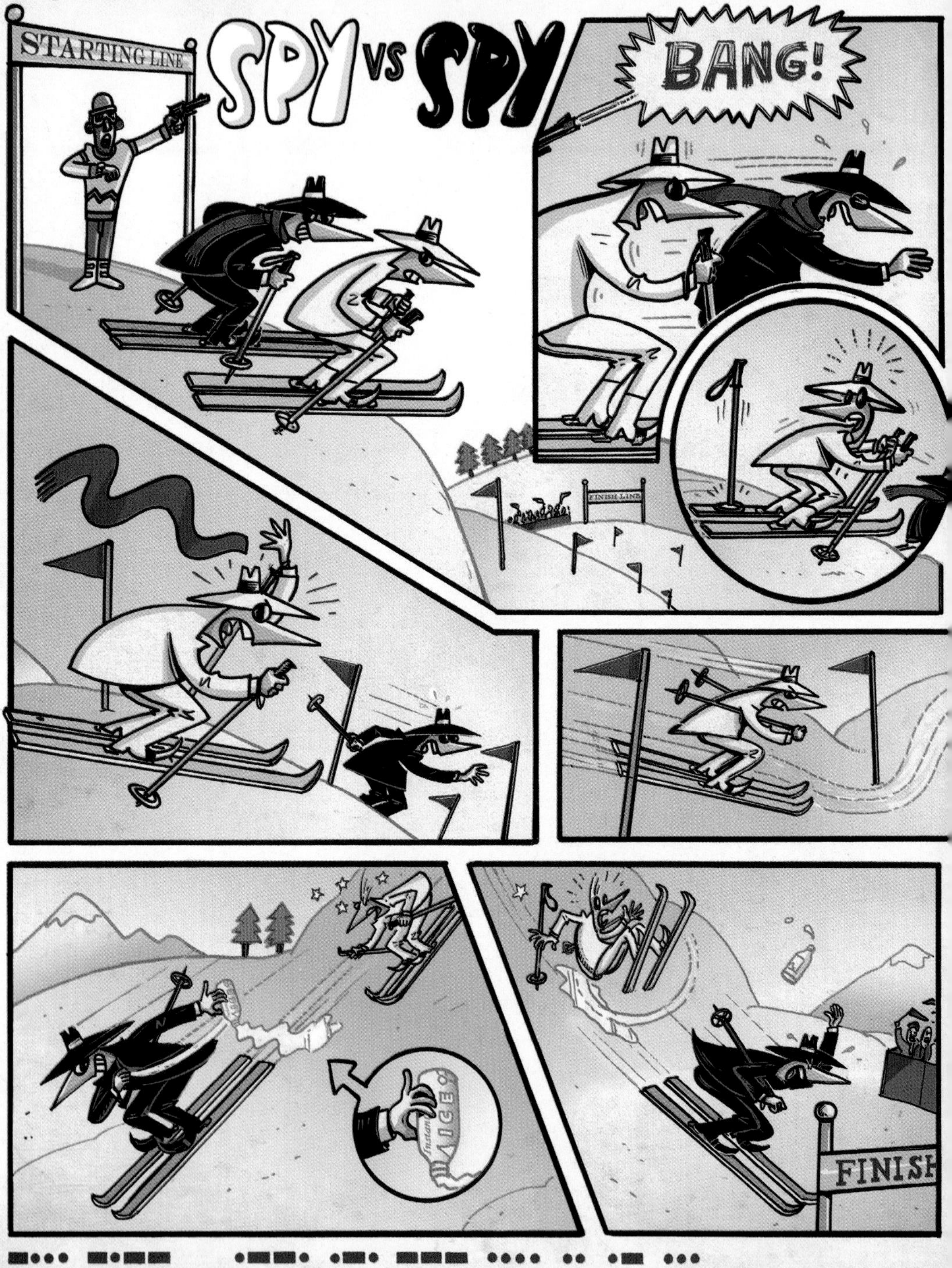
STARTING LINE
SPY VS SPY
BANG!
FINISH LINE
Instant ICE®
FINISH

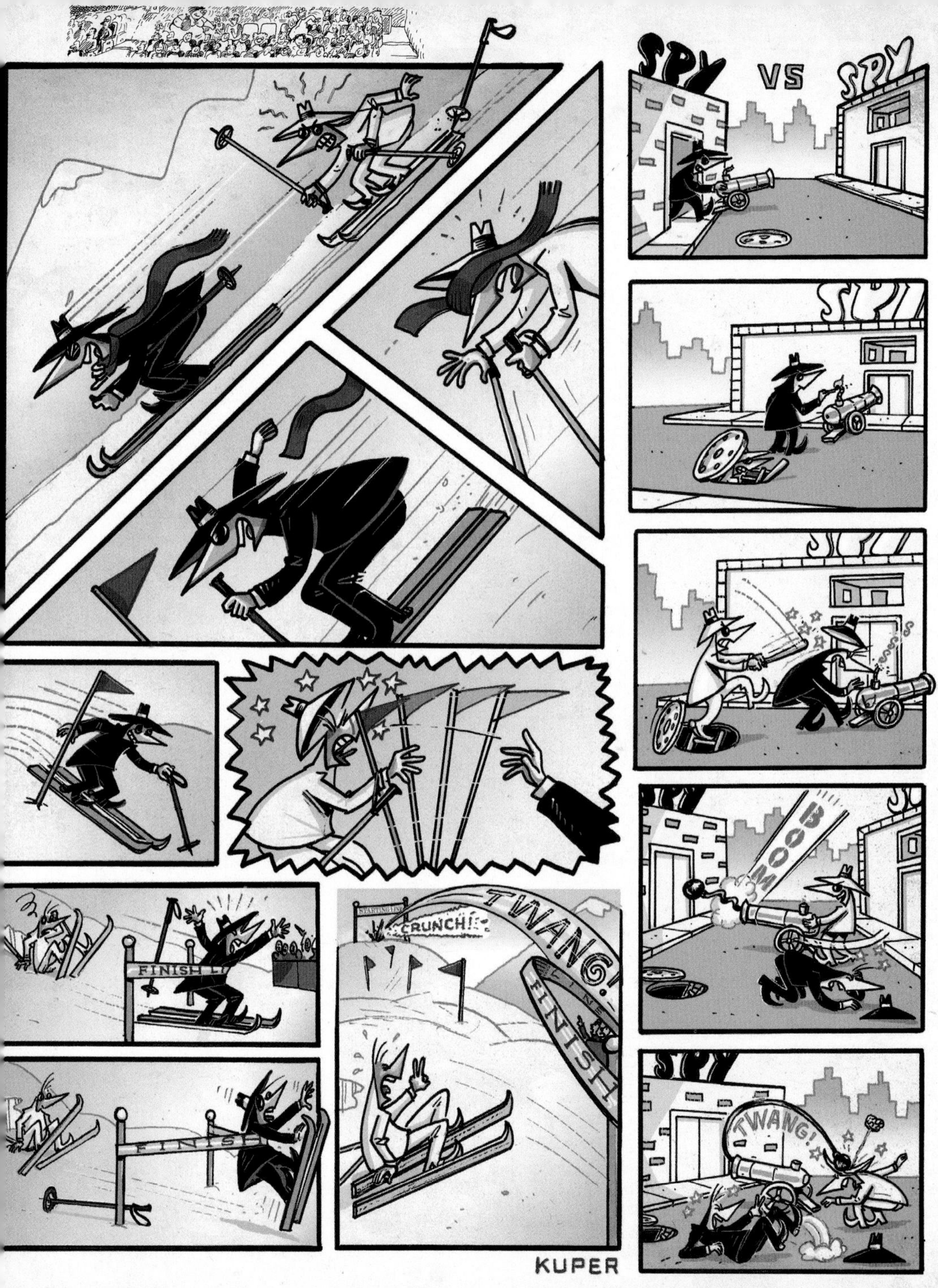
SPY VS SPY
FINISH L
FINISH
CRUNCH!
TWANG!
FINISH
BOOM
TWANG!
KUPER

SPY
VS
TOP SECRET
Booby Trap

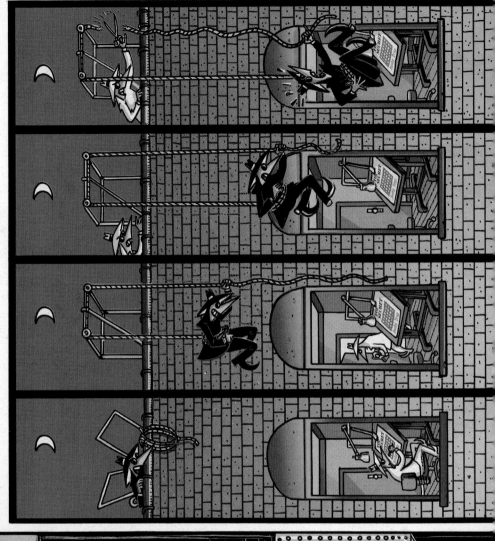

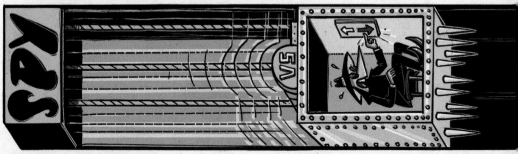

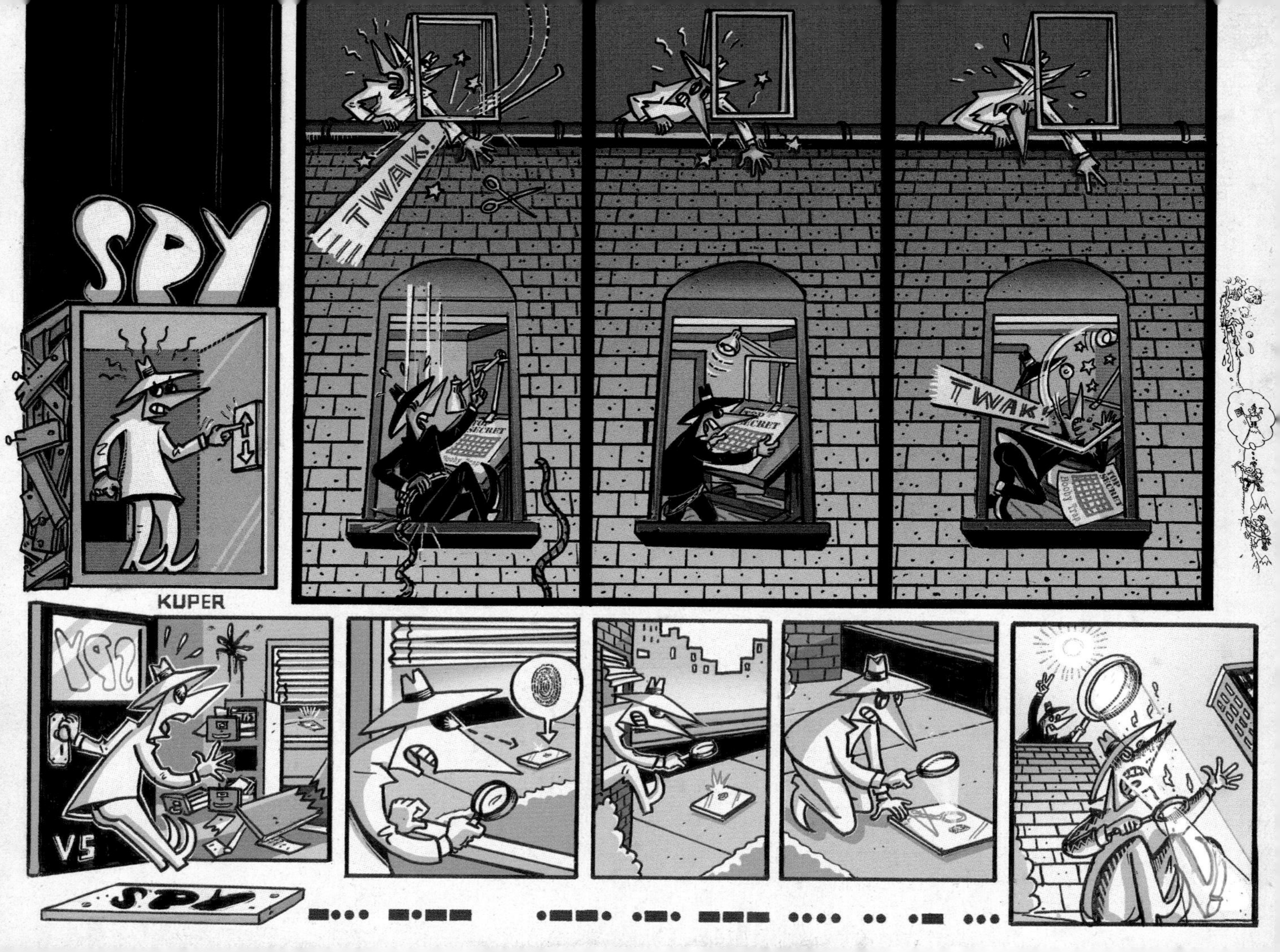
SPY
VS
SPY
KUPER
TWAK!
TOP SECRET
TWAK!
TOP SECRET
Booby Trap

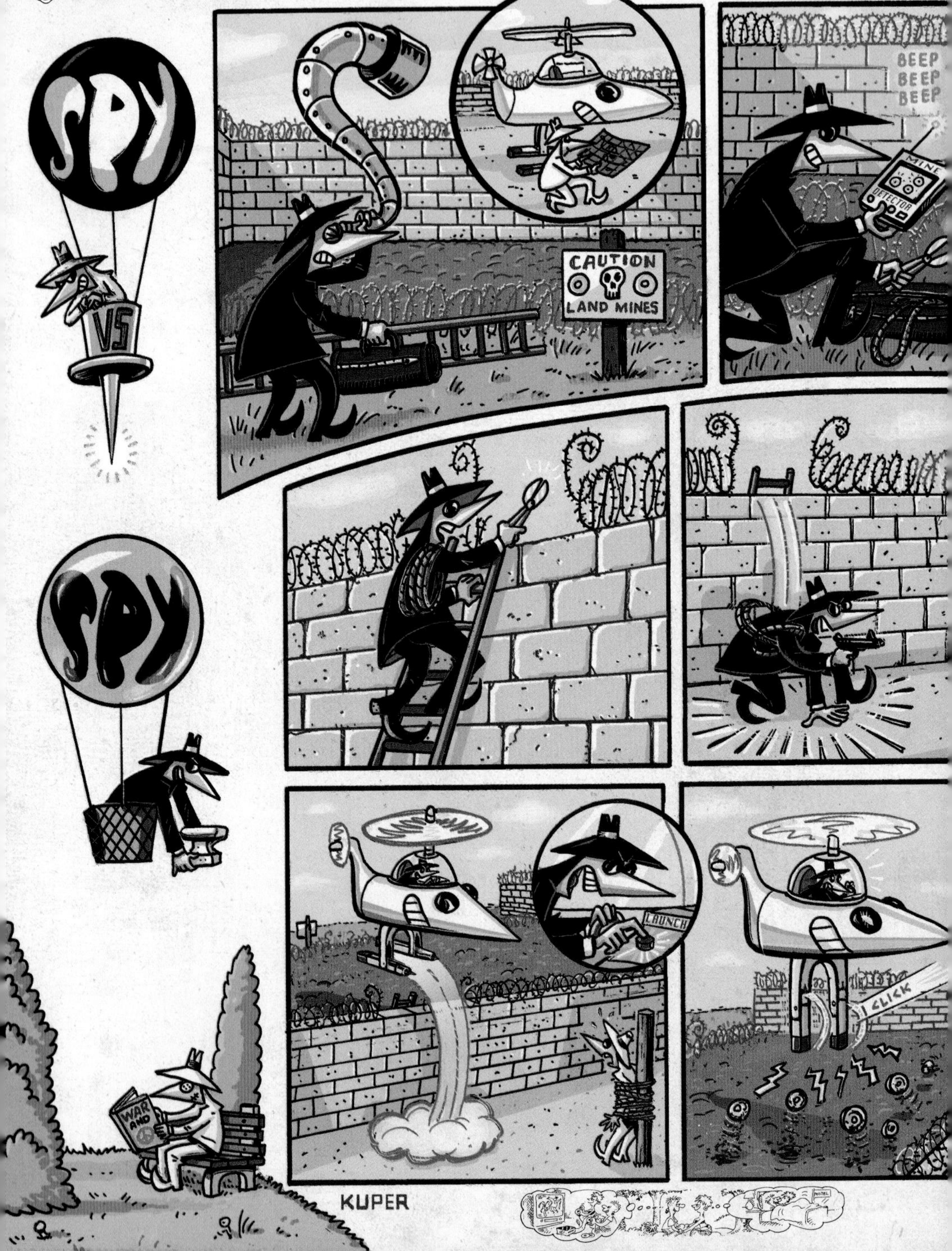
SPY VS SPY
CAUTION
LAND MINES
BEEP
BEEP
BEEP
MINE
DETECTOR
LAUNCH
CLICK
WAR AND
KUPER

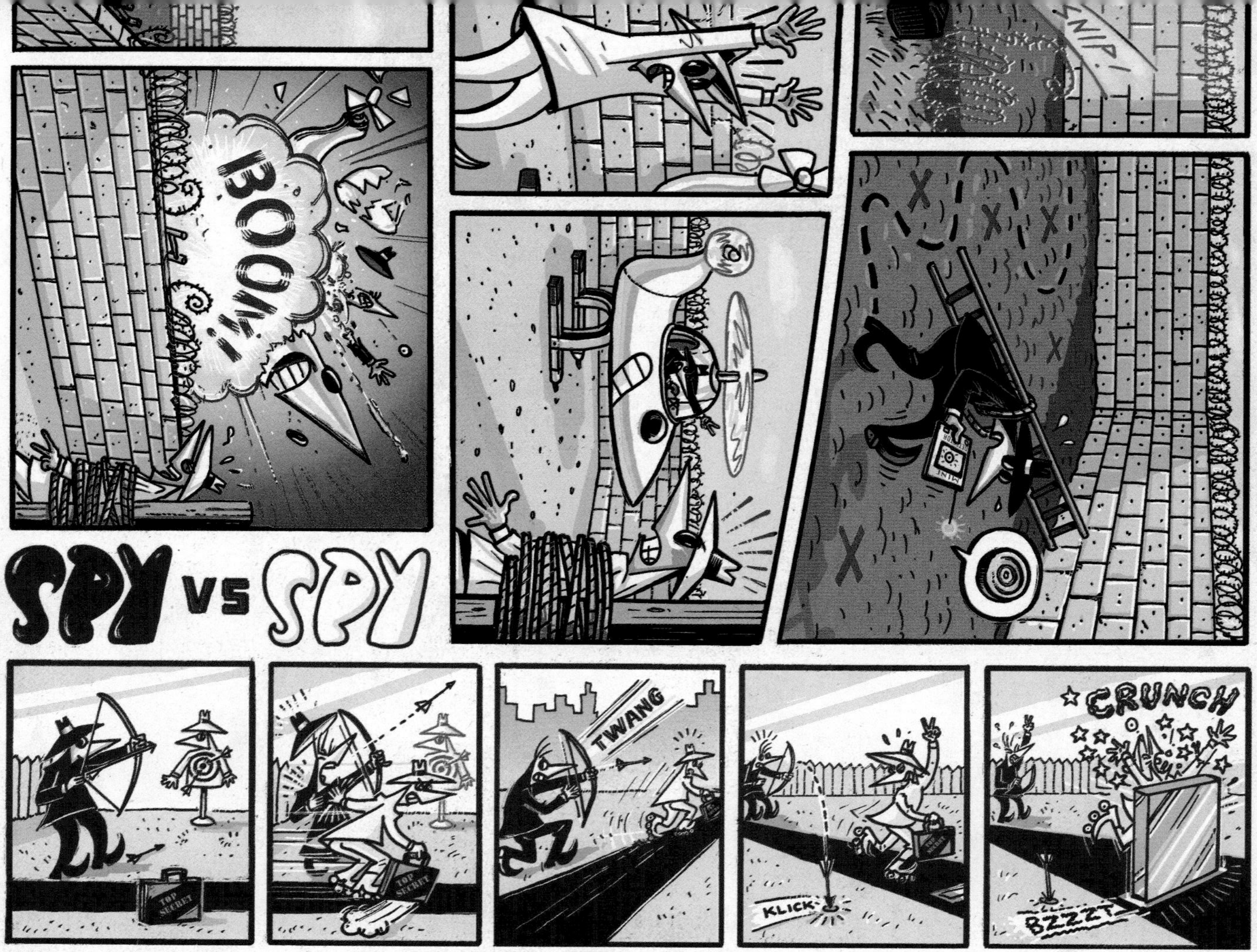
SNIP!
BOOM!
SPY VS SPY
TOP SECRET
TOP SECRET
TWANG
KLICK
CRUNCH
BZZZT

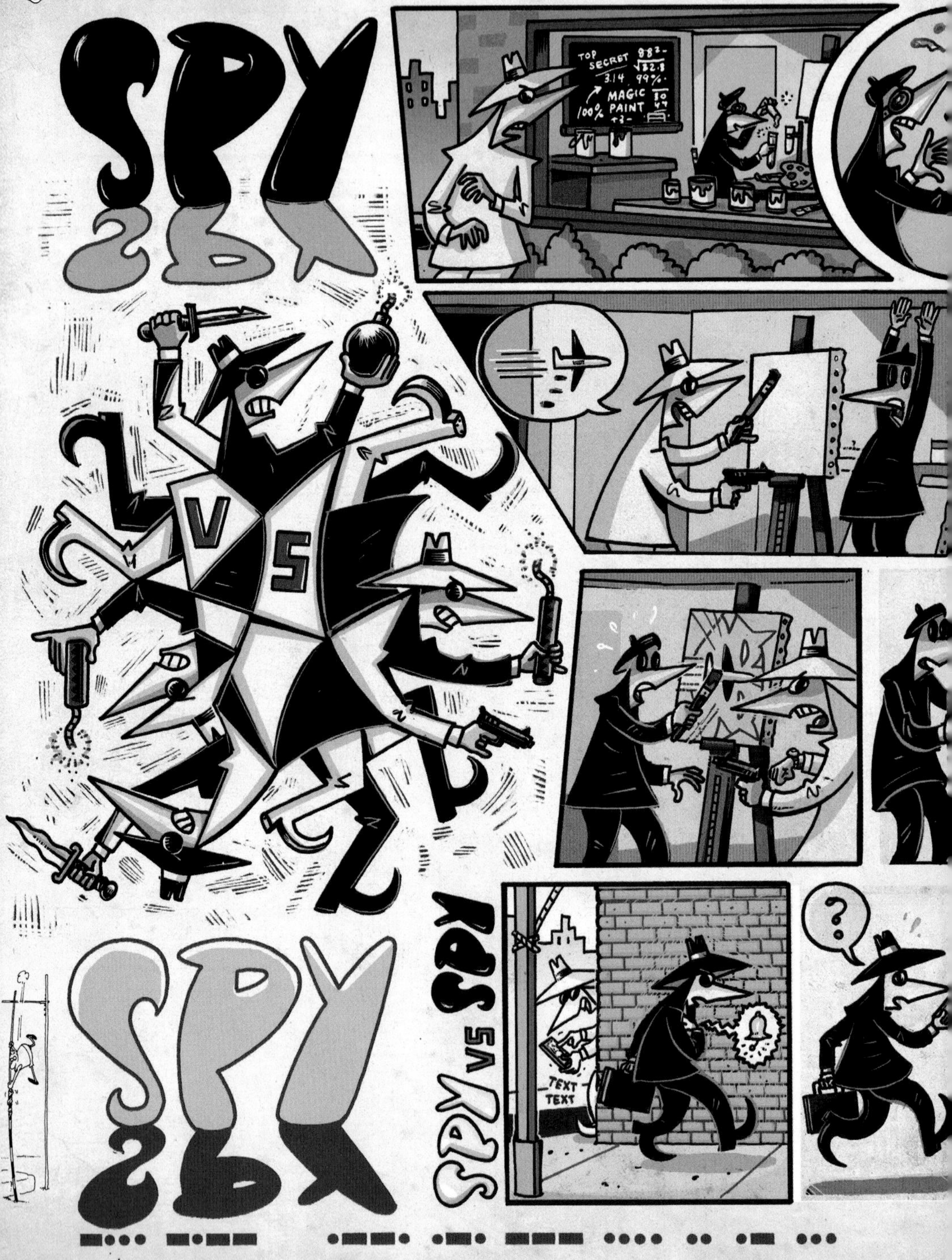
SPY
TOP SECRET
3.14 99%
MAGIC PAINT
100%
VS
SPY
SPY VS SPY
TEXT TEXT
?

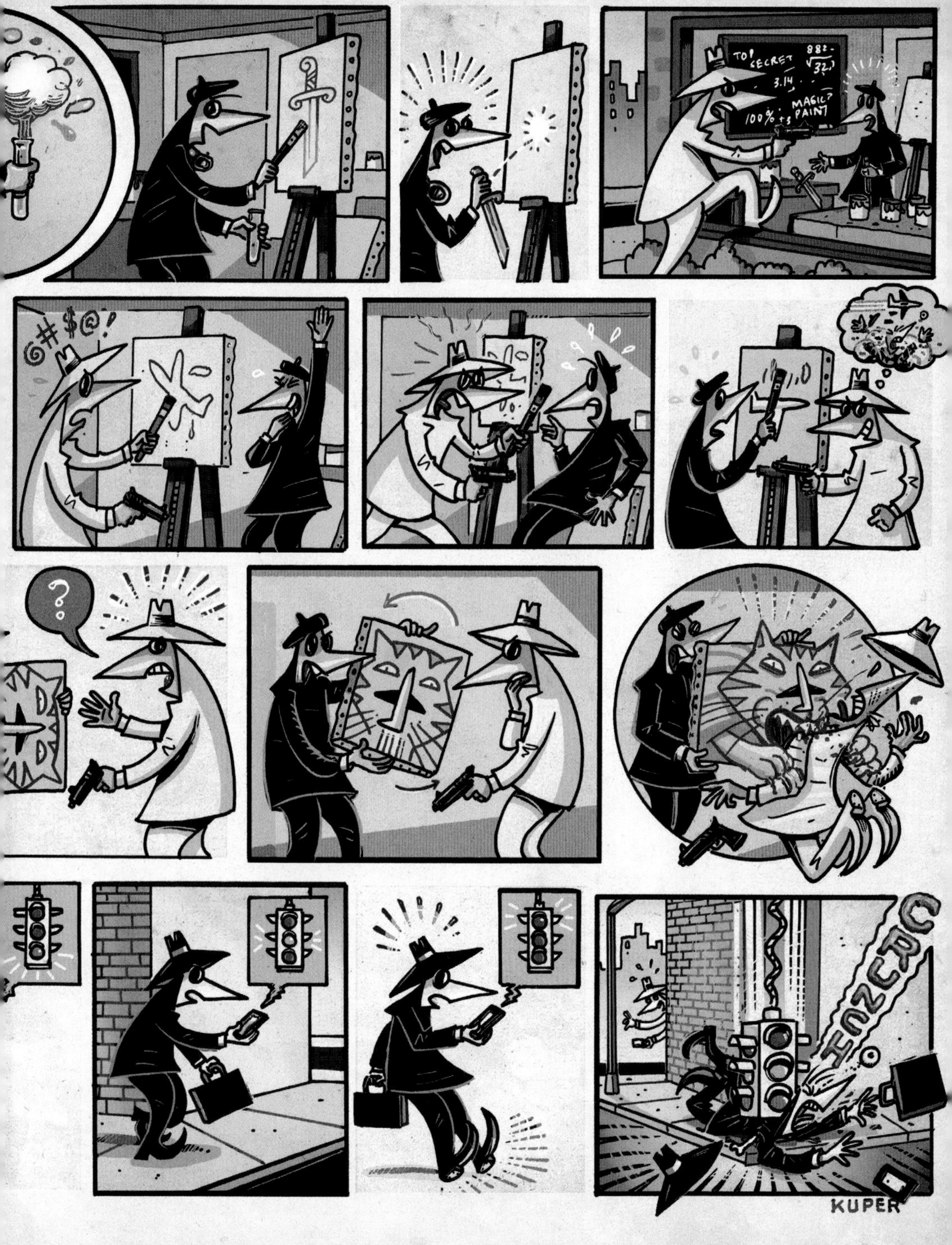
TOP SECRET
3.14
100%
MAGIC? PAINT
?
KUPER

JOKE AND DAGGER DEPT.

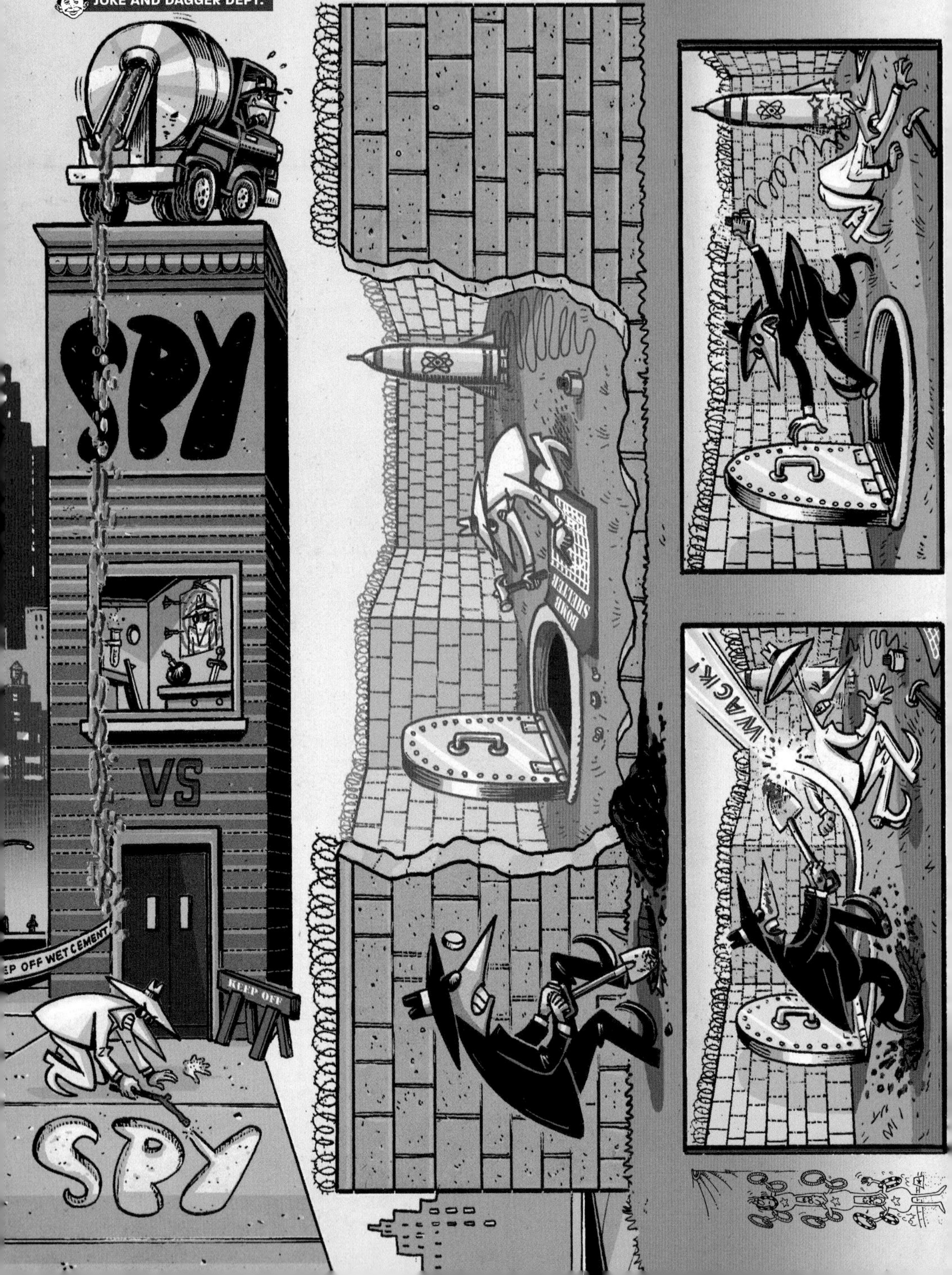
SPY
VS
SPY
EP OFF WET CEMENT
KEEP OFF
BOMB SHELTER
WACK!

BOOM!
CLICK
FLUSH
SPY VS SPY
Blind
RATTLE RATTLE
TAP TAP
RATTLE RATTLE
Blind
TRIP!
RATTLE RATTLE
RATTLE RATTLE
KUPER

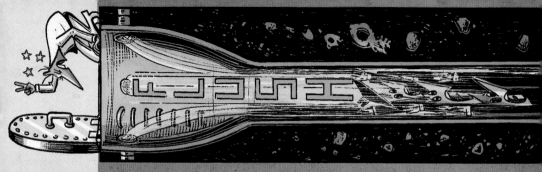

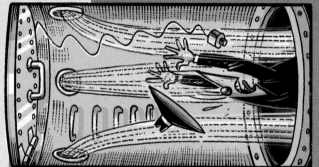

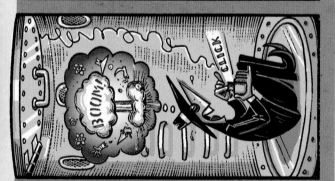

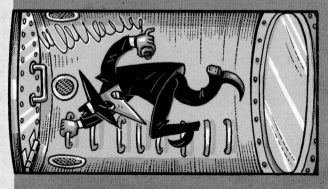

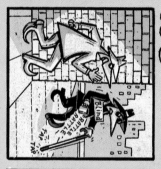

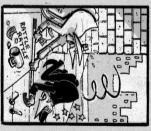

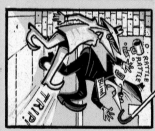

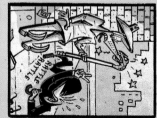

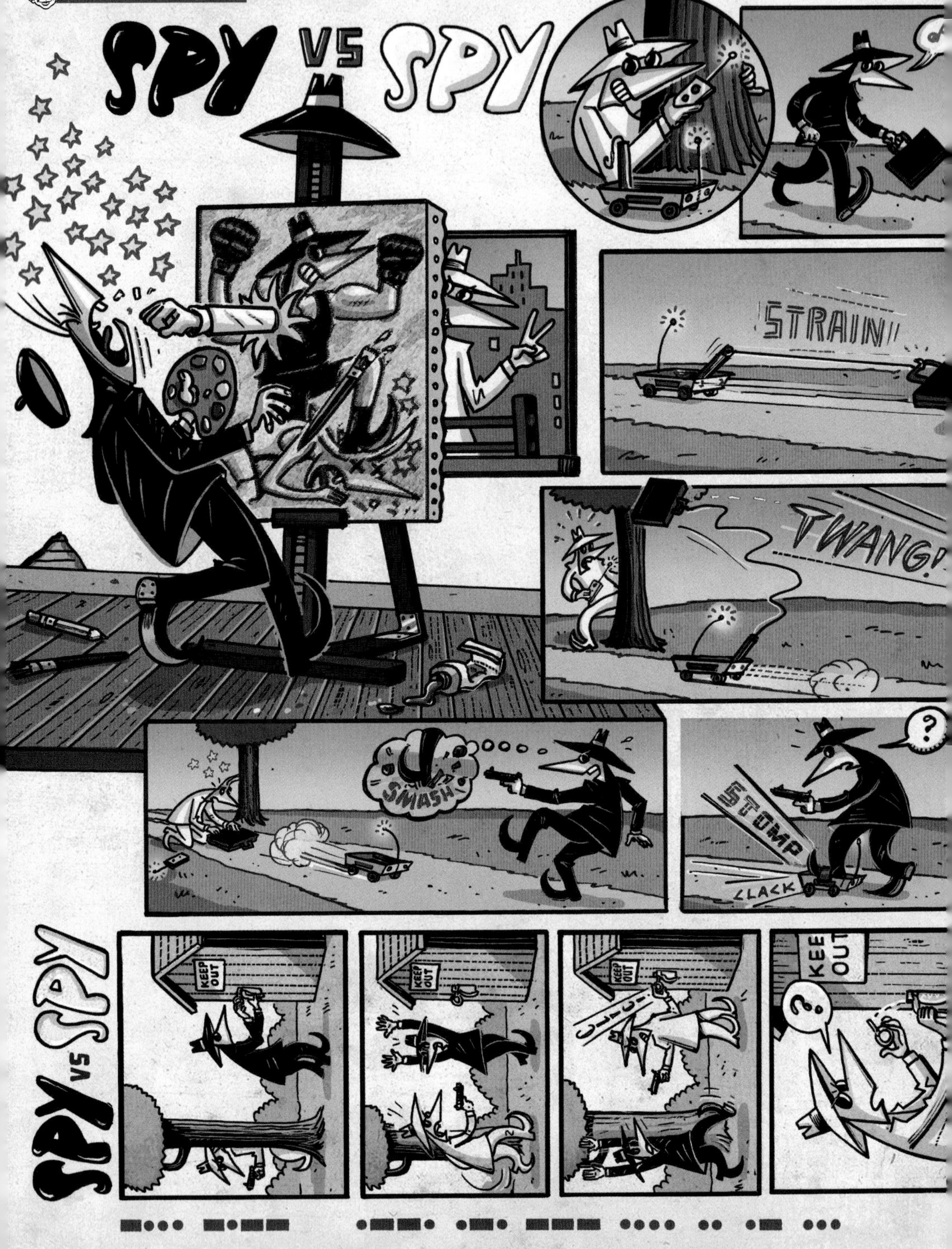
SPY VS SPY
STRAIN
TWANG!
SMASH
?
STOMP
CLACK
SPY VS SPY
KEEP OUT
KEEP OUT
KEEP OUT
KEEP OUT
?

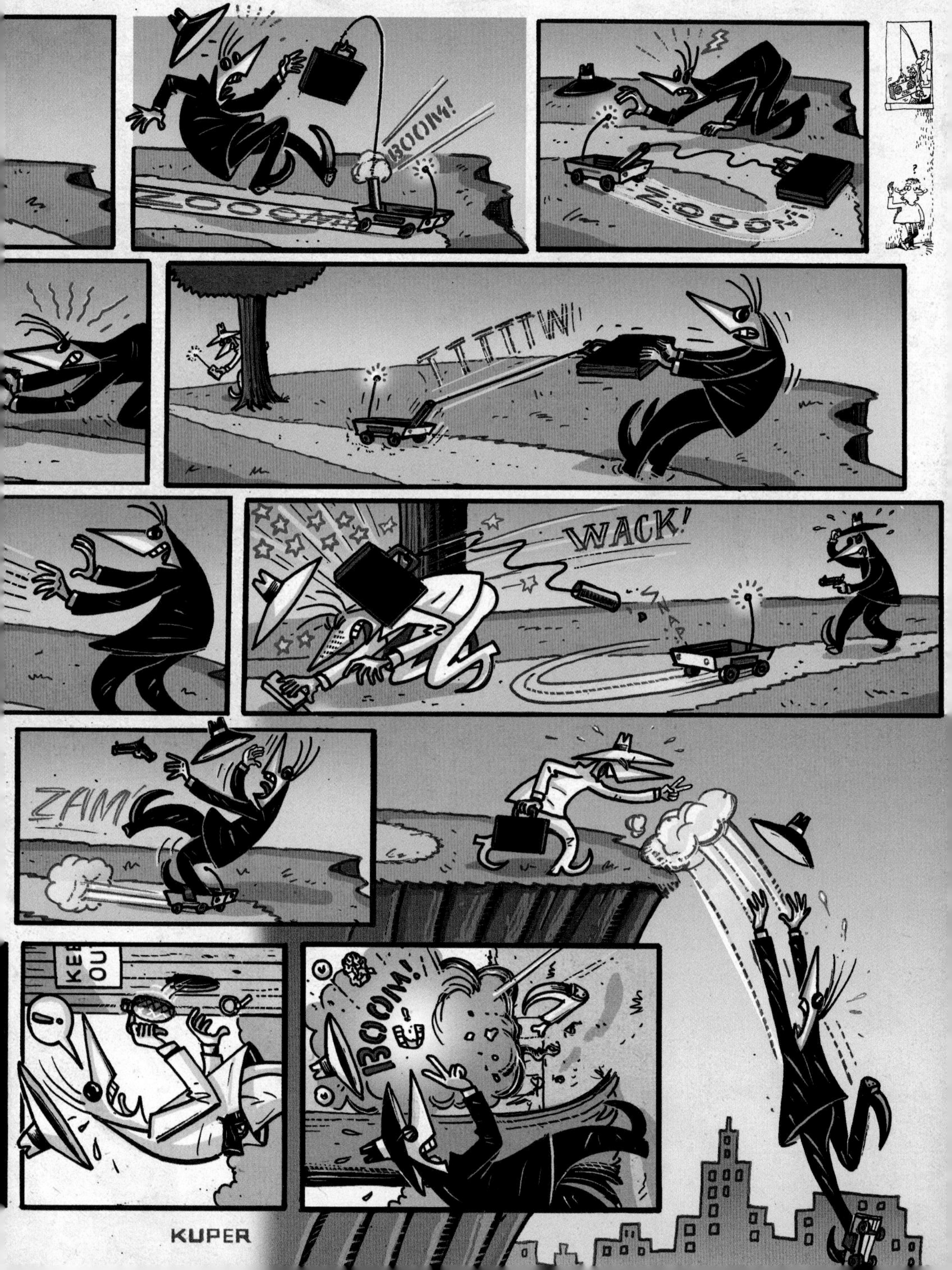

BOOM!
ZOOOOM
ZOOOOM
TTTTTW
WACK!
SNAP
ZAM
BOOM!
KUPER

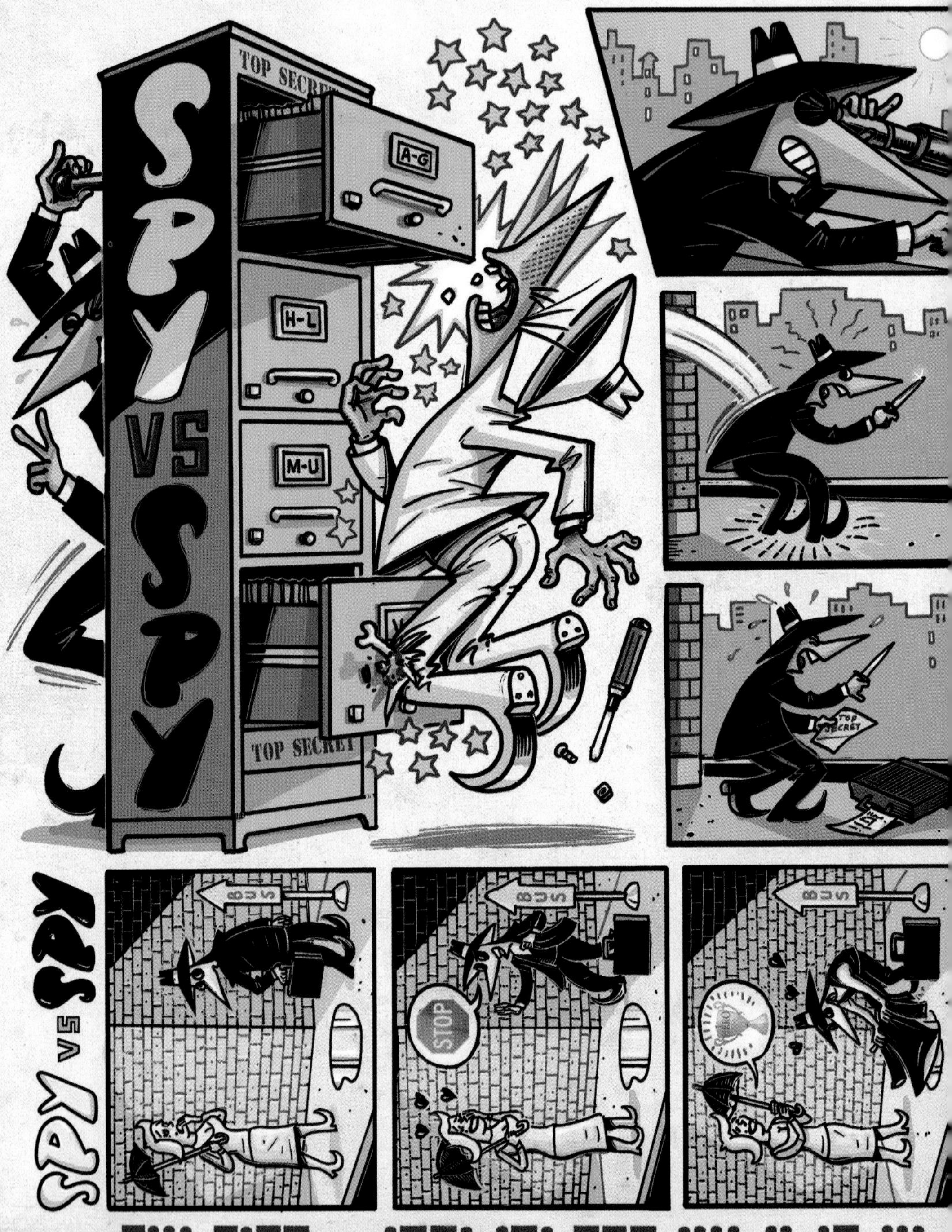
SPY VS SPY
TOP SECRET
A-G
H-L
M-U
TOP SECRET
TOP SECRET
SPY VS SPY
BUS
BUS
STOP
BUS
HERO

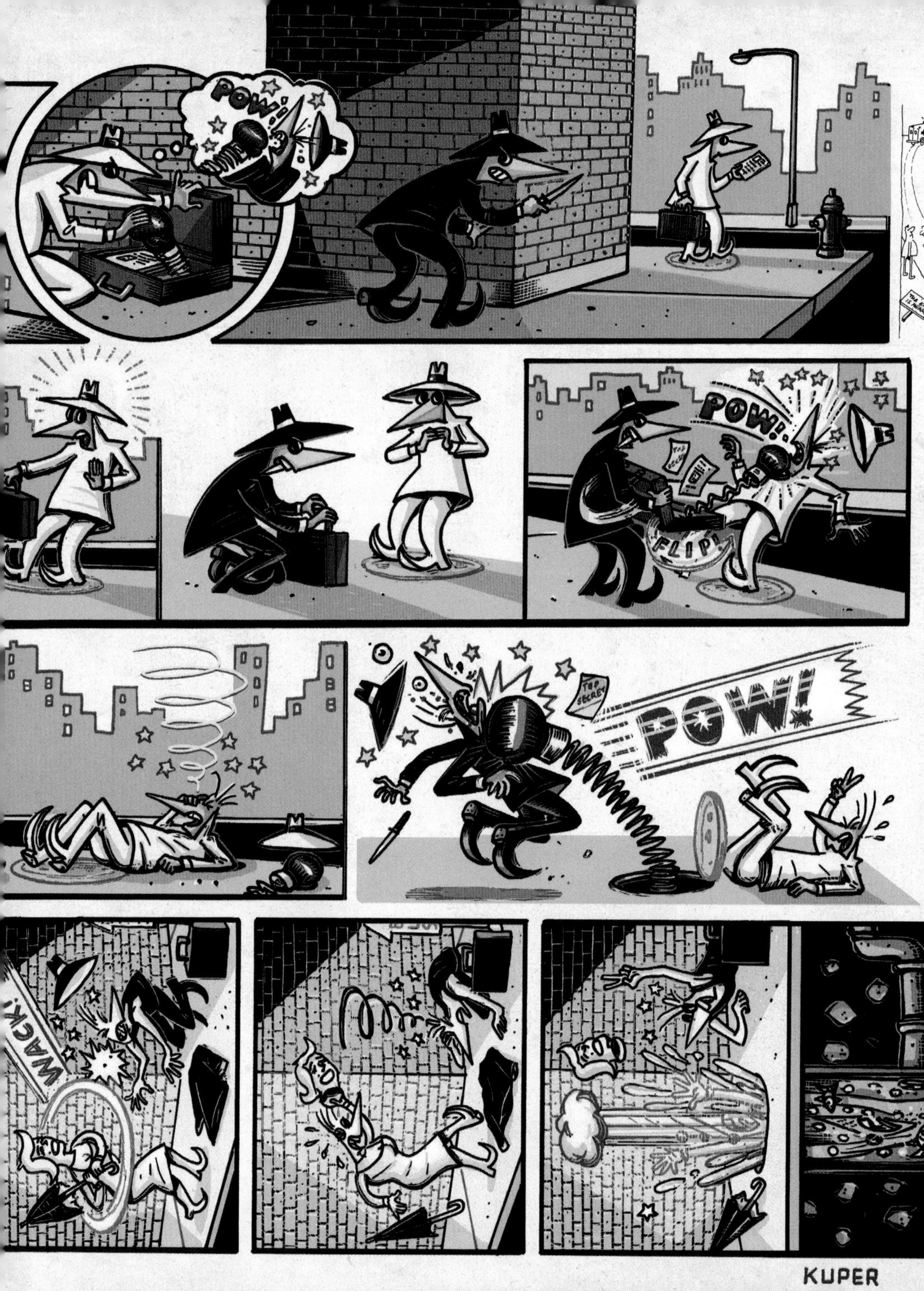
POW!
POW!
FLIP!
TOP SECRET
POW!
WACK!
KUPER

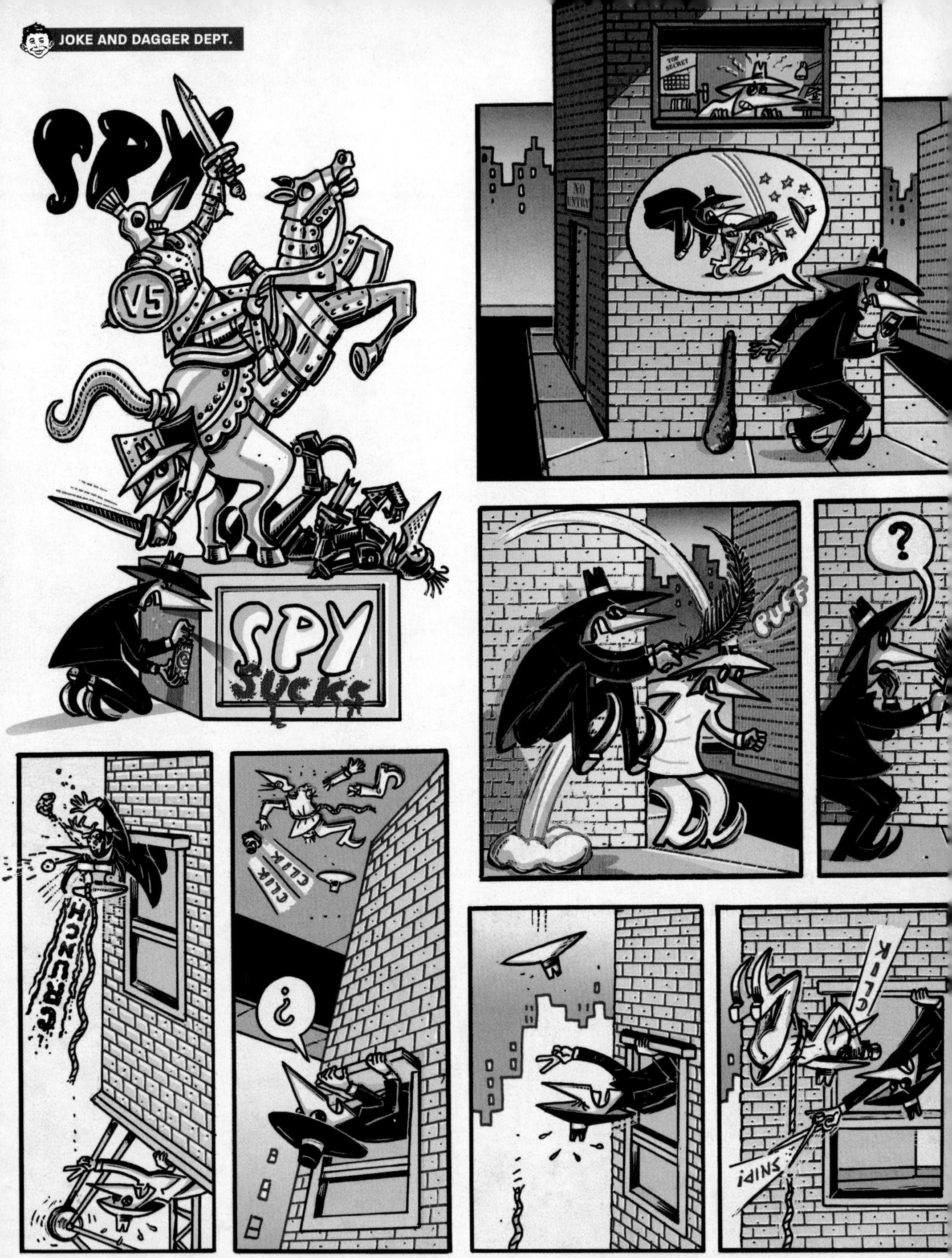
SPY
VS
SPY
TOP SECRET
NO ENTRY
PUFF
?
CLIK
CLIK
¿
SNIP!

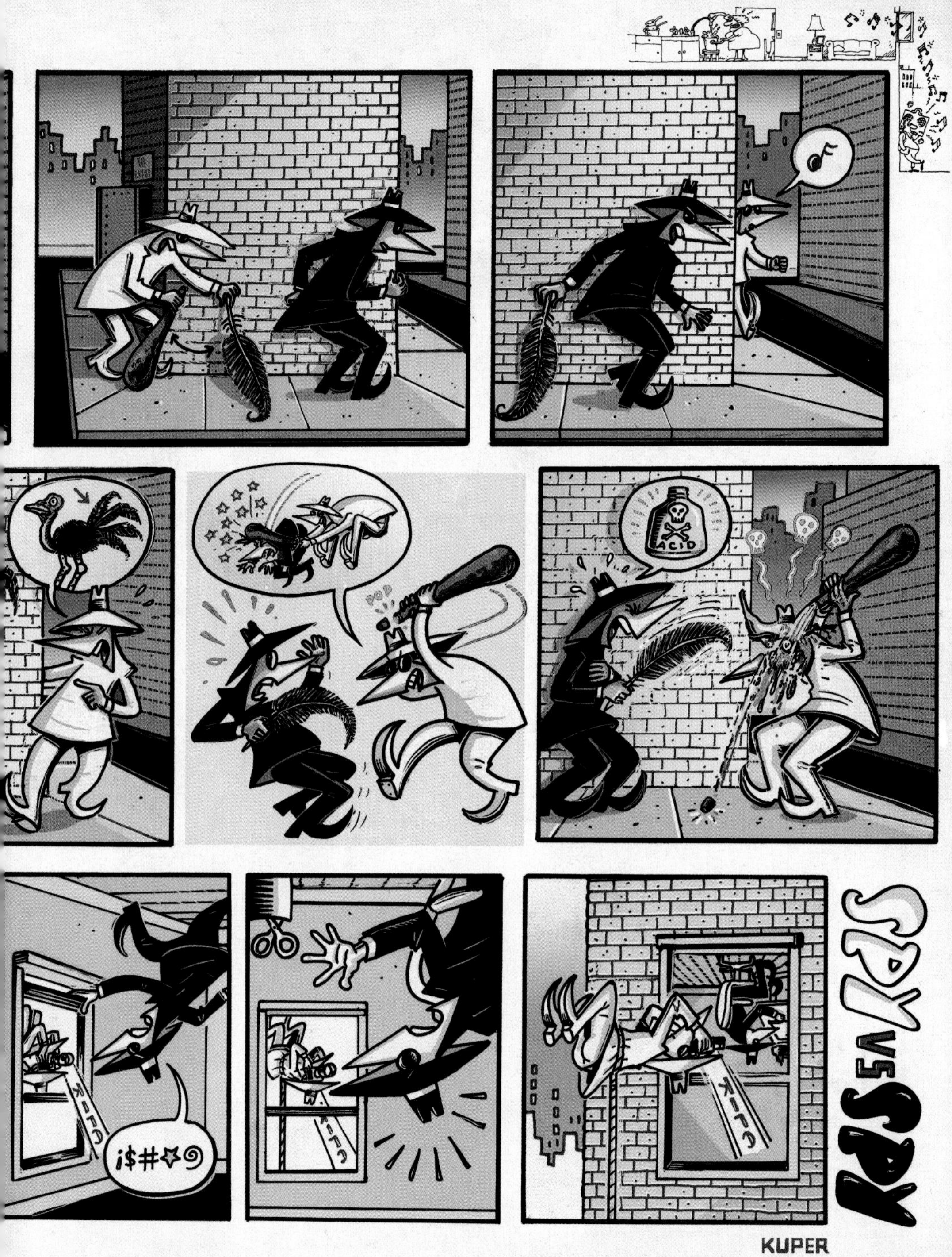
NO ENTRY
POP
ACID
SPY vs SPY
KUPER

SPY vs SPY

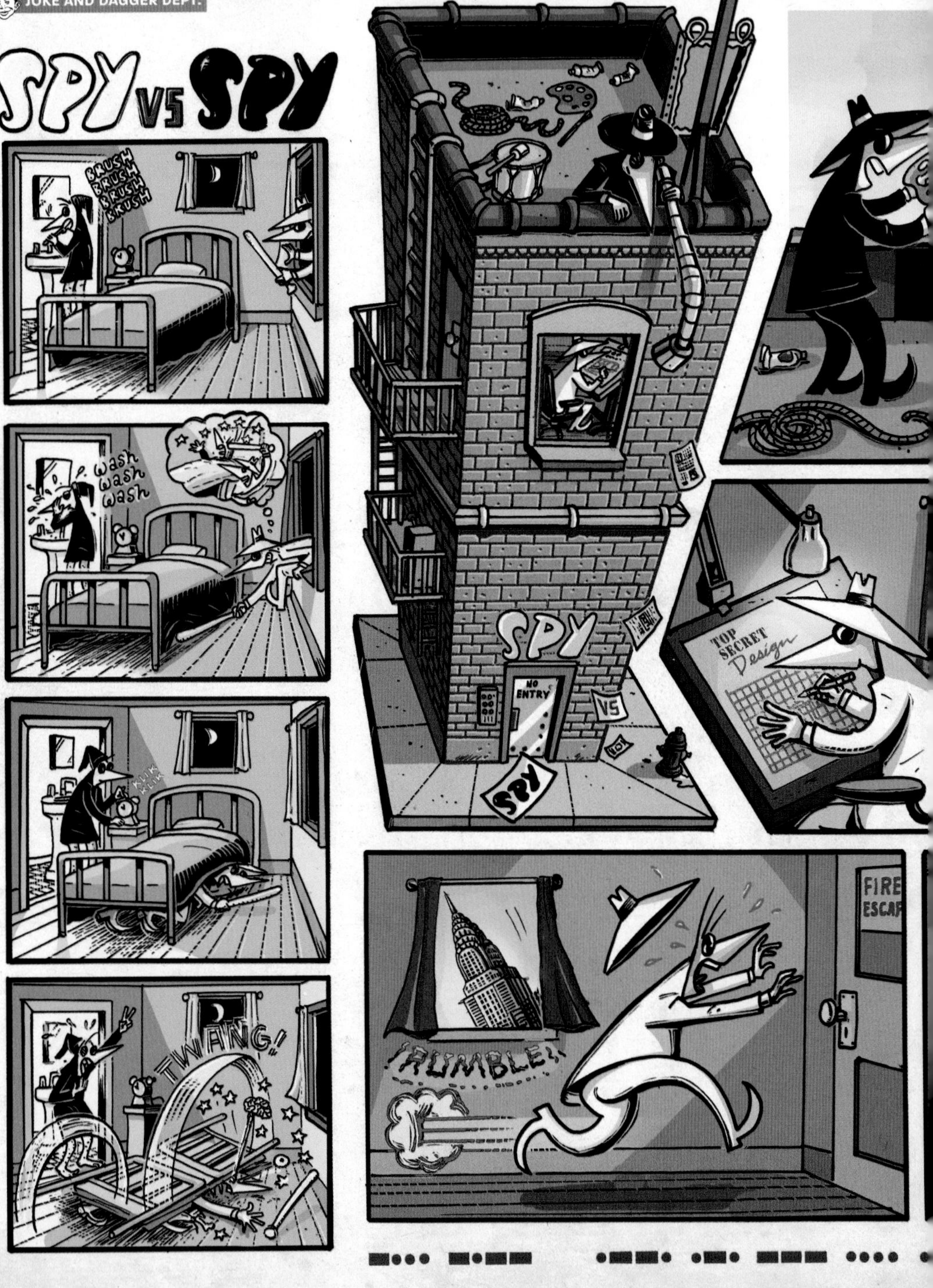
BRUSH BRUSH BRUSH BRUSH
wash wash wash
KLIK KLIK
TWANG!
SPY
NO ENTRY
VS
SPY
TOP SECRET Design
RUMBLE
FIRE ESCAP

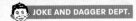

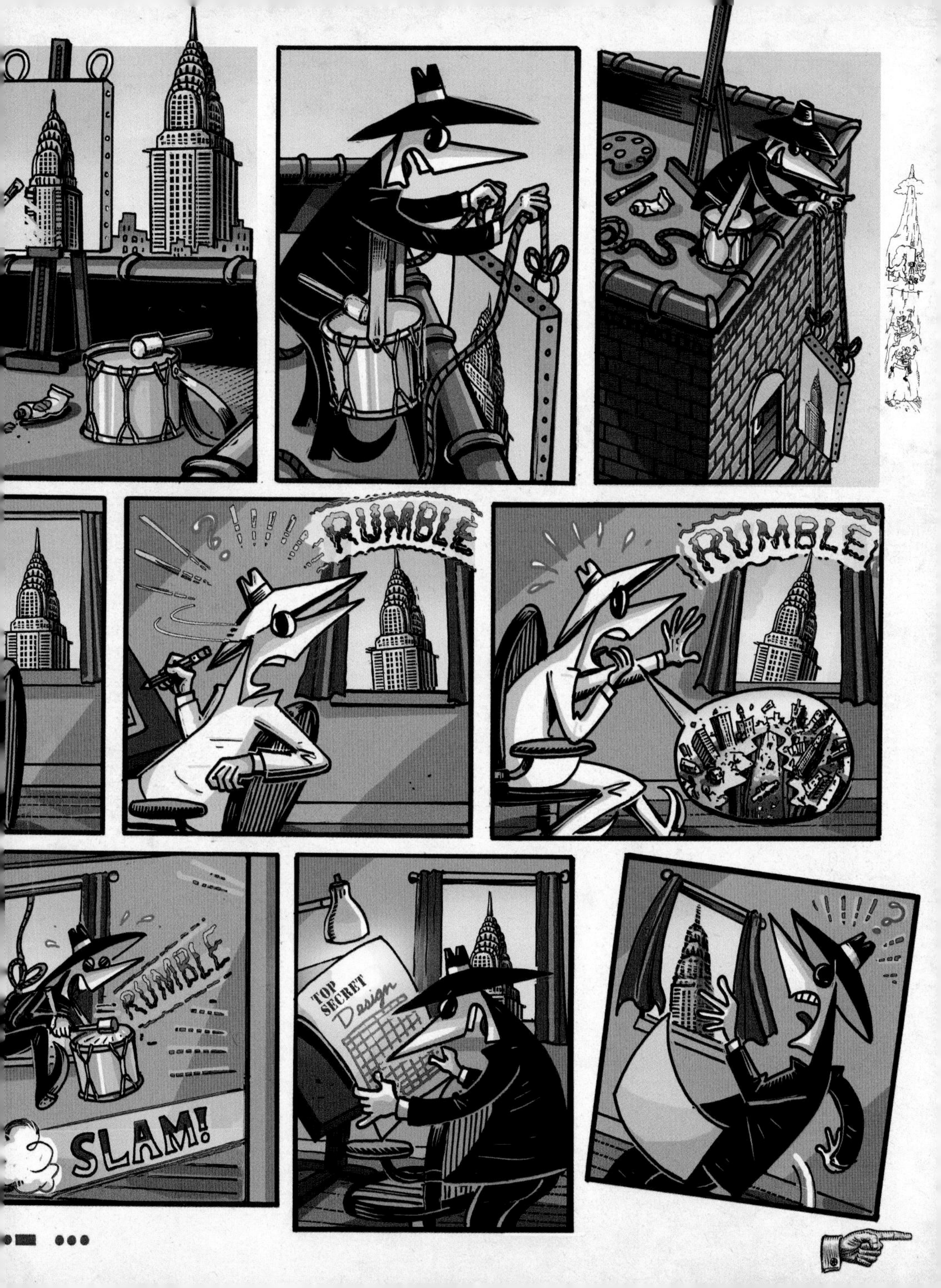
RUMBLE
RUMBLE
RUMBLE
SLAM!
TOP SECRET Design

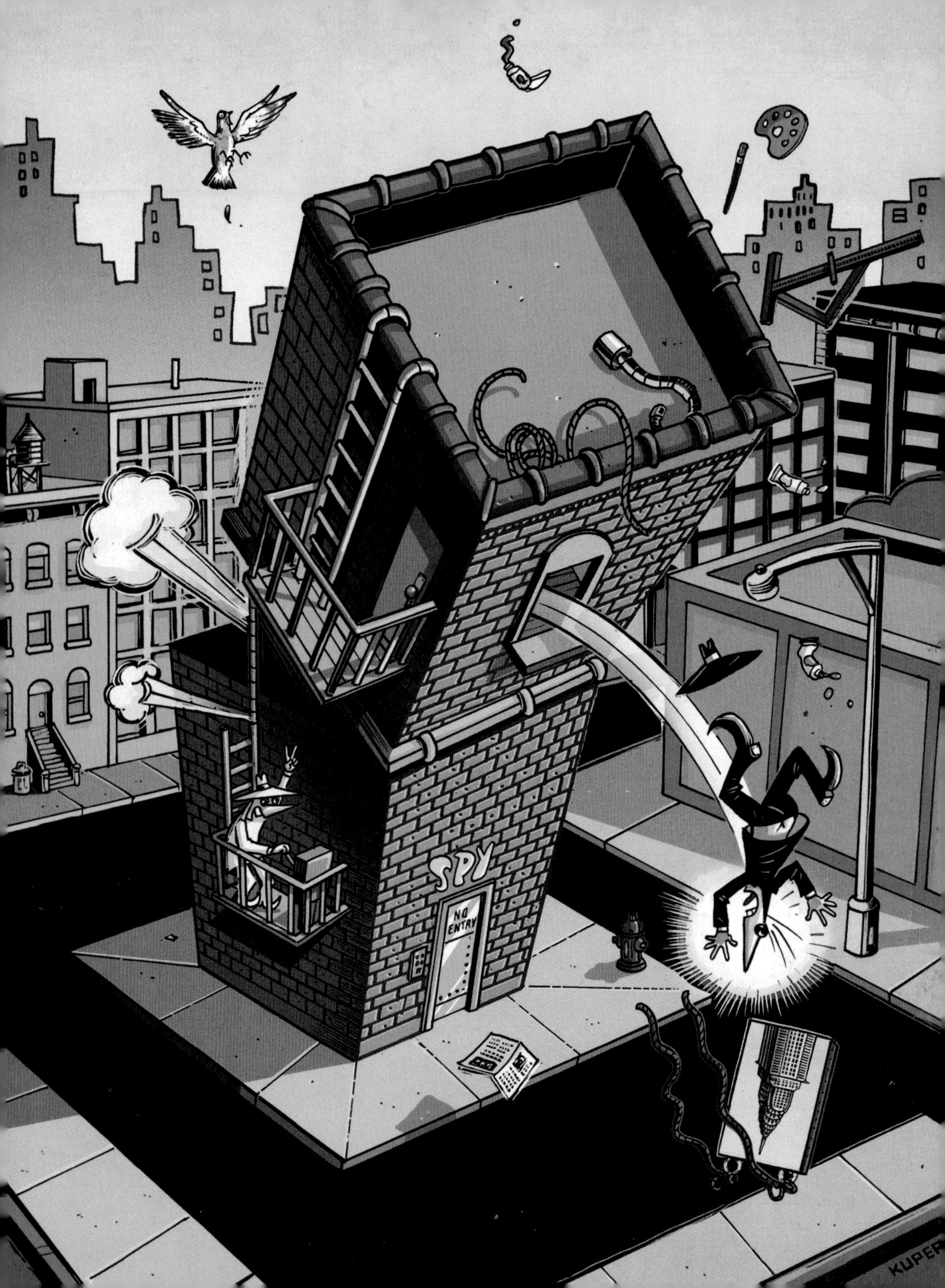
SPY
NO ENTRY
KUPER